Finish
Carpentry

Finish
Carpentry

CLAYTON DEKORNE
& TED CUSHMAN

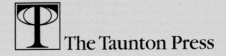

The Taunton Press

The Taunton Press, Inc., 63 South Main Street,
PO Box 5506, Newtown, CT 06470-5506
e-mail: tp@taunton.com

Editor: Peter Chapman
Copy Editor: W. Anne Jones
Indexer: Jay Kreider
Jacket/Cover design: Alexander Isley, Inc.
Interior design: Lori Wendin
Layout: Cathy Cassidy
Illustrator: Chuck Lockhart
Photographers: Ted Cushman and Robin Michals unless otherwise noted

For Pros/By Pros® is a trademark of The Taunton Press, Inc.,
registered in the U.S. Patent and Trademark Office.

Library of Congress Cataloging-in-Publication Data
DeKorne, Clayton.
  Finish carpentry / Clayton DeKorne, Ted Cushman.
      p. cm.
  Includes index.
  ISBN 978-1-56158-818-3
  1. Finish carpentry. I. Cushman, Ted. II. Title.
TH5640.D45 2008
694'.6--dc22

                          2008024805

Printed in the United States of America
10 9 8 7 6 5 4 3 2 1

Acknowledgments

B ooks, like houses, always represent the combined efforts of many, many people. Among the many fine tradesmen who have taught us over the years, we need to recognize a few who actively helped make this book a reality:

New Jersey carpenter Anthony "Smokey" Saduk, one of the best all-around craftsmen we know, generously gave of his time to help us illustrate production techniques, along with his colleague John Tetti. Massachusetts remodeler Chuck Green, well known to readers of the *Fine Homebuilding, Journal of Light Construction,* and *Remodeling* magazines, pitched in with some lessons from his long experience. Neal Gilberti, of Upper Darby, Pennsylvania kindly demonstrated his efficient precision with custom wainscotting. And we can't forget Ken O'Brien, formerly of Troy, Michigan, and lately of Phoenix, Arizona, who allowed us to photograph the mocked-up models he uses to sell his custom built-up Victorian and Craftsman-style trim treatments.

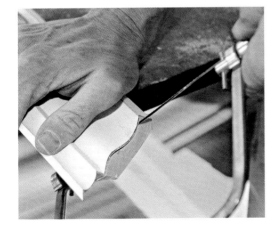

Further appreciation must be extended to a select group of expert tradesmen we have had the opportunity to work with, and who have provided tremendous inspiration, including Sal Alfano, Karel Bauer, Charles Berliner, Jim Boorstein, Butch Clark, David Crosby, Jed Dixon, Don Dunkley, Steve Ferrell, David Frane, David Gerstel, Mike Guertin, Carl Hagstrom, Jim Hart, Will Holladay, Don Jackson, J. Ladd, Mark Luzio, Craig Savage, and Dave Severance.

Finally, deep gratitude must be extended to Robin Michals for her photography and to Peter Chapman, our editor, without whose dogged persistence this book would not have been possible.

Contents

Introduction

The trade of finish carpentry is in a state of rapid change, a change that might be as profound as the changes that took place a hundred years ago at the dawn of the 20th century.

According to Mark Erlich of the Carpenter's History Project, carpenters in the early 1900s were beginning to realize that the idea of a "master builder" was becoming obsolete. In his book, *With Our Hands: The Story of Carpenters in Massachusetts,* Erlich tells about Connecticut carpenter J. W. Brown, who, upon looking over 50 years of transformations brought on by the industrial revolution, concluded that the "carpenter" of the mid-19th century—an artisan who trained for a lifetime—had, at the start of the 20th century, become simply a "tradesman" who would always be uncertain if he would ever be in a position to hire his own apprentices.

The journeyman carpenter of 1900 had to adapt to a completely new vision of his occupation, formed on the one hand by "lumpers"—piece workers who focused on specialized parts of a whole house—and on the other hand by a new breed of all-purpose carpenter in rural America who taught himself to design and build houses from pattern books, local tradition, and natural ingenuity. Aspiring master builders had to embrace new identities as contractors who managed at least four distinct

handcrafting, than tradition would suggest. Today's carpenter doesn't have excess time to perfect his technique at tuning a joint. Time and money set his pace; if you want to stay in business, you're bound by a schedule and a budget.

But even within that narrow window, you have the opportunity to do good work. Indeed, it's the ability to achieve quality within the bounds of time and money that defines excellence in the carpenter's trade. That's where we hope this book will come into play, presenting the basic skill sets required to practice the trade, showing a few short cuts, and describing some of the practical realities of fitting new materials into old houses.

Carpentry is still a tradition, and the carpenter working in 1900 would recognize the trim elements, the joints, and even some of the methods we present here. But this is not your grandfather's carpentry book. In fact, carpenters even 30 years ago didn't have the powerful tools or machinery on-site that

carpentry trades: framing, finishing, stair building, and sash-blind-door making. This fracturing of the trade, a symptom of growing from "guild" to "industry," set the pattern for modern homebuilding.

Now, a century later, the finish carpenter is typically a specialty tradesman—subcontractor or employee—who walks on to the job facing a narrow window of time in which to knock out his work and move on. Carpenters do far more assembly, and far less custom

we have at our disposal today. Cordless tools, plate joiners, portable power planers, and pneumatic nailers were at best prototypes—dinosaurs compared to today's nimble versions. In the new century, advances in equipment are revolutionizing trim carpentry along with the rest of the building industry, and new tools vastly improve the precision with which you can join, shape, and fasten materials.

While many of the ideas we present have been with the trade from the beginning, we have also tried to capture some of the most exciting recent advances. Far from destroying the finish carpentry trade, new tools and materials offer the modern tradesman new opportunities to do fine custom work. For example, computer-controlled CNC routers, and engineered wood products like MDF and finger-jointed rail stock allow today's carpenters to offer affordable custom wainscoting that is actually more resilient to dimensional change than the panel stock cut from old-growth timbers. Working alone, and without a machine shop of his own, a modern finish carpenter can give a whole house a trim package as personal and as artful as any 19th-century craftsman. Your handiwork can still be the final touch that makes a building produced with machines feel like a home built for people.

Getting Started

Getting the right gear is a fun first step to setting yourself up in the carpentry trade, and it's where we begin this book. But, if you really intend to do this work for a living, the proper tools and equipment are just one vital component of what you need to succeed. There's an entire realm that lies beyond the scope of this book, which is usually described as the "business" of building, and should come first. We strongly encourage the carpenter starting out in this trade to spend time wrapping his or her head around effective ways to direct coworkers and trade partners, to foster the patient indulgence of clients, and to manage contracts, insurance documents, and money carefully. In day-to-day operations, these business dimensions are inseparable from the physical and logistical orchestration of tools and materials. For this, there is no better source than David Gerstel's *Running a Successful Construction Company* (Taunton Press, 2002). This book distills years of Gerstel's hard-won experience running a small construction firm and should be considered a tool as valuable as all the others.

Setting Up On-Site

The first thing to do on a trim job, before you even unload the truck, is to scope out the conditions. You're looking for potential dangers, such as open stairwells or exterior doorways that the general contractor should have railed off, or any hot-wiring that might be in the finish carpenter's work area.

Beyond protecting the crew, you should also scope out the living space to determine what needs to be "roped off" from dust, noise, or traffic. Where will all the jobsite traffic be routed? Where will materials be stored? Where will you set up a staging area? And how will your daily work impact clients and neighbors?

Jobsite protection

You are also looking to protect existing materials from misfortune. In new construction, the finish carpenter comes on-site near the end of the project when finish flooring, finish stair treads, painted walls, and all cabinets, countertops, fixtures, and appliances may already be in place. These need protection from dust, scratches, and dents. Remodeling work ups the ante: You not only have to protect installed materials but also an owner's belongings, which can include expensive artwork and antique furniture. Protecting this sort of thing begins with a general awareness. If you see it, talk about it with the client. Encourage them to remove items that are in danger of toppling due to vibration. Especially cover up sensitive

Even within a sealed workspace, the best way to control dust is at the source. Chuck Green relies on a Festool® vacuum (right) hooked directly into the shroud of his chop saw to pick up the majority of sawdust. In addition, he runs a Ridgid® air-filtering unit (far right) that constantly pulls air through a cloth filter to remove the dust from the air that is kicked up by routing, sanding, and other dust-generating activities that are difficult to control.

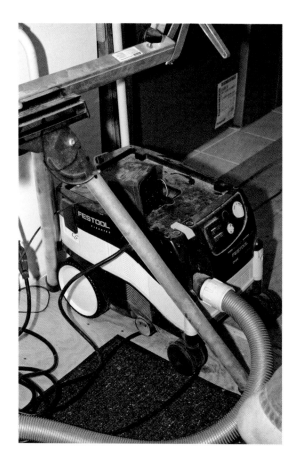

Caution: Electrical

While open electrical boxes that the electrician is still working on are obvious hazards to the finish carpenter, *any* finished wiring in the walls and ceiling poses a hidden risk. Every carpenter should carry some type of voltage tester. The least expensive type is a simple receptacle tester, which is designed to check if a circuit is wired correctly but can also simply tell you whether a circuit is powered—an essential check before opening or dismantling an electrical outlet that's in the way of baseboard or wainscoting. A more versatile option is a non-contact voltage "sniffer" (shown here), which detects whether voltage is running though any wire in the vicinity of your work. Bear in mind that it may not detect power in a line buried deep into the wall or ceiling, so take caution when ripping into these with a reciprocating saw.

electronics. While you will make every effort to control dust and vibration, you may also have to address the issue in the contract.

Whenever possible, it's always best to isolate the work area from the occupied parts of a home. Consider these options:

Tape Temporary protective materials should be fastened in place firmly, but gently. Avoid duct tape and ordinary masking tape, which will leave an adhesive residue on finished materials. Instead, use a low-tack "blue" tape whenever taping to finished surfaces. Even blue tape can bake on if left in place in sunlight for an extended period—for example, 3M®'s Long Mask®, although designed for an "extended application," is rated for UV exposure only up to seven days.

Plastic sheeting A roll of ordinary polyethylene sheeting should be a standard item on any job. If the poly will be up for a while, use 6-mil material as a minimum. Thin poly, when used

as a dust shroud over doorways or to create a duct wall, will shred the first time the end of a board is rubbed across it or will rip at fastening points with each change of air pressure.

Static-cling wrap A thin plastic does a good job of keeping dust out of cabinets. The easiest to use is 2-mil static-cling wrap, such as Dust Doc's red-tinted Multipurpose Protection wrap (http://dustdoor1.com/surface-protection/multipurpose.asp) or Poly-Tak™'s Window Mask®.

Dust walls and doors The best protection against dust involves some isolation of the workspace (in very dusty conditions you'll also want to depressurize the space by exhausting air out a window with a strong fan). Two good dust protection options that have a strong track record in the field are Dust Doc's Dust Door (www.dustdoor1.com) and the ZipWall® system from ZipWall® Barrier Products (www.zipwall.com).

Safety Essentials

For anyone in the trade for the long haul, protecting the eyes, ears, and lungs is not just the dull stuff of tailgate meetings with an OSHA representative. Ultimately, wearing annoying personal protective equipment is an essential means by which carpenters are able to sustain their livelihoods in the trade.

Hearing Protection

When selecting hearing protection, look for a Noise Reduction Rating, or NRR. This number equals the decibel drop you can expect by wearing a set or earplugs or earmuffs. However, the effective reduction may be less than the printed NRR, depending on how the hearing protection fits, its air pressure, and other variables, so there's no reason to obsess over a difference of a few NRR points. Aim for an NRR of 25, and choose the protection that's most comfortable to wear.

Don't wear ordinary glasses as eye protection. Carpenter Chuck Green, who depends on eyeglasses to improve his vision, invested in a pair of ANSI-rated frames with shatterproof prescription lenses.

Eye Protection

Regular eyeglasses won't stop a projectile kicked back from a tablesaw or the flying miter return kicked out of a chop saw. In fact, there's a risk that the eyeglasses will shatter and compound the damage. Look for eye protection that complies with ANSI Z87.1 rev. '89. Any safety glasses that comply will be stamped with those letters and numbers, or at least Z87.1, somewhere on the frame.

Dust Masks

Plain paper, nuisance dust masks are only appropriate for dust that isn't likely to cause scar tissue to build up in your lungs. They'll work as well as a bandana tied around your mouth, which can make breathing much more pleasant on a dusty jobsite. But for finishing or gluing up materials with solvent-based coating and adhesives, reach for a half-face respirator with a replaceable filter cartridge.

With an NRR of 29 to 33, foam or flexible plastic earplugs typically offer the greatest protection. Earmuffs offer a much lower NRR (17 to 23), though top-of-the-line models are as high as 29.

Several manufacturers provide components for creating "dust walls" to isolate dusty work areas. These systems typically consist of a set of spring-loaded poles that support polyethylene sheeting against the ceiling, and a long zipper that is taped to the poly. Open the zipper, slit the poly, and you have a sealable door in and out of the work area.

Tarps Poly and plastic tarps don't make good drop cloths because they get very slippery with a layer of sawdust on them. A true canvas drop cloth works the best and does a better job than plastic of relaxing at edges and in corners and staying put.

Self-adhesive films These are available for sticking to floors and stairs, but they vary widely in quality and effectiveness. A lightweight plastic works okay for temporary protection of a carpet from boot traffic. A heavyweight cotton-lined film, such as Pro-Tek^{SM}'s FloorLiner®, or a paper/poly masking will hold up a bit longer. On a trim job, you usually want something that can protect against damage from material that might inadvertently be dragged across it. The longer the job, and the more trades on the job, the more protection you'll need.

Rosin paper and lauan Rosin paper works okay on hard floors for short jobs. Make sure the floors are clean before taping it down. Use a low-tack tape at edges where the tape might need to bond to the finish floor, and use duct tape in traffic where the tape only sticks to the paper itself. Rosin paper shreds easily and only protects against dirt—not against spilled liquids or a dent from a dropped toolbox (or worse, the cast-iron sink brought in by a plumber). For maximum protection, cover well-sealed rosin paper with sheets of lauan and duct-tape the seams in traffic. Over the course of a long job, dust gets under the lauan at the edges, which is not a problem if it's only sawdust. But, if the dust is abrasive, keep in mind that it will grind its way through the paper and scratch the floor if it's allowed to accumulate under the lauan for an extended period.

Jamb guards Doorjambs, thresholds, stair newels, island cabinets, and any other outside corners are vulnerable to being bashed by a heavy toolbox or scratched as an air hose coupling is dragged across them. Plywood, old carpeting (beware scratchy stiff backings on glossy surfaces), and moving blankets are all good options for protecting these surfaces. Specifically for doorjambs, a snap-on rigid plastic protector or a quilted protector with spring-steel clips will solve the problem of temporarily securing the material to the finished surface.

The Staging Area

On a busy jobsite, the trim carpenter has to stake out a staging area that will become, in essence, a small on-site shop. This "shop" needs to have an assortment of hand, power, and portable stationary tools that you can get

Tight quarters are a fact of life on renovation sites. Here, the kitchen being renovated has been sealed off from the rest of the house using a Dust Door, as Chuck Green sets up to trim windows amid cabinet boxes and paper-wrapped countertops.

On some jobs, you can set up the cutting station strategically to make use of windows for cutting long stock.

to easily, and it should accommodate a stockpile of finish materials—both to acclimate them to the indoor environment and to keep them organized over the course of the job. (For more advice on choosing and handling materials, see Appendix A on pp. 215–238.)

Every site is different, and often the trim carpenter is crammed in between boxes of cabinets or hunched in the garage. Remodels are notoriously cramped, and the options for where you can set up are often limited. In a big, new house, look for the room with the highest ceiling and set up the saw near the center of the room to make it as easy as possible to flip long lengths of trim. A strategically placed workbench near an open window also provides extra room for handling long stock.

Miter-saw bench

The heart of the on-site shop is usually the miter-saw bench. While there are a number of commercially made miter-saw stands on the market, a surprising number of professional trim carpenters opt for just a simple plank on sawhorses: It's not beautiful, but it's easy to break down and inexpensive. Commercially made saw stands offer extendable material supports, but the plank option offers a more versatile work surface.

The defining virtue of any workbench is stability. Planks warp easily and they will rock unless screwed down to the sawhorses. One solution that keeps the plank flat is to screw it to the web of a wood I-joist. Banded plywood offers a flat and relatively light alternative that's easy to transport.

Supporting long material An important part of the bench setup is the stock supports. Here again, simple is better. Some carpenters prefer

The TrakRac is one of dozens of commercially made miter stands available that offer support for long stock, and set up and break down quickly. The "top" however, is usually limited to a saw table on which the saw is permanently mounted. No other workspace is available on the bench.

A tall bench, such as that used by Smokey Saduk and crew, is more forgiving on one's back over the course of a long day. The bench top is fashioned from a stout plank screwed to the web of a wood I-joist to keep it flat and rigid.

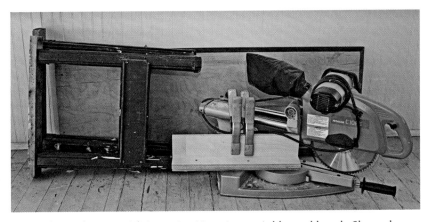

For any large chop saw, it's important to set up a stable workbench. Shown here is one of the simplest: A pair of folding sawhorses with a piece of banded plywood laid over the top works well for small jobs. While easy to transport, this setup is low, owing to the short folding sawhorses. It works for a short job, but on a longer one, your back will appreciate a taller workbench.

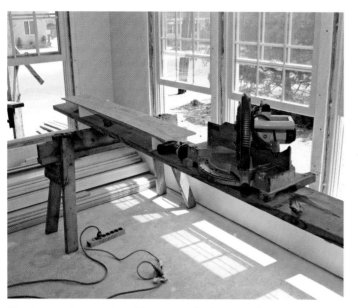

Most carpenters get by with support for long stock on only one side of the saw—usually to the left of the saw. **Smokey Saduk** sets up his cutting station with a stock support screwed to the workbench. **Clayton** uses a simple L-bracket clamped to the end of the bench.

to attach supports to the bench, so that setup is automatic. An elegant, but low-tech alternative is a pair of L-brackets that attach to each end of the bench with spring clamps and nest together for transport.

Even with stock supports, thin material tends to bow when sitting on the saw table. It's important to get in the habit of pressing the material against the saw table when cutting to straighten out any bow or flex that might affect the cut. Remember that the saw is set up to cut at angles in relation to the table and the fence, so make sure the stock is always perfectly aligned to both.

On-site storage A workbench can also double as a storage rack for keeping materials organized, flat, and accessible. Acclimating materials is critical to the long-term performance of the trim (see Appendix A on pp. 215–238), but keeping the materials organized is just as

important. It's worth taking the time at the beginning of the job to sort material according to size and the order it will be installed.

Getting around on-site

Be sure you think through how you're going to get at your work. Strapping on a pair of kneepads to crawl around the floor to install baseboard is the easy part. For overhead work, every carpenter should have an efficient way to work up high. And don't skimp on ladders. Opt for sturdy Type 1A (rated for 300 lb.) or Type 1 (rated for 250 lb.) stepladders. Fiberglass ladders of this class tend to be lighter and last longer over the long haul than wooden models. Obviously, safety is the paramount issue here. But there's also an argument to be made for quality. Overstretching or working on the balls of your feet will tire you out quickly, and the chance for making a sloppy mistake is reduced by working at a comfortable height.

For large jobs, Clayton sets up a workbench designed by Burlington, Vermont, carpenter J. Ladd that also functions as a lumber rack. The rack helps keep trim stock organized over the course of the job, and keeps it off the floor, promoting air circulation that helps the materials acclimate to jobsite conditions. The bench breaks down easily and remains reasonably portable.

A folding aluminum "drywall bench" provides a safe and convenient work platform, while a site-made bench accomplishes the same task. While both carpenters could easily have reached the window head without these stepstools, getting a leg up on the job allows them to control the quality of their work and keeps them from tiring out as quickly.

The challenge of working overhead is often not so much getting to the work as it is keeping all the tools you need at hand. Smokey Saduk relies on a heavy-duty fiberglass ladder outfitted with a simple, site-made toolbox that slips over the top.

Selecting Miter Saw Blades

Some manufacturers still provide a generic steel blade with the tool, but some are now savvy and provide a decent carbide blade. Plan to use carbide blades only, which not only have teeth that will stay sharp for hundreds of cuts but also thicker plates that are less likely to warp.

A high-quality 80- or 96-tooth, 12-in. diameter blade achieves a glass-smooth cut with no tearout on finish materials. A thin-kerf blade cuts faster than a thick blade and has vents and expansion slots to prevent the plate from warping. But a good thick-kerf blade will last longer in service.

Tooling Up

Most trim carpenters organize their shop area around the miter saw—arguably the most important trim tool of all. Let's look at this tool and some of the others you'll need with you on most finish carpentry jobs.

Miter saws

On-site, this tool is typically called a "chop saw," though technically a chop saw refers to a similar machine used in the commercial trades that uses an abrasive blade for cutting steel pipe and channel stock.

Chop saws for a trim carpenter come in a variety of styles, with blades ranging in size from 8½ in. to 15 in. in diameter. There are four general types:

- A **standard chop saw** pivots from a single point. Typically, this saw is used to cut miters across the width of a board by swinging a turntable to the left or the right. When cutting, the face of the board lies flat on the saw table with the edge of the board held tight against the fence. However, depending on the cutting capacity and the width of the material, a standard chop saw can also cut a bevel—an angle across the thickness of a board—by standing the board on edge and holding one face against the fence.

- A **compound miter saw** can cut miters like a standard chop saw, but the blade and motor assembly can also flop over to one side, allowing you to cut a wider bevel with the face of the board on the table. You can also cut a miter and a bevel at the same time—

The table of a standard power miter saw swings through an arc at least 45° to the left and to the right of straight crosscut. While primarily made for cutting miters, it's possible to cut a bevel on small stock by standing the board on edge, as shown.

a compound miter—which is typically used for joining crown molding.

- A **sliding compound miter saw** can cut miters, bevels, and compound miters like a compound miter saw, but the blade and motor run on a rail, allowing you to pull the blade forward to cut wider stock.

- A **dual-compound miter saw** functions like a compound miter saw, but the blade and motor assembly can flop to either the left or the right, allowing you to cut bevels and compound miters in either direction. The key advantage here is that you can cut a board with the miter and bevel oriented the same way it will be installed, which saves much head scratching. Also, with this saw you don't have to turn long material around, which can be a distinct advantage when working in a confined space. All of the dual-compound saws we are aware of are sliding saws with a 10-in. or 12-in. blade, so they offer large cutting capacities as well.

A compound miter saw can cut both miters (by adjusting the table) and bevels (by adjusting the angle of the blade). However, it's not always necessary to take the time to adjust the bevel setting. Here, Smokey Saduk "back-cuts" baseboard (cutting a slight bevel to relieve the end that will butt a wall) by propping up the end on a piece of scrap.

A sliding compound miter saw extends the capacity of a compound miter saw by allowing the blade to slide along twin supports to increase the width of the cut. Unlike a radial arm saw, this blade cuts on the push, affording a safer, more controlled cut. (Photo by Scott Phillips, courtesy *Fine Homebuilding*, © The Taunton Press, Inc.)

A dual-compound miter saw that can cut a bevel to the right or the left of a straight cut provides full functionality. This is most useful when cutting bevels or compound miters in tight quarters where it's difficult to flip the material end for end.

All compound miter saws, regardless of brand, will eventually develop some slop, particularly in the bevel adjustment that bears a lot of weight. When setting an old saw back to zero, don't rely on the stop. Instead, square up the blade to the table.

On the face of it, a dual-compound saw, which offers the widest range of angle-cutting options, might seem like the most versatile saw. However, all the bells and whistles come at a premium price. These tools are also big—most weigh in at around 60 lb. How often a tool must be moved plays a strong role in choosing which is the most appropriate.

There's a strong argument for owning more than one chop saw. Besides a 12-in. compound saw for crown and other complicated work, it's handy to have a 10-in. standard chop saw for extensive baseboard and casing jobs. This saw is portable enough to move conveniently around the house, cutting where you are installing, and even working right on the floor to save time and steps. If you anticipate doing a lot of framing and decking work, you'll probably spring for a big sliding compound or dual-compound saw.

Portable tablesaws

The other mainstay of the on-site shop is the tablesaw. Not that long ago, the only real professional option in a portable tablesaw was the Makita® 2708—an admirable 8¼-in. tablesaw that weighed only 38 lb. and had a surprisingly strong motor, but a rather crude fence. This old standby has since been upstaged by new models from its maker, as well as models from Bosch®, DeWalt®, and Hitachi®.

The primary innovation of the newer saws is a better fence. The Bosch and DeWalt models are exceptional, allowing cuts up to 25 in. (wide enough, that is, to rip any width from a 4x8 panel stock). Both also allow fence adjustments that are accurate to read right off the table and that stay parallel to the blade, saving the extra step of taking out a tape measure to set up each cut. This can be a real boon to

Measure and Cut

When measuring and marking a straight cut or bevel, it's much faster simply to mark the length with a caret rather than drawing a line all the way across the face of the board. Then, before laying a finger anywhere near the trigger, drop the blade right onto the board aligning it with the caret mark. If the caret is placed 1 to 2 in. from the edge of the board, you can bring a tooth of the blade right down onto it.

Miter Adjustments

When changing the angle settings on the miter table, get in the habit of turning the knob to lock it down. It's not necessary to tighten the knob a lot, and it's not necessary to unscrew it much either. There is a point on the thread where a half turn will lock the table down and a simple half turn in the other direction will free it up. Find this point, then always lock and unlock that simple half turn. It won't take any more time, and it will save you the grief of unknowingly bumping the handle and then miscutting the angle.

The new-generation portable tablesaws, including the Bosch 4000 shown here, can cut material up to 25 in. wide, making it possible to rip full sheets of plywood. This model also includes a fold-down rolling table that makes this bulky tool easier to lug around.

Safety Isn't Optional

There's no reason to take chances around a tablesaw. Use a pushstick to keep your hands away from the blade. It's astounding how frequently professional carpenters feel they have a license to avoid basic safety precautions because they are well practiced at their job. But the more you use a tablesaw without a pushstick, the greater statistical probability there is for a mishap.

On a cramped jobsite, Chuck Green sets up his tablesaw only when he needs it. He does this by using DeWalt's low-tech, but highly functional folding tablesaw stand, which is representative of the portable table options available for a number of 10-in. tablesaws on the market.

improving production, but it only works if you can really trust the measurements of the saw.

Another practical innovation of the new-generation portables is an enclosed blade housing that makes dust collection possible. This is an absolute necessity when trying to rip MDF in an occupied home.

Many portables come standard without a stand. It's tempting to keep the saw as portable as possible and just plunk it down on sawhorses, but this is not always a great idea. At the very least, screw it to the sawhorses to reduce the risk of it sliding off as you push stock into the blade. In many cases, an optional stand is available but most portables must be bolted on and this will increase the profile of the tablesaw, making it that much bulkier and less portable. Several notable exceptions are the folding stands available from many saw manufacturers. The slickest is the "gravity rise" wheeled stand sold with Bosch and Ridgid tablesaws, which can also be adapted to fit tablesaws made by other manufacturers.

Several aftermarket saw stands are also available that provide a wide surface for cutting up sheet stock, and extension tables for picking up long material. While these are undoubtedly useful, you'll need the room on-site, and they will easily double the price of the tablesaw.

One table option worth mentioning is the Black & Decker® Workmate®, which has a top that spreads apart in two pieces to function as a vice. By itself, this small, fold-down workbench provides a very stable work surface for any number of carpentry tasks. But it's also a good alternative for supporting a bench-top tablesaw. A mounting block can be permanently bolted to the tablesaw and then quickly

The Black & Decker Workmate excels in cramped quarters. Combined with adjustable stock supports to handle long pieces, the Workmate's clamping table works well for securing materials in place for coping, routing, and planing tasks. When finished, the table collapses into a relatively flat, easy-to-haul package.

fit into the Workmate table vise to hold the saw securely.

Portable planers

Though not as essential as a miter saw or tablesaw, a thickness planer opens up a trim carpenter's world and should be considered by the serious trim contractor. With access to one, you are no longer confined to commercial board thicknesses, which is most useful in old houses where you need to match existing work. There are a number of portable models that make thickness planing a viable option, but be aware that not all portable planers are

A portable planer can quickly pay for itself when you're working in old houses and need to match the thickness of existing materials.

created equal, and even the best portables have limitations.

The largest stock that will go through most portable machines is 12 in. wide by 6 in. thick, and the most they can take off in a single pass is about ³⁄₃₂ in. The number of cuts per foot determines the smoothness of a board's surface. Since you get more cuts per inch from a faster motor or a slower feed rate, these are generally the first variables to look for when shopping for a planer. Most portable machines run at 8,000 rpm at a feed rate of 26.2 ft./minute. With two blades on the cutterhead, this makes for about 51 cuts per inch. Compared to similar-capacity but much heavier shop machines, this is a bit low. A shop-size Delta® DC-33, for example, is rated at 82 cuts per inch; a Powermatic® 100 is rated

Thickness Planer Tips

A thickness planer can be a lifesaver, particular when matching existing trim work in old houses. When planing any stock to size, follow these basic rules:

- Pay attention to the direction of the grain when feeding boards into the planer. If the ends of "feather grain" are visible on the face of the board, keep the ends of the feathers pointed toward you when planing the pith side of the board. Keep the ends pointing away from you when planing the bark side.

- Don't take off more than $3/32$ in. per pass. A portable machine can't handle much more. Taking off less ($1/16$ in.) may take a little longer to get to the thickness you want but will produce a smoother surface.

- Remove stock from both faces if the board is kiln-dried. If the case hardening is removed from only one side, the board will often warp.

If you're working with wild grain, the only option you have to stop chatter and tearout on a small planer is to reduce the depth of cut. On larger machines, you can reduce the feed rate, as well.

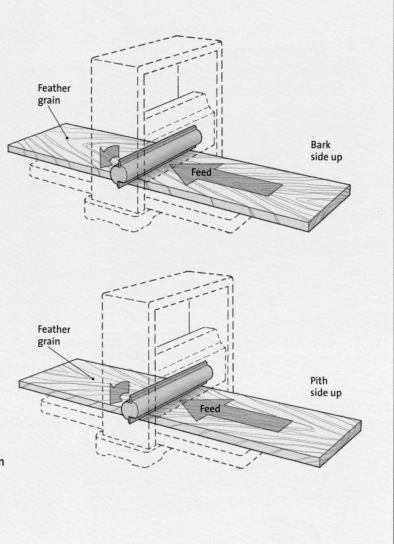

Feather grain

Bark side up

Feed

Feather grain

Pith side up

Feed

at 73. Nevertheless, the surface produced from the portable planers is respectably smooth.

Air nailers

Hammers are by no means obsolete, but with an air nailer on-site, they certainly don't get used by trim carpenters nearly as much these days. Not only does an air nailer (or cordless nailer) dramatically speed up the job, but it also improves quality because it drives the nail with a single stroke. Instead of having to hold the nail in one hand and the hammer in the other while clamping the trim material in place with your knee or elbow, pneumatic nail-

Trim Nailers, 15- or 16-Gauge?

Trim nailers typically shoot either a 15-gauge or a 16-gauge nail. The stouter 15-gauge nails are similar in diameter to conventional "bulk" 4d, 6d, or 8d finish nails and have a finish-nail head. To accommodate this head, they are typically collated at an angle, which means the magazine is also angled. But the angled magazine also makes it easier to get into corners.

A lighter 16-gauge nail can fold up in hardwood or near a softwood knot, and 16-gauge nailers usually have a straight magazine, which makes these tools better suited for shop assembly work, not trim work on-site.

ers give you a free hand to hold the material. Once you have it where you want it, you don't have to worry that your hammering will bang it apart. The action of the tool driving the nail is so fast that the piece has almost no chance of slipping. Plus, you can drive a nail with an air nailer in tight spaces where you could never swing a hammer.

You also don't need to predrill because the blunt tips on the nails are less likely to split the wood, even when driven near the end of a board. There are no hammer marks, and because most air nailers have rubber tips to protect the work, the drive tip leaves no mark either. Air nailers automatically set the nails, so you don't have to go back and do it by hand. While many nailers have an adjustable nosepiece, often the most reliable way to control the depth of the set is by adjusting the air pressure.

Compressors Compressors come in a wide range of sizes and capacities, but for running

Brad Nailers

While not suited for securing 1x stock, there are plenty of situations on a trim job that call for thin stock (5/8 in. or less) and small moldings that require a shorter nail, or "pin." An 18-gauge pin is also less likely to blow out, split the end of a board, or ruin the tiny miter return at the end of a window stool or the termination of baseboard, chair rail, or crown.

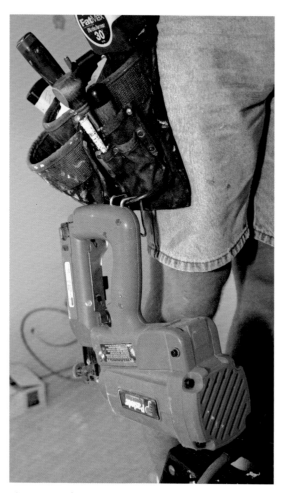

The Paslode® weighs just 5 lb. It's capable of setting a 2½-in.-long, 16-gauge nail into a red oak trim piece. To control the depth of drive, a thumb wheel that lengthens or shortens the safety provides enough range to set a 1-in. to 1¼-in. brad nail in the thin edge of pine clamshell or the full-length nail in oak. New models from Paslode and other manufacturers are even smaller.

many nailers are drawing too much pressure (a frequent problem with framing crews running underpowered rigs).

Cordless nailers A cordless nailer has become an essential instrument for many trim carpenters because it means the end of dragging a hose around, worrying about the connector snagging on (and marring) doorjambs, or throwing the client into a conniption when the compressor kicks on.

The Paslode Trimpulse—the original and best-known cordless nailer available—runs on both a fuel cell (a small aluminum canister filled with MAPP® gas) and a 6-volt ni-cad battery. One fuel cell drives about 2,500 nails. A single battery charge is good for about 4,000 shots. Recharge takes three hours after an initial conditioning charge of 24 hours. Except for a loud pop and the constant droning of a fan, using the Impulse isn't much different from an air nailer without the hose.

Instead of a gas-fueled piston, DeWalt's recent entry to the cordless nailer competition uses a self-contained on-board mini-compressor and air tank powered by an 18-volt battery (the same platform that runs other cordless tools), thus dispensing with the gas canister. The DeWalt has plenty of power and an accurate depth adjustment for setting nails and a flywheel keeps the air tank topped off well enough to keep up with bump-fire nailing: you can make time with this tool. It's quite handy for small to midsize jobs, but it's noticeably bulkier than a standard trim gun, and a little heavy for all-day production work. On big jobs, you'll also need a couple of spare batteries on hand (the gun drains them fast); but, then again, you don't have to worry about running

a trim gun, a small, hand-carry model is what you want. These typically come with 1½-gal. to 4-gal. tanks and electric motors in the ¾- to 2-hp range. For trim work, you don't need to be too concerned with sizing the compressor. Trim nailers don't take a lot of air, so you're unlikely to wind up in a situation in which too

DeWalt's cordless nailer packs about the same power as the Paslode and provides a more ergonomic depth-of-drive control. Best of all, it saves the expense of having to buy fuel cells. But weighing in at 8 lb. (due largely to its big 18-volt battery), it's noticeably heftier and bulkier than the more streamlined Paslode. (Other battery-driven models are in the works as we write.)

out of fresh fuel cylinders—and you don't have to put up with the Sterno®-like smell of MAPP fuel.

Power and Hand Tools

Beyond the shop setup, a carpenter's lifeblood lies in the assortment of power tools that he or she fills the truck with and the toolboxes full of hand tools. Throughout each chapter in the rest of this book, we have identified each of the power and hand tools that can come in handy, and a few that are essential, for completing each task.

Buying power tools

While a good carpenter can do wonders with inexpensive tools, there's a limit. In general, you get what you pay for in power tools, and professional carpenters owe it to themselves to invest in the best tools they can afford.

This is especially true in power tools where the cost is often in unseen features, such as

Choosing Toolboxes

Inevitably, trim carpenters will accrue a number of toolboxes, either for carrying power tools (such as a "drill" box, which includes a wide variety of drill bits, hole saws, and other drill accessories) or for specialized collections or hand tools. Keep in mind that metal boxes aren't always the "best." While metal is durable, it's nice to have a number of sturdy plastic boxes with recessed handles, which allow the boxes to be stacked easily in the back of the truck or on-site. Boxes with protruding top handles can be very limiting in cramped quarters.

Power Tool Ratings

Bigger isn't always better when it comes to a trim carpenter's power tools. Yet the tool industry is obsessed with big numbers. Here are some myths about the typical numbers used to sell power tools.

Amps

A tool's amp rating indicates the electrical current load the motor can carry for an indefinite time without degrading the insulation and other electrical components. In a UL-rated tool, the motor is tested to verify that it operates at or below a specific temperature when current flows through it. Strictly speaking, an amp rating indicates the maximum allowable continuous current a motor can handle without exceeding temperature limits. In other words, a tool's amp rating measures how effectively a motor cools itself, not how powerful it is.

Horsepower

Horsepower is a mathematical expression of the relation between speed and torque. Depending on the torque figure in the equation (either sustained or stall torque), horsepower is reported as either a continuous running or peak rating. Most manufacturers of portable power tools list peak power—the highest number—but if a motor were continuously operated at the load required to measure maximum output, the tool would quickly burn out because of the high current being pulled through the motor. Manufacturers justify this number by claiming it shows the "available power" to muscle through a knot, or another short-lived, high-demand application. But if the horsepower rating depends on stall torque, a tool is unlikely ever to exhibit maximum power before it trips a breaker. It's simply not a realistic number.

Watts Out

A few manufacturers report watts out as a measure of motor power. Watts out is derived from horsepower by multiplying peak horsepower by 746 (1 hp = 746 watts). As a result, watts out numbers are higher than horsepower figures (for example, a 3-hp electric motor—measured at peak power—delivers about 2,220 watts out), but it's no more reliable as an indicator of sustained power than peak horsepower or stall torque.

When buying power tools, look to other features, such as how it feels in your hand, how heavy it is, and how smoothly it stops and starts. Generally, control carries the day in trim tools over raw power.

the quality of the electric motor windings and insulation, bearings, and gearing. However, before investing a lot of money make sure you understand the tool ratings. Most of us obsess about size thinking bigger is always better.

But while durability and cutting capacity are favorable features to have on your side, lots of power isn't the chief requirement for a trim carpenter's tool.

Cordless Power Ratings

For the professional carpenter, a cordless drill/driver may be second only to the miter saw as the most often used tool. Certainly, screws are not used too often for show. But behind the scenes, bugle-head wood screws secure blocking and backing, and are invaluable for tacking things in place and fashioning jigs. While they are now commonplace tools in a professional's arsenal, there is also plenty of misunderstanding about cordless power.

Voltage is not an indication of a cordless tool's power any more than amps is a measure of a circular saw's power. The voltage defines the number of the number of cells wired together in a battery, and each cell is rated at 1.2 volts. This determines the amount of power available, and can give an indication of runtime. But the real measure of power in most electric tools is *torque*—the rotational force that, for example, keeps a large-diameter drill bit spinning fast enough to cut efficiently.

Yet high torque can be misleading, too. For any tool, there is no single measure of torque, but rather a range of torque measurements corresponding to the speeds at which a tool operates—from the fastest no-load speed to a complete stall. Torque is always related to the speed of rotation. The torque of a universal motor goes up as a load is applied and the speed of rotation slows down. The more you load a motor, the slower it runs until it stalls, at which point the torque is at a maximum. When most toolmakers publish a torque rating (which is now common for cordless drills), it's nearly always the stall torque, also known as breakdown torque—the highest reading possible. At the stall point, a tool is drawing the maximum current, and is generating the most heat. In short, stall torque reflects the very worst possible condition for operating a tool.

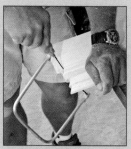

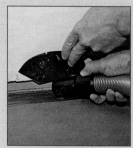

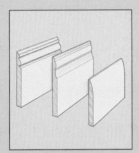

34 | One-Piece vs.
Three-Piece
Baseboard

35 | Basic
Cuts

38 | Baseboard
Layout

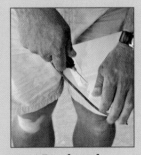

43 | Baseboard
Joinery

Running Baseboard

You'll find **baseboard trim** in almost every room, in
almost every house. Applied at the intersection of the
floor and the walls, baseboard serves several purposes.
Aesthetically, it adds definition to room edges and wall bases
(especially important for large formal rooms), and it supplies a
visual horizontal baseline to ground the vertical trim treatments
applied to doors. Baseboard also plays another, more mundane,
visual role: It masks the joint where floor materials meet wall
materials, hiding the ragged edges of carpeting or the rough-cut
ends of floorboards and drywall. Finally, baseboard also has an
important functional purpose: It protects the walls from life's hard
knocks, such as the bumps and blows of boots, furniture, and
vacuum cleaners (or, in homes occupied by families with vigorous
lifestyles, skateboards, and hockey pucks).

Applying baseboard is often a good task for a carpenter's helper
to train on—it's repetitive and relatively straightforward, and it
provides plenty of practice in taking accurate measurements, making clean cuts, and assembling basic joints. But that's not to say
that baseboard has to be simple, or that it doesn't offer its own set
of challenges (especially in old houses where all the floors are out

of level, and none of the corners are square). Like all trim work, baseboard demands due attention to prep, layout, joinery, and proper fastening.

Baseboard Toolkit

There's no substitute for a whole truckload of tools. You want all the firepower you can get sitting in the driveway where you can access it when you need it. But no one wants to unload the entire truck every day. For baseboard work, here are the items to unload first.

Chop saw

A miter saw (commonly referred to as the *chop saw* on-site) is essential for cutting base stock. Among pros, there are two general approaches to choosing a chop saw for baseboard. Some production guys still opt for a simple, 10-in. straight-cut saw with no bells and whistles, set

up on the floor. The idea is to chop and go. You're only bringing the stock you need into the room, dicing it up, and moving to the next room, instead of constantly going back to a cutting station. The Makita LS1030N and Delta 36-070—the descendants of some of the first chop saws—are two old-time favorites for this work. At about 30 lb., they are relatively easy to lug from room to room.

Running baseboard on your knees is a killer on the lower back and knees, so anyone who isn't young enough to still feel immortal will prefer an upright cutting station (see "Miter-saw bench" on p. 12). You'll need plenty of space to work—either room on both sides of the saw for cutting both ends of long stock, or head room available to flip the stock end for end, so you can cut both ends of a long run.

The chief advantage of a larger 10-in. or 12-in. miter saw is the increased cutting

A simple chop saw can be used to cut bevels, as well as miters, if the trim is short enough to stand vertically against the fence.

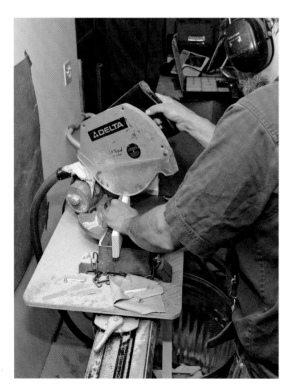

When setting up a cutting station for baseboard, make sure you have enough room to maneuver long stock.

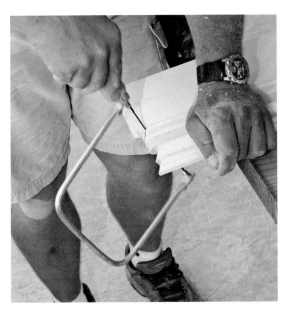

A basic, traditional coping saw is still the standard tool to cut precise curves for a tight joint in profiled baseboard or crown.

A jigsaw is not an essential baseboard tool … until you have to cut out for an electrical outlet. It can also come in handy for cutting the straight portion of the baseboard when coping single-piece profile material.

capacity and the ability to cut a bevel on wide stock for coped joints and outside miters (see "Baseboard Joinery" p. 43).

Coping saw

For coping one-piece profiled baseboard or base cap moldings, the traditional tool is a simple coping saw. Its C-shaped body and very narrow blade allow it to twist and turn as it follows the profile. In general, the stiffer the back, the better. Typically, the blade has 12 to 18 teeth per inch (the more teeth, the finer the cut), and these should face down (toward the handle) so that it cuts on the pull, keeping the thin blade in tension.

Jigsaw

Nothing's more aggravating than a cheap jigsaw. Don't try to save money here; pony up for a good one that will hold a line, includes

orbital action for better control in different materials, and has a built-in blower so you can see where you're cutting.

At the very least, a pro-grade jigsaw is needed for cutouts to accommodate outlets. But many professionals rely on a jigsaw to speed the production of coped joints (see "Coping with a jigsaw" on pp. 160–161).

Kneepads

Kneepads are awkward to wear but, for the less agile of us, essential gear if we want to stay active after a day of kneeling on subfloor. These days, kneepads come in a wide range of different types. One of the recent revolutions of the past 10 years are kneepads with replaceable gel pad inserts, using materials that are similar to those that have improved running shoes and football helmets. The gel provides better support and has a better "memory" than

Making Cutouts for Baseboard Outlets

In old houses, it's common to have electrical outlets located on the baseboard, and if you're installing wainscoting, it may be less visually disruptive to relocate outlets in the baseboard area than to have them interrupt the wall panels. Here's what to do in these situations:

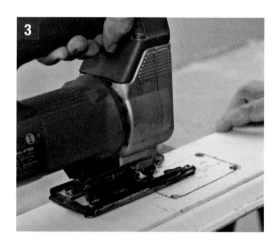

1 | Use an electrical box to mark the cutout.

2 | Drill out the corners.

3 | While it's only necessary to drill one hole, it's easier to drill all four so you're not turning tight corners with the jigsaw.

4 | If you're using plastic boxes (which work best in this situation), shave off the little protrusions for a clean fit. (With metal boxes, you may have to drill a couple more holes to make room for any protrusions at the edges of the box.)

5 | Insert the box into the cutout.

Knobby-kneed guys like author Clayton DeKorne find kneepads a must-have on any baseboard job.

A "molding chisel" (right) features a flat blade for slipping behind trim stock without excessively marring the edges. The other end of this model includes a Japanese nail puller, which has a sharpened claw that can bite into the nail shank, making it possible to grab the nail at any point along its length. On the left is a more standard Japanese-style "cat's paw," with the sharpened claw on both ends; this larger tool is useful when you need to pull bigger nails, but you must take special care to avoid damaging the wood.

the old-fashioned felt-cushion or low-cost foam rubber variety that tends to be pressed down, and loses its loft, in a short time.

Wall scraper

Scraping down the wall with a stiff, 3-in. drywall knife is the quickest way to clean up the inevitable mud drips and buildup of drywall mud found at the base of walls and floors. Taping knives come in a variety of styles. Look for one with a stiff blade that can be sharpened on a grinder. Red Devil® makes a line they refer to as "wall scrapers" to distinguish them from their thinner, flexible taping knives. Hyde also makes a 12000 "bent chisel" scraper that's a useful configuration for this work. The blades on these models have enough meat to stand up to a grinder, so you can sharpen the edge. This will allow you to shave the clumps of drywall mud off the wall at the base of corners and other places the tapers have left a substantial buildup.

Molding chisel

A molding chisel is a short, wide pry bar, similar to a flat bar but thinner in section. Because these are thin, they are better than flat bars for prying off trim without gouging the edges. A

good choice is the Hyde® 45600 or 45605 pry bar, which has a very thin, sharp, stiff blade that can easily be slipped behind moldings. Another useful version is the Shark® 10-in. pry bar, which has a very thin, wide blade with a sharp edge that holds up well to repeated sharpening and includes a Japanese-style cat's-paw on the other end.

Nail set

A medium ($\frac{1}{16}$-in., sometimes specified as a $\frac{2}{32}$-in.) nail set works well for setting most finish nails. Carry one even if you are running an air nailer. There are times when you may get ahead of the compressor and the air system won't have the power to fully set the nail. Or, you may hit a knot or a particularly dense stud, and a nail will be left standing proud of the surface and need some persuading to sink it home.

Pin punch

Every trim carpenter should keep a pin punch within arm's reach to drive nails through the board. This is a good way to remove a piece of trim you may want to save without dinging the edges with a flat bar—a lifesaver for a piece of trim that has to be removed after you've already nailed it in place. Unlike a standard nail set, which is tapered, a pin punch has a straight shaft, so it won't wedge into the board, get stuck, or create too large a hole when you push a nail all the way through. A ⅛-in. straight punch will drive even a larger 10d finish nail.

Nippers

Along the same lines as a pin punch, a pair of end-cutting pliers, or "nippers," should be a standard item in any trim carpenter's nail

A pair of end nippers are one of the few tools author Clayton DeKorne keeps in his nail bags at all times. They're useful for pulling a nail through finish material from the backside. Like it or not, this is not always just a task for salvaging existing trim in an old house. Even in new work, it's likely that work will have to be taken apart and repositioned from time to time.

bags. Once a piece of trim has been pried off and has a bunch of finish nails sticking though the backside, you can pull finish nails through from the backside with the end-cutters without marring the face.

One-Piece vs. Three-Piece Baseboard

In traditional old homes, baseboard often consists of a classic assembly built up out of three separate moldings: a square-edged, flat "base molding" (usually 3/4 or 5/4 stock), with a profiled "cap molding" mounted on its top edge and a simple "shoe mold" (often a quarter-round, though traditional shoe molding is taller than it is wide; occasionally, a small cove molding may be used as well). The flexible shoe molding is tacked along the bottom edge to cover the meandering joint between the baseboard and the floor.

In the simplest older houses, you may find baseboard that consists of only the square

A pin punch is typically sold as a mechanic's tool for driving steel pins. But it is a trim carpenter's secret defense in the face of change orders, allowing you to drive a finish nail through the newly installed board. The resulting hole can be filled as easily as any set nail when the piece is reinstalled.

Traditional Three-Piece Baseboard

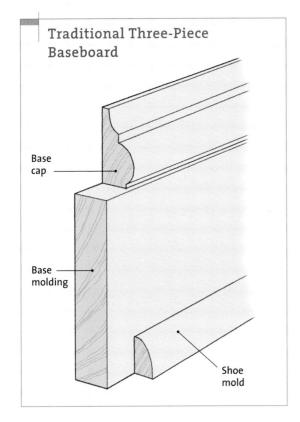

Base cap

Base molding

Shoe mold

One-Piece Baseboard

Simple clam shell represents the most basic single-piece base stock available. A step up in price and quality affords single-piece profiled stock that mimics the look of traditional three-piece baseboard.

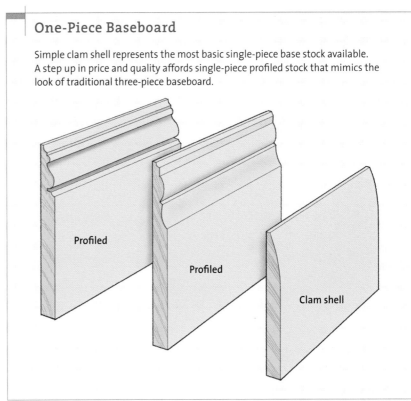

Profiled

Profiled

Clam shell

base molding, with no cap or shoe. In modern times, the whole base-molding plus cap-molding assembly has been widely replaced by a one-piece baseboard, generally of ¾-in. material. Instead of a cap molding, the material is manufactured with a simple profile at its upper edge. At the low end, tract houses typically get a very simple "clam shell" baseboard; for a little more money, you can have a wider baseboard with an ogee profile, or perhaps a half-round bead.

Traditionally, carpenters chose three-piece baseboard for reasons that are as good now as they were back then. Large heavy moldings cost more than small moldings; you can get the same, or better, looks for less money using a three-piece assembly. And for heavy, complex trim looks, three-piece baseboard is less work when all is said and done. Yes, you have to nail on three pieces, but it is much easier to get nice tight joints with three pieces of relatively small

and flexible molding than with one large piece that must be scribed to fit.

Basic Cuts

At its simplest, baseboard joinery involves a lot of simple square cuts and butt joints. You can make these cuts with the piece lying down on the miter saw or, if the stock is not too tall, standing up on the saw table. With short base stock, the standing-up method is a good way for apprentice carpenters to learn the ropes; since the baseboard gets cut in the same position it will be installed on the wall, it's easy to visualize.

Miter joints

At outside corners, baseboard gets a basic outside miter joint. For typical 90° corners, you can stand the material against the fence of the miter saw, set the miter at 45°, and simply chop down through the board. The mating

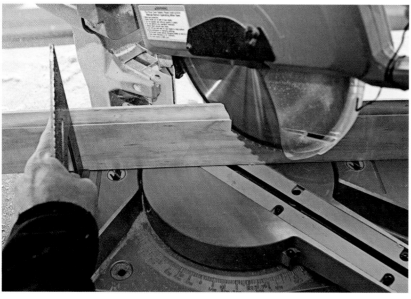

Short baseboard stock can be chopped or beveled in a miter saw standing up. Even if you have a compound miter saw, this technique will save time. But you must be careful to keep the board square to the table or the bevel will not be square to the face of the board. As a check, brace it against a Speed Square®, as shown.

If the baseboard is wider than can fit under the saw blade, it will need to be beveled on a compound miter saw.

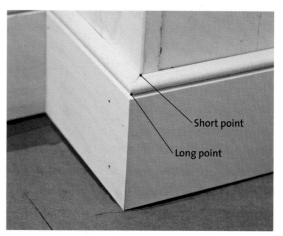

A miter has both a *long point* (the pointed tip) and a *short point* (the angled heel), terms that prove essential for communicating with other carpenters about the joint. The terms, abbreviated LP and SP, respectively, also serve as shorthand for writing out a cut list.

piece receives the same cut, but with the opposite miter angle. Glue and a couple of carefully placed 4d finish nails complete the joint.

Coped joints

For inside corners, it's best to cut a coped joint. One side of the joint is a simple square cut, butted against the wall; the other side you cut to hug the profile of the first (see "Cutting coped joints" on p. 44).

The coped joint has two advantages. First, it minimizes the effect of wood shrinkage, because the first, square-cut piece—the one that runs past the joint and butts to the wall—can shrink all it wants without widening the space between the boards at the joint. With a simple miter cut, by comparison, both cut ends would be able to shrink away from the joint, so any gap created by shrinkage will be twice as large. Second, even when the boards do shrink and the joint opens up slightly, the eye will

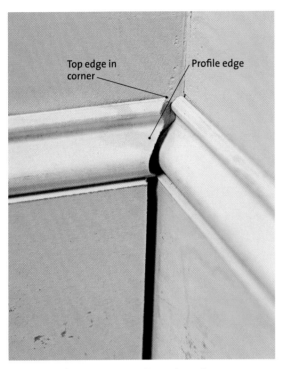

Every coped joint starts with one board cut square and butted into the corner. The end can be relieved to accommodate the buildup of plaster or mud that's common at the bottom of wall corners. The only part that will be seen on this end is the end of the top edge. The coped piece is cut to key with the profile on the underlying board.

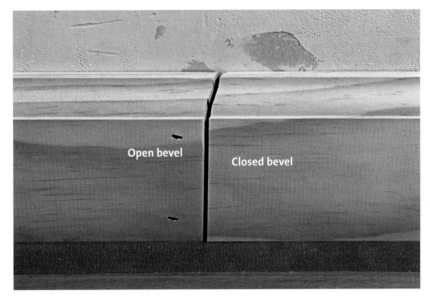

A scarf joint starts with a simple bevel cut on the end of one length. The long point of this first piece goes against the wall, creating an "open bevel." A second piece with a matching bevel is cut next. With this piece, the short point of the miter goes against the wall, effectively "closing" the bevel.

not detect any crack in a coped joint as readily as in a miter joint because there is wood right behind the gap, where the square-cut piece extends past the coped end of its mate. Cracks in a carefully coped joint are scarcely noticeable.

Scarf joints

The other important joint in baseboard work is a "scarf" or "lap" joint—the joint in the middle of a run of baseboard that you have to make if one piece of molding is not long enough to reach all the way between two corners. Scarf joints in baseboard are made with a beveled square cut. For small moldings, you can set

the molding upright against the miter saw's fence, swing the miter arm left or right (30° is a good bevel for scarfing baseboard, but some carpenters use 45°), and chop down through the board. If the molding is too large to stand up under the saw blade, you need a compound miter saw to cut the bevel. You have to lay the piece down flat on the saw, set the miter arm at 0°, set your 45° or 30° bevel on the saw's bevel setting, and chop down through your piece on the bevel angle.

A scarf joint requires two opposite bevels to match up: an "open bevel," with the newly cut wood facing away from the wall, and a "closed bevel," with the fresh cut facing into the wall.

Prepping for Baseboard

Baseboard, obviously, is applied on the floor—where dirt, grime, and debris collect. There's a tendency to jump in and get to work, which for most carpenters means cutting wood and shooting nails. But nothing is more maddening than starting to nail off a nice long run of baseboard only to find you've trapped an errant drywall screw or a glob of mud behind your new work.

Start with a good vacuuming. It's especially important to get down and clean along the floor perimeter. Take a crevice tool and dig into that crack between the drywall and the ends of the floorboards; that's where lumps of drywall mud, screws, nails, and trash are hiding.

While prepping the area, take a close look at the wall base, the floor, and especially the corners, to see how straight and regular everything is. Wall bases and corners are awkward for drywall finishers to get into—if there's slop on the job, that's where it will show up. When in doubt, go ahead and stick a 2-ft. square into the corners and lay a 6-ft. level or straightedge against the walls to check for humps or dips.

Some carpenters carry a 6-in. Surform® wallboard plane—a sort of pocket cheese grater—for knocking down the high spots on drywall. Even better, especially for baseboard, is a stiff drywall knife or scraper. Simple but

effective, this tool can be handled like a large chisel to shave down high spots and plane them flat, leaving a clean, sharp edge that requires, at most, a minimal touch-up. Sharpen the edge on a grinder, so it can be used to shave the irregular spots smooth. Use the scraper in one hand and the nozzle of a shop vac in the other hand.

Baseboard Layout

There's no hard and fast rule about where to start laying baseboard, but it helps to approach the job with a defined strategy.

Production procedures

The first rule in increasing efficiency is to make sure you have enough material on-site at the beginning of the job. Having to run out for a few missing sticks will destroy any efficiencies you may have gained while running that trim in the house. Start by taking a close inventory of the material dropped off at the site (and take this opportunity to organize it and sticker it properly so it can acclimate to jobsite conditions, particularly if it has been dropped haphazardly on a damp garage slab, as is often the case). Document any shortfalls in inventory and send this in writing to the job supervisor. This will help in getting the material ordered. Also note the name of the model and neighborhood if you're working in a development. Oftentimes the takeoff is just wrong, particularly in a new model, and your accounting for the stock can help the builder get the quantities corrected.

For efficiency in running base stock throughout the house, measure as many runs as possible, cut those pieces all at once, and then install them. Start by identifying any outside corners, and plan to measure and cut

Step one on any baseboard job should be scraping down the wall with a stiff drywall knife to clean up drywall mud and check for under-driven screws that might interfere with the baseboard fitting tight to the wall.

these first. If it's a production job, work with a helper. Have that helper rough cut the boards to length, and lay them around the room as you mark out the studs on the floor. The helper should proceed through the whole house, as you follow cutting the baseboard to fit and tacking in place. When the helper is done, set them up nailing off the runs and filling the nail holes in preparation for paint.

Taking accurate measurements

Measuring accurately requires focus and an orderly workflow. While every room is slightly different, some guidelines will help make the work flow smoothly and improve accuracy.

As a rule, keep your tape measure in its pouch and instead mark the board directly off the wall whenever possible. For outside corners, for example, butt one end hard to the wall in one corner and let it run past the outside corner on the other. Then mark the short point of the bevel for the outside corner directly off the wall. Keep in mind that it's always easier to have the opposite end of an

Where Baseboard Meets Door

Before running baseboard, figure out what trim stock you're going to run for door casing (if that hasn't been defined already). Primarily, you want to make sure that the baseboard doesn't project farther from the wall than the door casing. Visually, three-piece molding works best when teamed up with heavy door casings—otherwise, the deeper profiles of the cap and shoe moldings tend to terminate awkwardly in fussy, labor-intensive returns or simple, inelegant snubbed-off ends.

outside corner abut the wall, rather than butt another piece of baseboard. This allows for some adjustment in length in case the outside corner bevel needs adjustment to fit precisely.

Next, measure all the pieces that have square cuts on both ends, bending the tape into the corner. For long runs, cut the board a fat $\frac{1}{16}$ in. long. This way, the board will have to be bowed slightly to fit into place, but it can be easily pushed against the wall (or "snapped into place," as is often said) for a snug fit.

To speed measurements, butt one end hard to the wall in one corner and mark the length directly off the wall (left). This won't work for a space enclosed by end walls, however, so keep a tape on hand (above).

A long run of baseboard between two walls should be cut slightly more than 1/16 in. long (but not more than 1/8 in. long). The board will have to be bowed slightly to fit into place, but it can be easily pushed against the wall for a snug fit.

To get an accurate measurement at an inside corner, trace the profile of the baseboard with a piece of scrap to represent the board that butts into the corner (right). Now withdraw the scrap and measure to the profile line (below). This gives you a more definitive point than you can get trying to fold the tape measure into the corner.

Don't cut it too long, however, or you may crack the drywall tape in the corner when the piece is pushed into place.

To measure the pieces that butt into these fixed lengths (prior to cutting and installing them), hold a scrap of baseboard in the corner, and trace its profile onto the wall. Then measure to the pencil line of the profile. Note that if you are coping the inside corner (see "Cutting coped joints" on p. 44), the pencil line on the wall will be the short point for the cope.

Take care during this initial measuring phase to check the tilt of the baseboard. If the wall is out of plumb or there is a heavy buildup of drywall mud at the base of a corner joint, the baseboard will tip back. Unless you consider this, you may end up with an ugly gap in the corners. While you're measuring in old houses, make it a habit to check for square between the floor and the wall with your Speed Square. If the base is more than 1/8 in. out of plumb, make a note to cut the pieces that butt into the corners at a slight angle.

Some pieces you can't measure precisely until after other pieces are installed. A common example is a piece that gets coped on one end and butts into a door casing on the other.

Take Note • The long point measurement for the reverse bevel on a cope is the length of the actual wall. The short point measurement, which you actually mark on the face of the board, is 3/4 in. shorter than this (when using standard 1x stock).

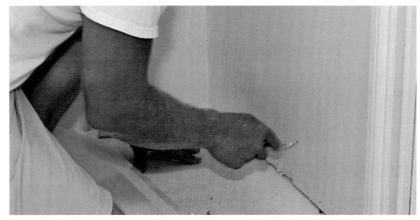

To verify the stud layout and establish solid nailing for your baseboard, first knock on the wall with the handle of an awl and then push the tip through the drywall. Make sure test holes fall below the top edge of the baseboard so they will be covered.

In this case, cut the cope first, leaving the end a ½ in. long, and then come back later to mark the cut line for the butt end using a scrap piece of the door casing.

Establish the stud layout While you're on the floor measuring, take the opportunity to mark the stud layout. (In baseboard work, the real time killer is getting up and down, so as a rule, plan to do as much on the floor as you can in one area before you get up.) In a drywalled interior, the easiest way to find the stud layout is by rapping on it with the handle of an awl. When you think you hear it, push the tip of the awl through the drywall to make sure you've found solid nailing. Be sure you make your test hole where it will be covered by the baseboard. Studs near outlets are the easiest to find. When you've found one stud, you can mark out the remaining studs on a 16-in. layout, checking every other one with the awl.

Finding the stud layout is a lot easier in a newly drywalled interior than it is in an old house with plaster-and-lath walls. The plaster is denser so it's harder to discern the difference between the cavity and the stud; the stud layout is more likely to be irregular; and when you push the awl into the wall, it's difficult to distinguish between a lath and a stud. In this case, establish a hole with the awl that's

obviously between two pieces of lath. The lath usually runs parallel to the floor, so this height should be consistent around the room (but be forewarned that the lath heights can shift when a piece breaks on a stud; pay attention when you demolish old plaster walls and you'll begin to get a feel for how it was done). Then do your best to establish one stud. It may take a lot of trial and error, and you may end up with numerous holes in the wall before you find one. Pull a tape to mark the remaining ones, but don't take the stud layout for granted. Test every one so you're sure. Many old houses were framed by eye because the carpenters didn't have to worry about stud layouts breaking perfectly on the drywall and sheathing layout.

A wall outlet will tell you where a stud falls (check inside the box by removing the cover plate if in doubt). With one stud location known, you can mark out the remaining ones on a 16-in. layout, checking periodically with the awl to make sure the framing layout is consistent.

Watch Out for Pipes!

A word of caution: Make sure you have a reasonable idea of what's in the walls when you're marking the stud layout for baseboard. If you're installing baseboard on the other side of a bathroom wall, find out where the pipes are, and mark this so you can avoid causing a leak. If you're uncertain where the plumbing layout falls, look around in the basement or poke your head into the crawlspace. On a slab home, you may have to walk the first and second floors, identifying the water fixtures, and then make your best approximation of where the water risers come up.

Order of installation

When planning your strategy, think out the order of installation before you begin. First look for any box-outs—a chimney, a plumbing chase, or a jog in the wall. In the overall scheme of a room, it helps to cut the baseboard that goes around these first. It's easier to get the outside miter or bullnose right if you don't also have to worry about coping an inside corner at the wall on the same piece. That said, once the outside corner fits, you might have to cope the opposite end.

Ideally, each run of baseboard between inside corners has a cope on one end and a square cut on the other. This is dictated by the order in which you install the pieces of baseboard, which itself depends on where you start.

As a rule of thumb, start on the wall opposite the main entryway to the room—the place that will likely get the most traffic. Most rooms have one primary door where people will most commonly enter or pause to look into the space. The idea is that, from the vantage point in this place in the room, the coped joints should still look good even if the wood shrinks or the walls move. If a coped joint is viewed at an oblique angle, the viewer will look right past the open joint, not straight into a gap if the joint should open up. This is a primary reason to cope a joint in the first place.

Baseboard Joinery

Laying baseboard is traditionally the place for new trim carpenters to get their chops, literally. Except for restoration or remodeling work in crooked old houses, most baseboard won't pose real problems, and unless the clients get down on their hands and knees, any imperfections in the work at least won't be in their face.

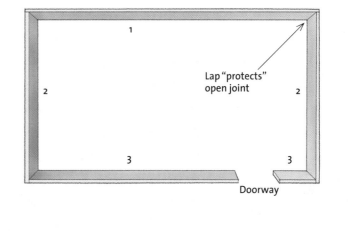

Installation Strategy

There is no absolute order of installation, but a safe strategy is to start on the wall opposite the door that's used the most often. This way, occupants won't be looking into an open joint if the wood shrinks back.

Lap "protects" open joint

Doorway

Viewed at an angle, a coped joint looks acceptable, **whether it is open or not.**

Inside corners

Never miter inside corners. Even in a new house, most corners are hardly ever exactly 90° because of the buildup of drywall mud, so an inside miter will be surprisingly difficult to make look right from the start. But inside miters are also vulnerable to shrinkage and building movement, so they will look even worse six months after you leave the job. Instead, join inside corners with a butt joint (for flat stock) or coped (for profiled stock).

Cutting butt joints

Ordinarily, butt joints are a no-brainer: These are straight, square cuts across the board. Set the miter saw table at 90°, and the bevel at 0°, and chop away. Unless your chop saw just fell off the tailgate of your truck, there should be no trouble.

A simple butt joint starts with a "square" cut, placed in the corner, with a second square cut butting it.

A very slight bevel on the square cut that goes into a corner will provide some relief if there is a buildup of drywall mud in the corner. To relieve the end, prop up the end of the board on the miter saw. This technique is quicker and just as reliable as adjusting the bevel setting on the saw.

If there is a big buildup of drywall mud in the corner, it's usually easier to backcut the piece that dies into the corner than to excavate the mud. A 1° or 2° bevel is often sufficient. Since it's not a precise angle, the fastest way to make this cut is by propping up the end of board with a piece of scrap wood.

Cutting coped joints

Although it requires some practice to execute, a coped joint is simple in concept. One side of the joint is a simple square cut that butts to the wall, with the covering piece sculpted to match, hugging the profile of the first piece. Coped joints are often viewed as fussy to make, but they're easier than inexperienced carpenters make them out to be. And the standard of visual perfection they make possible is well worth the effort.

The real beauty of a coped joint is that when the wood moves (as it will from seasonal moisture changes), the joint will still look good. A cope might shrink back a little, but the profile of the board behind the coped edge can still be seen. You don't ever see an open void, so any gaps are less noticeable. In our mind, coped joints are essential to high-quality trim work.

Start with a reverse bevel To execute a cope, first cut the end on the angle that bisects your corner (45°, in the case of a square corner). In this case, the long point is at the back. The short point of the bevel reveals the outline of the curve you must trace to make the pieces match.

Cut this reverse bevel a fat 1/16 in. long. This will give you a little extra if you wander slightly over the edge of the pencil line that defines the profiled edge with your coping saw, and the resulting sharp knife-edge will bite into the meeting piece when it's "snapped" into place.

Follow the profile Trace the profiled edge that is revealed by the reverse bevel by running the side of a pencil lead along it. The darkened edge will help you see the line when following it with a coping saw. Next, cut along that curve, using the coping saw. Hold the saw at the correct angle by imagining this saw as the piece of wood that will meet the coped joint in the corner.

Keep in mind that you want to remove all of the wood beyond the profile edge so the matching piece can slide right past mating perfectly. It can be overcut (or "backcut") behind the profile. In fact, this is desirable, so the profiled edge forms a sort of knife-edge to intersect tightly to the underlying piece.

Use a delicate touch to work the coping saw. There's no need to force it roughly through

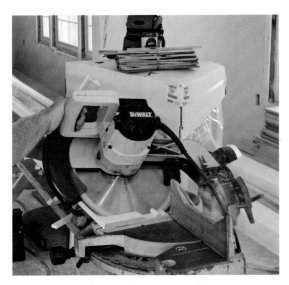

The first step when coping baseboard is to cut an open bevel (also called a reverse bevel) on the end of the baseboard to reveal the profile.

Trace the profile with a pencil **to darken the edge.**

Follow the profile with a coping saw. While the saw can turn a corner, it will be necessary to start the cut at several places and come at the profile from different directions.

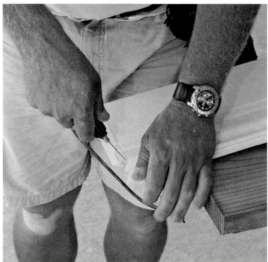

Take Note • Be extra careful once you've coped the end of a piece of MDF baseboard. The leading edge is thin—and will be fragile no matter what material you're using—but with MDF, a whisper can cause the fine edge to crumble or flake.

Take Note • To get the cutting angle right for a coped joint, some carpenters draw a square line on the bottom edge of the baseboard. That's only necessary if you're coping the entire cut by hand, but most carpenters prefer to use some sort of power to speed the job along.

the cut. Rely on a sharp blade and a smooth stroke to do all the work. Also remember that the blade is kept in tension by cutting on the pull stroke, so relax a bit when you push the blade back up. No cutting action is taking place on this return stroke. Most blades snap when they're pushed too hard and they kink.

Cut the flat If you're only coping a small base cap, the coping saw will do it all. But on a one-piece baseboard, the final step is to cut the long flat run. This can be done relatively quickly with a handsaw. Or for a precision straight cut (preferred with hardwood base stock), you can cut partway with the miter saw and just finish off the end of that cut with the handsaw.

Fine-tune Inevitably, the first pass with the saw will leave a few bumps that prevent the "knife edge" along the profile from meeting crisply with the mating piece. Check the fit with a scrap of the same stock. The corners in the profile may need to be cleaned up with a utility knife and the curves and flats eased back with sandpaper.

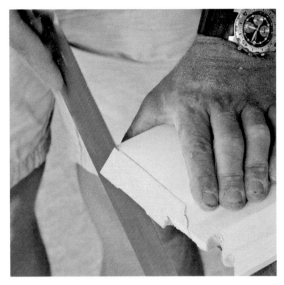

Once the profile is cut, the straight portion of the baseboard can be cut out quickly with a handsaw.

The straight section of baseboard can also be substantially cut out with a miter saw (center), leaving only a small portion to remove with a handsaw (above).

To fine-tune a coped joint, test-fit the sculpted (coped) end against a piece of scrap (top). Carve out any discrepancies you find by hand using a utility knife and a piece of sandpaper (above).

Cutting outside miters

The baseboard wrapping an outside corner will most often be mitered. But in most houses, a hard corner is rarely a perfect 90°. It's worth checking with a framing square. If it's off, find the exact bevel angle by drawing the corner right on the floor using scrap baseboard stock

Beaded Baseboard Options

Beaded baseboard can be coped, and for an out-of-square inside corner, it's the most forgiving joint. However, the tight curve on the bead is hard to navigate with a coping saw. If the inside corner is square, the best option is to use a modified miter joint. In this case, the flat part of the baseboard can be square cut to minimize the effect of wood shrinkage, which would open up if the entire joint were mitered. The only part actually mitered is the top bead. The left side was cut with a handsaw and the other side as described below.

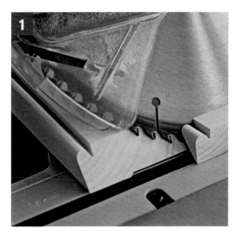

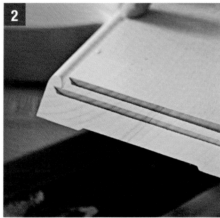

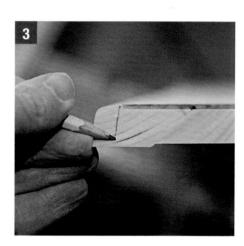

1 Start by cutting a reverse bevel, just as if you were mitering the whole joint or starting a coped joint.

2 Adjust the saw to cut straight (no bevel), and cut the butt joint through the flat section of the baseboard, stopping the cut at the bead. (If the joint is to be coped, a second straight cut can be made, extending into the bead.)

3 Draw a straight line down the face of the bevel, transferring the point at the base of the bead to the long point of the bevel. In this case, a straight line is "scribed" by using the middle finger to guide the point of the pencil at a consistent (parallel) distance from the top edge.

4 Complete the cut with a coping saw or other handsaw. The end of the straight cut made with the miter saw will also need to be completed with a handsaw, to remove the material left by the curved saw blade.

5 The completed joint looks like a miter, but will be much more dimensionally stable.

as a template, following the procedure outlined in the sidebar on p. 50.

Miter joints can be finicky, but they aren't that difficult to fix. If the joint is tight at the back or at the front, a few strokes of the block plane may be all it takes to bring the two faces into full contact. If the tip of one face stands a little proud, the block plane or even a piece of sandpaper or emery board may serve to flush up the edge.

Bullnose corners, which are increasingly common with the advent of drywall accessories that make these easier to execute, are a bit more involved than a miter (see the sidebar on p. 53).

Cutting scarf joints

Scarf joints are used to join two boards in the middle of a run of molding, when one piece won't make the whole distance. We'll tell you how to cut scarf joints, but if at all possible, we recommend you try to avoid them. They not only take time to cut, but it can also be difficult to make a scarf joint disappear. If the board is at all cupped or the wall is anything but totally flat, the joint will stay visible without a lot of laborious sanding. And there is always the likely chance that the material will shrink or the building move around it, causing the paint over the joint to crack.

A simple scarf joint consists of an open bevel (typically a 45° or 30° cut), covered by a matching closed bevel on the mating piece. It's a simple joint: Cut one piece with the long point against the wall. The break should occur over a stud, so you have good nailing to secure it. Then measure to the short point of that cut (the long point of the best piece) and cut that without adjusting the saw. For both bevel cuts, the boards are cut with the back on the miter

saw table. By not adjusting the saw, you eliminate the chance of cutting matching bevels that are slightly off. You need an accurate saw, and when you're cutting each bevel, hold the board firmly to the table and the fence—any small creep can throw the cut out of whack.

Scarf joints typically appear in the middle of a wall, where they're often in plain sight. So the scarf is one joint that you want to make sure does not open up when the wood dries and shrinks. It's best to glue it, and then bury the outside ends of the run under a cope in the corners. That way, any shrinkage in the board will show up in the corners behind the cope rather than declare itself at the center joint.

To make a scarf joint, start by cutting an open bevel. In this case, the cut is about to be made on the right-hand end of a piece of the board.

Marking Uneven Outside Miters

Outside corners of rooms rarely end up being perfect 90° angles. Most often, the outside miter must be cut at an angle slightly greater or less than 45°. To find the exact angle, draw the corner on the floor using scrap baseboard stock as a template, as follows:

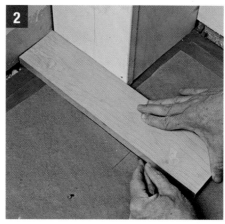

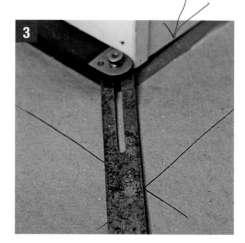

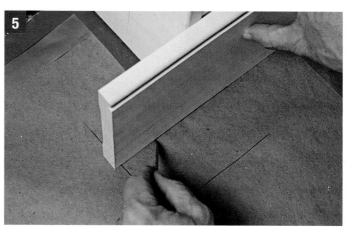

1 Hold a scrap of baseboard against the wall, letting it run past the corner. Draw a line on the floor along the bottom edge to mark the outside face of the baseboard.

2 Do this on both sides of the corner so that the two lines intersect.

3 The intersection of the lines establishes a corner that runs parallel to the outside corner. Use a bevel square to establish the angle of the bevel cut.

4 Use this angle to set your saw by laying it on the miter table and reading the angle when the saw blade is parallel to the blade of the bevel gauge. The angle on the miter table will give you the angle for your bevel setting.

5 Position the piece of baseboard stock you intend to cut with the end running long, past the outside corner on the wall. Mark the front edge of this board on the floor.

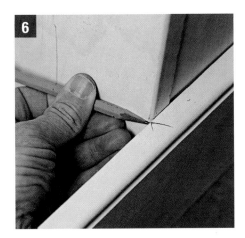

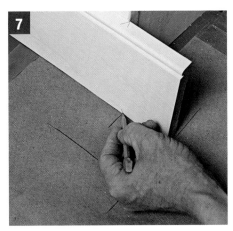

6 While this board is in place, mark the short point off the wall to establish the length on this side of your corner.

7 Then position the opposing piece of baseboard stock and mark the long point of your bevel cut off the mark you made on the floor. Also mark the short point of the bevel where the board intersects the wall (shown as a caret on the top edge of the baseboard).

8 You're now ready to cut the outside corner: Start by drawing a reference line for the long point of the bevel across the face of the board. This gives a positive indication of the exact outside corner as you cut.

9 Cut the bevel using the bevel setting you found with the bevel gauge, and make sure the blade doesn't cut past the caret you marked off the wall corner on the top edge of the board.

10 The finished joint.

Secure the board to the wall over a stud for solid nailing. **Keep the nails away from the bevel, so you leave unobstructed nailing for closing the bevel with the matching piece.**

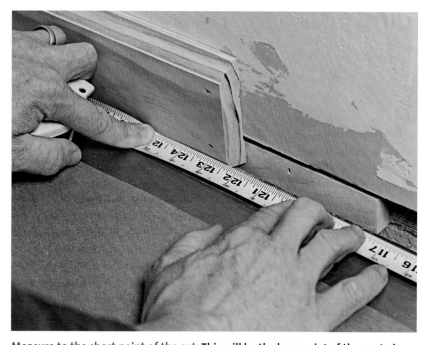

Measure to the short point of the cut. This will be the long point of the next piece.

Miter returns

Occasionally, it's necessary to terminate a run of baseboard, using a miter return to trim out the profiles neatly, rather than simply chopping the board and treating the end grain. A miter return does just that—it turns the corner and dies into the wall.

To execute the return, cut a bevel on the end of the board, with the short point against

Without adjusting the saw, cut the closed bevel. This time the cut is made on the left–hand end of the baseboard: same saw setting, different end.

Close the bevel using glue to join the end grain of the two scarfed pieces and nails to secure the joint.

Bullnose Corners

"Bullnose" drywall corners, made by installing a specialty rounded corner bead at wall intersections, add a touch of style to rooms, but they create a new wrinkle for the baseboard trim carpenter. To wrap a bullnose corner with baseboard, use small segments, one mitered to the next. For a typical 3/4-in.-radius bullnose, a small, center segment just 3/4 to 7/8 in. from short point to short point will do the trick. Each end of this small piece must be cut at a 22 1/2 ° bevel where it joins to the long baseboard runs on either side of the corner.

The only tricky part of this detail is getting accurate measurements, since there is no one point on the wall that tells you where the short point of each miter goes. Finish carpenter Smokey Saduk starts by mocking up a corner with baseboard scraps and uses this same mockup for all the bullnose corners in the house. The final length of the baseboard on each side of the corner is established by the short points of the 22 1/2 ° miters on this mockup.

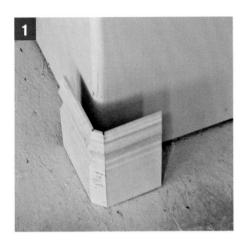

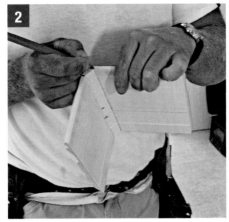

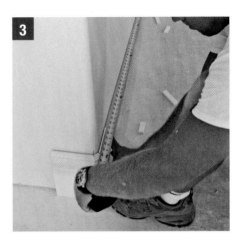

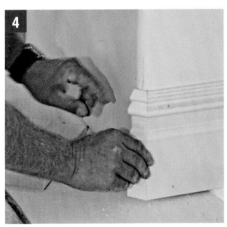

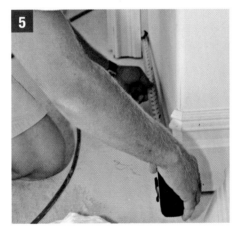

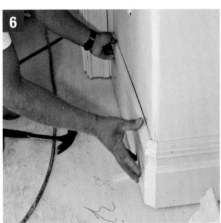

1 | The corner mockup.

2 | Mark the short points of the 22½° miters on the mockup in bold.

3 | Use the mockup to measure the length of one sidepiece.

4 | Cut and install the first length, and then the centerpiece.

5 | Measure the length for the third piece to the long point on the centerpiece.

6 | Adjust the cut if necessary until it fits perfectly.

the wall and the long point on the face of the baseboard. This bevel will be "closed" by a small piece with a matching bevel that's only as long as the material is wide. This means that the piece is small, and there is a strong chance that the tooth of the miter saw can kick it into oblivion (or worse, fling it at an unwary person standing nearby). You can do a couple things to help avoid this.

First, never make a bevel cut on this tiny return piece with the board standing vertically. The blade is more likely to fling the offcut when it falls over (and in this case, it's the so-called offcut that you want to keep). Always use the bevel cut on a compound miter saw.

Second, clamp a narrow board against the fence that spans the blade. Then, chop down, but when the blade is all the way through the cut, release the trigger and don't lift the blade until it stops rotating. Usually, the offcut is flung into outer space when a tooth catches it as the blade is being lifted out of the cut.

Fastening Baseboard

Most baseboard can be nailed off with 2½-in.-long (8d) nails. Step up to 10d nails for securing 5/4 stock. Standard 1x4, one-piece stock should be fastened with one nail high at each stud, and one into the bottom plate.

For taller baseboard (wider than 6 in.), use three nails if you're working with MDF or MDO stock—the first in the middle of the board, the second at the top edge and a third into the bottom plate. If you're using wide, dimensional lumber, however, plan on having a shoe molding, and in this case forgo the third nail in the bottom plate and let the shoe mold pin the lower edge in place. This will reduce

the chances that wide solid stock may split with dimensional changes.

Outside miters should be secured with yellow glue, or a smear of fresh construction adhesive. Heavy stock can be pinned just to the corner studs, but a few brads driven across the joint may help to suck it together.

Most base cap and shoe molding can be nailed off with 1¼-in.-long (3d) or 1½-in.-long (4d) nails. Nail the base cap into the top edge of the baseboard, not into the wall. This will allow the base cap to "float" with the baseboard as it changes dimension with the seasons, and if the baseboard shrinks, it won't crack the paint between the baseboard and the base cap. Also nail the shoe molding to the baseboard. This will not only prevent an unsightly crack in the paint, but the primary

A 2- to 2½-in.-long nail works for most 1x baseboard. For 5x4 stock, upsize to a longer 3-in. nail.

Making a Miter Return

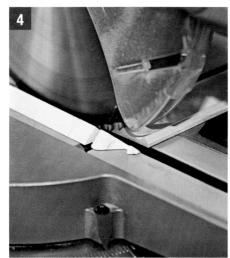

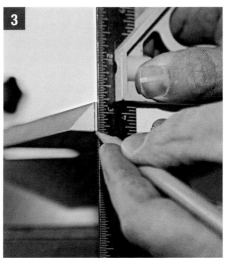

1 | Fasten the baseboard to the wall with the short point of the bevel against the wall.

2 | To make the small miter return, first cut an outside miter. In this case, the short point of the bevel is on the back of the board.

3 | Use a square to transfer this point to the front of the board.

4 | Cut the small return with no bevel setting, plunging straight down. To prevent the saw from kicking this delicate piece into the saw, hold the saw head down when you release the trigger, and don't bring it up until the blade stops.

5 | Fit the small return in the triangular void between the long point of the bevel and the wall.

When in Doubt, Draw It Out

Mathematically minded carpenters may be inclined to figure out all the angles for a tricky run of baseboard with pen and paper. But that's not always the easiest method for veteran carpenters. John Teti of Ocean City, New Jersey, handles a complicated run of base cap running down a set of stairs by drawing the pieces on the wall and test fitting each miter. Accurate measurements can be measured directly off the wall. The process of test fitting each miter can be painstaking, but the results are reliable.

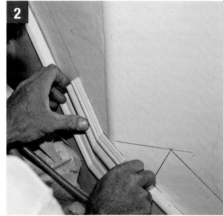

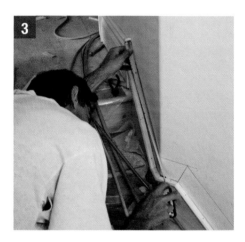

1 Tracing the outline of the baseboard on the wall, and drawing a line to mark the intersection points gives you a starting point to make approximate test cuts on small scraps.

2 Holding the test pieces in place, you can physically check your miter and bevel for a good fit.

3 With the angle and bevel dialed in, measure to your traced mark to find the length for the final piece.

4 One after another, each joint must be test-fit in a careful trial-and-error process.

5 The result of piece-by-piece cutting and fitting is a unique trim solution for a specific problem. You can find examples like this in almost any house, modern or historic; trim carpenters have been solving this kind of puzzle since the invention of the hammer and saw.

Cross nailing an outside miter will help keep it closed as the wood shrinks and swells in width. Be sure to align the nailer straight (parallel with one wall and perpendicular to the other), so the brad doesn't blow out the face.

purpose of this molding is to cover the gap between the perimeter of a wood floor and the wall. The floorboards must be allowed to shrink and swell independently of the trim work, and the shoe mold allows for a slip joint between the two materials.

Carpeted rooms, on the other hand, don't always get a shoe molding unless it's used to match the trim in the rest of the house. When carpet will be installed, it's a good practice to install the baseboard on temporary ½-in. blocks placed on the subfloor. This will allow the carpet installers to tuck the pad and carpet under the baseboard.

Almost without exception, professional carpenters have switched from hand nailing to air nailing for trim installations. Besides being faster, most carpenters agree that pneumatic nails hold better, doesn't bang the pieces apart, and automatically sets the nail heads.

A note about framing

No discussion of fastening trim is complete without a few comments on framing. If you

Nailing Baseboard

Most 1x baseboard can be nailed off with 2½-in. (8d) nails. Shoe molding base cap should be secured with smaller nails into the baseboard only so it will move with it as it shrinks and swells.

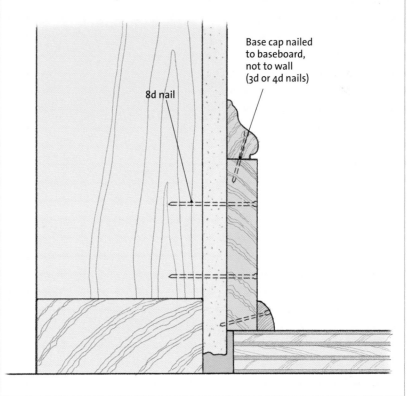

8d nail

Base cap nailed to baseboard, not to wall (3d or 4d nails)

The Rake Problem

When an angled molding intersects with
a horizontal molding, you'll likely run into a
classic "rake problem." There's no way the
profile of the horizontal base cap will line up
with the profile of the sloped run if it was
joined with a miter. In the old days, carpenters
facing this problem with crown molding on
the rake of a roof used two different molding
profiles to get the profiles to line up correctly.
Short of having a complimentary base cap
milled, it's best to insert a stop block here
to terminate each run and create a graceful,
yet practical transition.

"Carpet blocks" raise
the baseboard up ¹/₂ in.,
which allows room for
the carpet to be tucked
underneath.

Blocking for Trim

For standard 2¹/₂-in. door casing, the framing around the door opening still leaves a little "meat" for the end of the baseboard. If the casing gets much bigger, however, the end of the baseboard may need blocking.

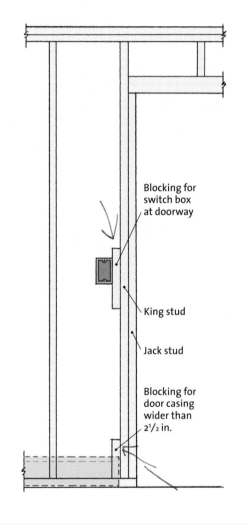

Blocking for switch box at doorway

King stud

Jack stud

Blocking for door casing wider than 2¹/₂ in.

Hand Nailing Tips

While air nailing works best, if you do end up having to hand nail baseboard or other trim, here are a few tips for avoiding the heartache precipitated by splitting wood:

- In softwood, blunt the nails before driving them by hitting them with a hammer on a hard surface. A sharp nail tip separates wood fibers, sometimes causing wood to split. Blunt nail ends punch through and cut fibers, which helps prevent splitting.

- A word of caution: Some carpenters like to use a little wax to ease the friction as the nail is driven home. While this helps the nail slip in, it's a disaster for the finish. Use caution on stain-grade work. The wax will seal the wood and cause it to take stain differently than the wood around it, leading to a blotchy job.

- In hardwoods, or for any nails located near the ends of pieces, pre-drilling is usually necessary. Use a drill bit slightly smaller than the nail diameter.

nail trim to walls, you're going to notice framing flaws. In particular, standard stud framing does not always provide you with solid wood behind the wall that will give your nails good holding power. "Good nailing"—plenty of solid lumber behind the walls for trim nails

to sink into—is one of the hallmarks of good framing.

For baseboard installations, there's one spot in particular where bad nailing is a frequent problem: the area next to the door casing. Typical door openings are framed with one "jack" stud and one "king" or "trimmer" stud on either side of the opening—that's it. If the door gets 4-in.-wide casing, the trim is already out past the "meat" of the doorframe. That means baseboard ends have nothing but drywall to attach to, above the wall plate. And even the wall plate may not offer much: its 1½-in. thickness is likely to be at least half obscured by a ¾-in.-thick hardwood floor, and

When butting wide casing, baseboard may not have solid nailing behind the ends. **One solution is to use a plate joiner to cut a biscuit that holds the end fast.**

a scant ¼ in. from the edge of your baseboard is not where you want to be placing your nails.

There are a couple solutions: With tall baseboard, consider using a plate joiner to place a biscuit between the end of the baseboard and the edge of the door casing. A second option is to rely on adhesive on the back of the baseboard, and at the butt joint between baseboard and door casing. A snug fit and a few judiciously placed toenails at the end of the baseboard into the casing help to hold the baseboard tight while the glue sets up.

But the easiest solution for the trim carpenter is to have solid blocking between each door opening frame and the nearest flanking studs—a framing detail that's high on a trim carpenter's wish list for the framing crew. It's an easy pick-up item for a carpenter's helper on the framing crew, and it will certainly save time and boost quality on the trim job.

62 | Window
Trim
Toolkit

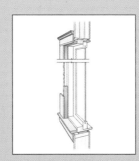

65 | Prepping
the Window

67 | Installing
the Stool

76 | Installing
Jamb
Extensions

81 | Installing
Window
Casings

85 | Installing
the Apron

Trimming Out Windows

Every house has windows—many windows—and they all need trim. Window trim's basic function is to bridge the gap between the rough opening and the window jamb. But the trim also helps to define the window's shape, add visual interest, and may give the window frame a sense of weight. At the low-end of the housing market, window trim has devolved into nothing more than a picture frame of flimsy "clam shell" molding tacked onto the jamb and the wall. That's too bad—even a low-cost window in an affordable home deserves more thought and a little care. People will look through that opening for decades.

Whether basic or upscale, window trim tends to be a good money maker for the finish carpenter. The work is easy to organize and to approach in a systematic way, the techniques are not too hard to master, and the carpenter's skills improve with practice. Once you hit your rhythm, you can efficiently trim out window after window, adding significant value to the house with each unit you complete. In this chapter, we'll look at a typical straightforward trim-out on a basic window unit, with sill, jamb extensions, casing, and apron.

Whether the window trim-out is simple or complicated, you'll always find that it's more efficient to mark your trim pieces

One of the key efficiencies in trimming out a window is to mark trim pieces directly from the window itself rather than use a tape measure. Here, Smokey Saduk is marking the length of the apron below the window stool.

directly from the window itself. Don't throw your tape measure away, of course, but always look for ways to avoid using it. Every length and every angle can be measured more accurately and marked more efficiently just by holding the pieces where they go.

Window Trim Toolkit

As with any trim job, a miter saw, a table-saw, and a nailer are indispensable tools (see Chapter 1). However, a number of additional tools will make the job of trimming a window much easier.

Framing square

Ideally, all window units should be square before you apply the trim. Use a framing square on the inside of a jamb to check. You need the legs of the square to be long enough to get an accurate reading. A little 6-in. Speed Square is not going to tell you if the center of the jambs is bowed inward.

Tri-square

On the other hand, a small 6-in. tri-square will come in handy for marking reveals: adjust the blade length to match the desired reveal. Then hold the square in place on the jamb and mark the end of it with a pencil. Some carpenters like to file a tiny notch right at the centerline of the blade at one end, which holds the tip of a pencil securely while you run the square right done the edge of a board. The result is a line that runs parallel to the board's edge—a trick that works well for laying out the notch of a window stool or establishing any parallel reference line. Others prefer to make a "reveal block" for marking the reveals on window and door trim.

Holding a pencil at the end of the blade of a small tri-square allows you to transfer any line that runs parallel to the board's edge. This technique can be used to lay out the notch on each end of a window stool, mark the reveal on casing, or establish a line parallel to one edge for applying profiled trim on a built-up casing.

Reveal Block

To mark the reveal for casing, carpenter Smokey Saduk relies on a simple reveal block—a jig made with two blocks screwed or glued together, with one block sticking past the other by the amount of the reveal. The two blocks form a step that can be placed right on the edge of the jambs and the edge marked off to establish the reveal.

Two square blocks of scrap screwed together make a handy pocket jig for marking reveals.

Handsaw

For trimming window shims flush to the wall, consider using a handsaw rather than trying to do this with a utility knife. The tool of choice for this is a Japanese handsaw that has longer teeth with no "set." A conventional "western" backsaw has teeth angled slightly to the left and right that will rake the wall and jamb when cutting the shims flush. In contrast, the teeth on a Japanese-style crosscut saw have sharply ground alternating bevels and a steep rake angle, so they sever the wood fibers, rather than tearing a narrow trough as a western backsaw does.

In general, Japanese handsaws are useful for occasional precision crosscuts, as well. They cut noticeably faster, owing to the thinner kerf and the steep bevel of the long teeth that slice rather than shred the wood fibers.

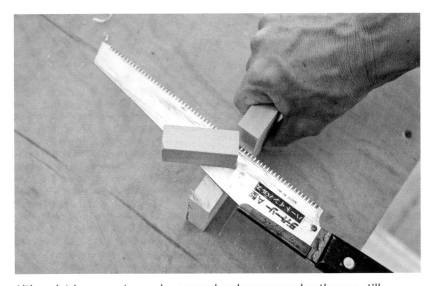

Although trim carpenters no longer use handsaws every day, they are still essential tools for occasional cuts, such as finishing the notch on a windowsill or cutting shims flush to the wall. This Japanese-style crosscut saw folds to carry easily in a tool belt until needed.

All Japanese saws cut on the pull stroke, so the blade is in tension as it is drawn through the cut. The blades can be made of thinner, harder steel since the blade doesn't need to be thick to resist bending. By contrast, western handsaws cut on the push stroke, so the blade must be thicker to resist bending, and made of softer steel, so it has a bit more flex to resist kinking if it binds on the push stroke.

Plate jointer

If you don't secure the facing pieces at the miter joints where the head casing meets the side casings, there's likely to be some movement there. You can simply glue the joint, or glue it and screw it, but the strongest method is to use a plate joiner.

All of the plate joiners on the market work in the same way. They are essentially small circular saws designed to cut a semicircular kerf into the edge of each piece to be joined. A football-shaped wood plate is inserted into the slots to produce an effective spline—sometimes called a "biscuit"—made of slightly compressed beech, which is crosshatched by

grooves to hold glue. This biscuit will swell in contact with any water-based glue to ensure a strong bond and a very tight joint. The grain of the spline lies at about 30° diagonal to its length, providing incredible resistance to shear. Trying to break such a joint usually breaks the surrounding wood rather than the spline itself. And biscuits serve to hold the faces of the pieces in the same plane as you make the joint, producing a nice, flush surface that will stay that way in service.

Router

A router is especially useful for finishing the edge of the windowsill. For this work, a small fixed-base router will suffice. Plunge routers are not necessary and are usually far too big and inconvenient for bullnose work. A D-handle

Most plate joiners on the market have a folding or a removable fence designed to rest on the top surface of the board and adjust for the thickness of the stock. However, a more efficient way to use these tools is to ignore the fence and reference everything off the bottom surface.

You don't need a plunge router with all the bells and whistles to bullnose the edge of windowsill stock. In fact, a simple fixed-base router is easier to handle. Instead, put your money into buying good bits that include carbide cutters and ball-bearing guides.

base, which has an on/off trigger, will provide better control than one with only a toggle switch.

Foam gun

Expanding foam is necessary for air-sealing windows, and it's also a useful "stabilizer" for setting preassembled jamb extensions (see the sidebar on p. 80). However, a foam gun allows you to buy the foam in larger quantities than purchasing single cans and affords far better control. The cheap plastic nozzles on single cans are usually incredibly finicky, and you pretty much have to do the work in one shot. Once the foam dries in the nozzle, the can is spent whether it's empty or not. A professional-grade stainless-steel gun cleans up easily, and the speed with which the pressurized foam comes out of the canister can be controlled.

Prepping the Window

Before you start to measure, cut, and nail the trim, take a close look at the window in its opening. Crosscheck the diagonal dimensions to see whether the unit was installed square; if it's out of whack, you know you'll have to fiddle with the joints accordingly. Be sure to operate the window to see if it works properly. Slightly out-of-square joints can be dealt with—you can make them look acceptable by fudging your casing reveals—but if the unit doesn't open and close, don't trim it out. If you didn't install it, bring it to the attention of the general contractor and move on until it's fixed. If you did install the window, it will be a pain to fix, but it will be ten times more time-consuming to fix after it's trimmed out on either side.

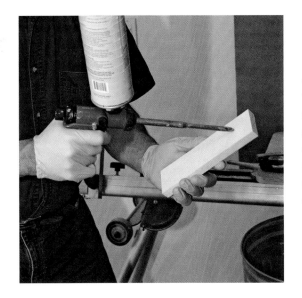

A professional-grade foam gun makes it far easier to control window sealant than individual cans sold with a screw-in plastic nozzle. Always check the flow on a scrap of wood, cardboard, or newspaper before hosing down the window.

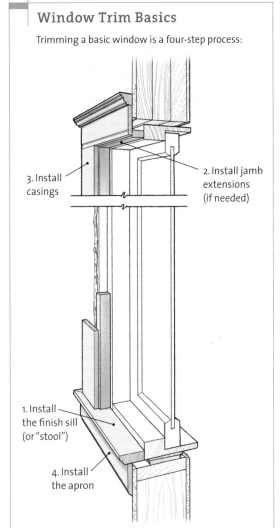

Window Trim Basics

Trimming a basic window is a four-step process:

3. Install casings

2. Install jamb extensions (if needed)

1. Install the finish sill (or "stool")

4. Install the apron

Airtight Window Installation

The gap between the rough opening and a window or door unit must always be sealed to stop airflow. The best way to do this is with a foam sealant that will expand to fill the contour of this narrow cavity. However, it's important to use a low-expanding foam sealant that is formulated for windows and doors. Ordinary foam sealants expand to 200% or more, which can exert pressure on the jamb to cause the window or door to bind.

Formulations for sealing windows and doors are sometimes called "nonexpanding foam," but this is a misnomer. Low-expanding foam sealants still expand to fill the cavity and cut off pathways for air leakage. However, the expansion drops off before the foam fully cures. The latest latex formulations work this way and have the added advantage of cleaning off with soap and water. Urethane foams, on the other hand, will stick and stay stuck to your skin, leaving a black stain that eventually wears off (this is why plastic gloves are usually provided with each can). If urethane foam gets on your clothes, consider it a permanent addition.

Too often, the "usual way" of sealing around a window or door is to stuff the cavity with fiberglass insulation, but fiberglass does not stop airflow very effectively. Some builders argue that the caulk under a window-nailing flange provides the air seal, while the fiberglass reduces heat flow. However, fiberglass is a poor insulator when crammed into the gap, and exterior caulk under the flange is not acceptable. Caulk may be used under the nailing flange on the sides and across the head as a secondary water stop. But, if the bottom flange is caulked, it can trap water that leaks through the window unit. Leave this flange unsealed so water can drain out.

Take Note • If a window has been shimmed too tightly, it's often possible to fix it by inserting a flat bar and levering out the jamb to free the shim. Then, using a chisel, try to split one shim out. This is often not pretty and can be extremely frustrating. After the top shim is out of the way, knock the jamb tight to the framing, using a wood block so you don't damage the window frame.

All windows must be air-sealed before trim is applied. That's not always a trim carpenter's job, but the window really should not be installed over an empty cavity. In many cases, it's to the trim carpenter's advantage to take on this job. It's too easy to do wrong.

Check the window for square first. On a large window, you may have to hold a straightedge along each jamb to gauge how straight the jamb is. It's easy for the window installer to overshim the window so the jamb bows at the center. To get the excess shims out, you may have to clip the nails by slipping a metal-cutting blade on a reciprocating saw between the jamb and the shims. Be conscious of the length of the blade and the depth of the wall studs. On a flanged window (or one that already has brick mold or other exterior casing installed), you may have to angle the reciprocating saw so the blade doesn't hit the flange.

If there are shims sticking out of the opening, cut them back carefully so they won't interfere with the casing. Don't just score the shims and snap them off, because they might splinter and fall out of the opening. Cut right through the shims with repeated strokes of your knife, or with a thin handsaw, so they'll stay intact—they are helping to hold the window firmly in place. If you're relying on a utility knife, this would be a good time to change your knife blade—it's hard to cut a shim cleanly with a dull blade.

Installing the Stool

A traditionally trimmed window includes a window stool—the bottom of the window opening that serves as the base, and may be wide enough to serve as a shelf for houseplants. As a convention, we prefer to call the interior trim the stool to distinguish it from the sill on the exterior that's sloped to shed water.

The stool butts directly to the bottom of the window frame. It projects into the room past the plane of the window casing and extends beyond the casing on each side. Typically, the stool is made from 5/4 stock: pine or poplar for paint-grade work, and hardwood like oak or maple for stain grade. Clear, quarter-sawn lumber is best: knots or flat grain can cause problems with fastening, as well as with painting or staining (see Appendix A, on pp. 215–238). Standard ¾-in. 1x stock is sometimes used, but because windowsills occasionally see rough service, we usually make them from solid wood, not MDF, which is more easily dinged and susceptible to incidental water damage.

Lumberyards stock 5/4 windowsill material with profiled edges in typical patterns, such as a simple bullnose or a classic ogee. But it's also easy enough to rout your own profile onto square-edged material. For a basic bullnose, the simplest way is to use a quarter-round roundover bit with a bearing that rests on the board edge, and to make two passes (one from each side). The quarter-round bit will typically leave a narrow flat strip in the center of the rounded curve, which you can quickly knock down and smooth out using 100-grit sandpaper.

A simple bullnose profile is easy to rout onto the edge of windowsill stock on-site. Here, Chuck Green uses a piloting bit to round over the top and bottom of a piece of 3/4-in. pine. The material slips into a sleeve in the bottom jamb of the windows, as will the extension jambs for these windows.

Establishing the Centerline of the Stool

A center mark on the window jamb and on the wall under the window helps with measuring and setting the sill and apron.

1 | Measure the window unit's width, divide by two, and mark that point on the window frame.

2 | Using a Speed Square, transfer the mark down to the rough sill . . .

3 | . . . and then onto the drywall below.

Take Note • Garnet sandpaper gives a smoother finish than most other abrasives because it is self-sharpening—the grit fractures as it abrades, offering new, sharp edges. It also stays much cooler than other sandpapers do, making it a good choice for power sanding when other abrasives might scorch the wood surface.

If you're routing your own material, you can rout the ends of the window stool—a fast way to treat each end. But, if you start with pre-routed stock, you'll typically have to cut and piece mitered returns, as shown on pp. 74–77.

Establishing the centerline

To lay out the stool, start by finding the center of the window frame and mark this on the bottom of the window units. Once the stool is cut, you'll use this mark on the window to position the stool. Because the window may not be centered exactly in the rough opening, you cannot use the sides of the rough opening as a reference point for accurately positioning the sill. Use your Speed Square to transfer that centerline mark down to the drywall beneath the window: You'll use the mark later to position the apron under the sill.

Figuring the length

The stool will extend past the casing on either side, a distance equal to the width of the cas-

Anatomy of a Window Stool

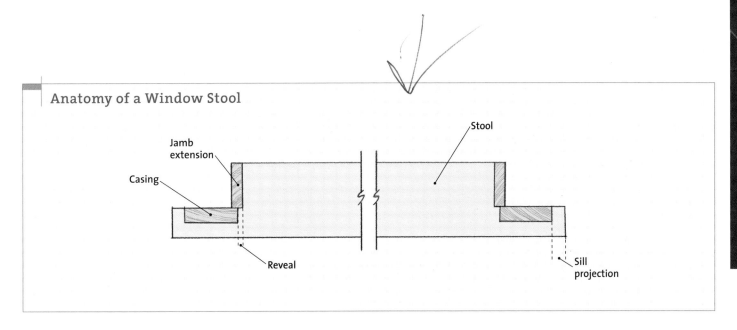

ing plus a small projection beyond the edge of the casing. A good rule of thumb is to make this projection equal to the distance the stool extends into the room past the face of the casings. So, if the stool extends 2 in. beyond the face of the casing, then the "ears" at the ends of the stool should project 2 in. past the outside edge of the casing. The finished length must also account for the reveal you have between the jamb and the casing, as shown in the drawing above.

If you are cutting a mitered return on each end of the stool, start with a piece of stock that is about a ¼ in. longer than the finish length, so you have a little extra for marking and cutting the end miters.

Cutting out for the ears

The stool needs to butt directly to the window frame and extend under the casing. If the window is flush to the wall, the stool piece will be a straight board. But, if the window does not fit flush to the inside wall, the window will need jamb extensions and the stool will have to be notched at each end so it can extend under the casing.

To lay out the notches, mark the centerline of your board and roughly position this over the centerline of the window. Hold the stool piece on the window centerline and mark it where the edges of the rough opening fall. Give yourself a little wiggle room here—this cut will end up buried under the ends of the jamb extensions so there's no reason to cut the notches tight to the rough opening.

Next, measure the distance from the face of the window frame to the edge of the sill piece: that's how much you have to take out of the corners of the piece. Transfer this measurement onto the board, and, using a tri-square (as shown in the bottom photo on p. 62), draw a line parallel to the sill edge. Or, if the stool is wide enough, you can use a Speed Square on the end. In either case, the two lines define the notch you have to remove from the corners of the stool piece.

You can make the parallel cut on the tablesaw. The square cut you'll make on the chop saw. For both cuts, you have to stop when you reach the corner, so be careful. For greatest accuracy, you could stop short and finish the cuts with a handsaw, but that's not necessary.

Measurements for a complex cut are best taken directly from the window onto the piece, where possible. Hold a piece of profiled 5/4 windowsill stock against the window opening and mark the edge of the window opening onto it (left). Then take a measurement for the depth of material to be removed so that the sill can slide into place against the window frame (right).

Minor overcutting at that corner will be buried underneath the casings. Now the piece can slide into the window's rough opening.

Making the end cuts

The next step is to cut the ends of the sill on a 45° angle, to provide for a mitered return into the wall at the sill ends. Mitering this termination serves two purposes: it shows side grain rather than end grain at the end of the board,

which makes for a nicer painted or stained finish and a cleaner look; and it also carries the front profile of the sill stock around to the side of the sill. The simplest way to lay out for the end cuts is to grab some scrap pieces of extension jamb and casing material, and trace their profiles onto the actual piece. Then you can trace the 45° cut mark onto the piece exactly where it will go—no measuring required.

With the top of the stool facing up, make the rip cut for the ears on the tablesaw, and then take the piece to the chop saw for the crosscuts, being careful to stop at the line. These stopped cuts are delicate to make on either tool. There's a risk of binding and kickback with the tablesaw, and some chop saws "jump" when you take your finger off the trigger. No matter how familiar you are with the tool, it's important to pay attention to what you're doing.

With the corners cut out, the windowsill slips into the window opening. At this point, the ears still sit about 3/16 in. out from the drywall, because the back edge of the piece needs to be profiled with a tongue that will match the factory groove on the window frame. When that's done, the ears will lie snug against the wall.

The Stool-to-Window Joint

Depending on the window unit, it may be necessary to rip the inside edge of the stool to match the window. For example, on the Andersen® windows shown here, the frame has a groove to match a corresponding tongue on factory-made extension jambs, so the back of the sill has to be profiled with a matching tongue. If the general contractor did not opt for the jamb extension kit, you may have to rip your own.

1 Use a scrap of the factory-applied jamb extension as a template to rip a matching tongue onto the back of the windowsill.

2 Set the tablesaw to the correct height for the first cut.

3 Use the scrap block to mark the location of the cut.

4 Two passes on the saw, adjusting the fence between cuts, remove enough material to outline the top of the tongue.

5 Holding the template block flush to the top face of the sill, mark the depth of the second cut.

Be sure to account for the width of the tongue when you rip the width of your stool in the first place, and carry it through when figuring the depth of the notches that define the ears. As the photos show, you can use a scrap piece of the factory jamb material as a template for marking the sill, and profile the sill edge to match with several passes on the tablesaw.

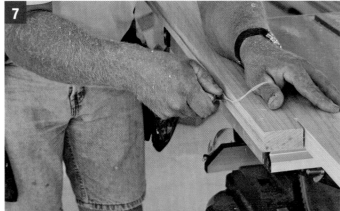

6 | Set the tablesaw for the height of the second cut and make one rip cut.

7 | Slice away the paper-thin edge of remaining wood using a drywall knife.

8 | Knock down the face of the tongue with a block plane for an easy fit.

9 | The piece drops snugly into place.

Cutting Stool Ends for Mitered Returns

Marking in place, using templates, and scribing allow precise layout for return cuts, eliminating the need to fuss with tape or remember any numbers.

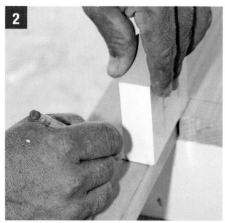

1 With the sill in place, trace the outline of the extension jamb onto it.

2 At the bench, place a scrap of window casing material onto the sill and trace its location.

3 With the Speed Square, trace a 45° diagonal from the outside edge of the sill to the corner of the window jamb.

4 Set the scrap of casing back onto the sill to check your marks.

5 Cut both ends of the piece on the 45° angle.

Fastening the stool

After cutting the 45° return, you can nail the stool in place. The actual return piece is easier to add once the stool is secured. Using solid blocks and shims, make sure the top of the stool is flush with the top of the window's bottom jamb. Square it to the window jamb, and attach it with long trim nails.

Making the stool returns

To make the mitered returns for the ends of the stool, start with a piece of stock long enough to cut comfortably on the chop saw—say 12 in. or 18 in. long. Rip the piece to the same thickness as the "ears" on your stool (See "Cutting the Stool Returns" on p. 77.) Then cut the matching 45° angle on the end of the piece, and cut

back square to make a triangle. In theory, the little triangle piece should mate up perfectly with the existing pointed end of the stool piece you've just nailed up. But, in practice, you may have to note any problems with the fit, and cut a second piece. For the sake of safety, don't try to shave down that little triangle using power equipment. If it doesn't fit, figure out what the problem is and cut a whole new piece.

Slide the butt end of some shim shingles between the blocks and the stool and mark the shims with a pencil before pulling them out to cut to length on the chop saw.

To help hold the stool up so its top face sits flush with the edge of the window frame, set the corner off cuts from the stool to serve as blocks, nailing them down with your trim nailer.

Slide the narrow ends of additional shims into the crack, and adjust the shims until the stool sits flat and square in position.

Shoot finish nails down through the top of the stool into the shims and nailing blocks beneath to hold the stool in place. Finish by trimming the thin shims back with a drywall knife.

The window stool shown here is nice and hefty, and the triangular off cut used to create the mitered return isn't as tiny as the piece you might have when you're mitering returns for smaller stools. Cutting those little pieces can be dangerous. When you're raising the chop-saw blade after making the cut, the carbide tooth on a spinning blade can catch the edge of that little triangle of wood and zing it across the room. But there is a way to be safer: Make a temporary wooden fence for your chop saw. Just pony-clamp a strip of ¾-in. pine or MDF to your saw fence temporarily. Run the strip right across the throat of your saw and cut right through the strip at the same time as you're trimming off the little triangle end. That way, the little piece of wood cannot fly out through the throat and go ricocheting around the place.

When a test fit shows that your return piece fits perfectly, put some glue on the face of the cut and fit it carefully to the main stool. A small finish nail into each side of the joint will hold it while the glue sets up and hardens.

Installing Jamb Extensions

In the simplest cases, you'll find windows installed with the jambs already flush to the drywall: the builder has ordered units that fit the wall perfectly, and all you have to do is run casing. But, more common, window jambs don't extend out as far as the wall surface; they need jamb extensions measured and cut to fit to bring the jamb out flush.

Cutting the Stool Returns

1 Rip a piece of stock the width of the ears.

2 Cut the board to rough length on the chop saw, and then cut off the very end of the piece on a 45° angle.

3 Test-fit the piece to the end of the stool.

4 Apply glue to the cut face of the piece and fit the return back in place. Nail the joint tight with gun nails through both edges of the corner.

5 A little light sanding with 100-grit paper smooths the joint and works some fine sawdust into the crack for a near-invisible joint, ready for paint.

Nails That Follow the Grain

Nailing together the stool return shown here provided an example of a common mishap with finish nailers and wood trim: wayward nails. Following the wood grain, the nail curved around and poked out the top of the sill. It's a reminder of why you make sure to keep your fingers away from the nailer when you're firing it. It's also the reason why in some situations, carpenters may pilot-drill and hand-nail instead of using the gun.

But this was an easy fix for carpenter Smokey Saduk. He used a pair of nippers to snip off the end of the nail near the wood, tapped the snubbed-off end back into the wood with his nail set, dabbed a little glue into the hole, and rubbed over the whole thing with sandpaper to work a little fine sawdust into the glue and hide the hole. After painting, none of this will show.

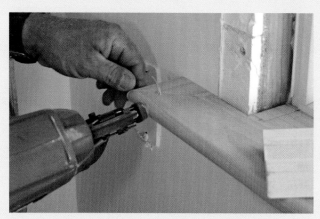

Occasionally a nail will follow the wood grain and pop out at some inconvenient place.

Snip off the end of the fastener with metal shears, using a Speed Square to protect the wood.

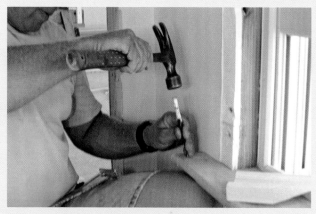

Use a nail set to nudge the tip of the nail back below the surface of the wood.

Smear a little glue into the small hole created, and sand some sawdust into the glue.

Jamb extensions can often be ordered from the window supplier in various widths, or you can make your own. There are several different kinds of manufactured jamb extensions, and window designs make various provisions for extensions. Andersen Windows, for example, supplies windows with a groove in the jamb, and jamb extensions with a matching tongue that seats the extension accurately in place. Harvey® Windows, a New England–based supplier, offers vinyl-clad windows with a sleeve at the jamb edge that receives ¾-in. jamb extensions. With either of these window designs, you can also make your own jamb extensions that will match up with the window jamb's profile.

To determine the width of the jamb extensions, hold a straightedge on the wall so that it spans the corner of the window opening. Measure from the straightedge to the window jamb and add ¹⁄₁₆ in. This means the jamb extension will project ever so slightly into the room, making it easier to apply the casing. Trying to bring your casing tight to the jamb when the wall is holding your casing out can be troublesome and leave messy results. But, if the jamb is a little proud of the wall, the worst that will happen is a small gap between the casing and the wall at the outside edge of the casing—easily remedied with drywall mud, caulk, or paint.

Always cut jamb extensions from solid wood, not MDF or plywood. Composite materials tend to split when nailed or screwed through the edge. When ripping the extension pieces to width, plan your rips so you end up with a factory-milled edge facing into the room. This way, each piece has one clean edge that doesn't require you to plane off the saw

Routing the Stool Ends

Instead of a mitered return, sometimes it's easier to cut square ends on the windowsills and rout (or sand) the ends to match the profile of the front. This will save a little time if you're doing a whole houseful of windows, and the visual result is acceptable for paint-grade work.

If you choose to rout the ends, do so before you cut out the notch for the ears on the stool. That way you can feed the router bit into the already routed front of the piece; when the router exits the piece at the back, the bit may splinter out some wood, but that's okay because that piece is going to get cut out anyway.

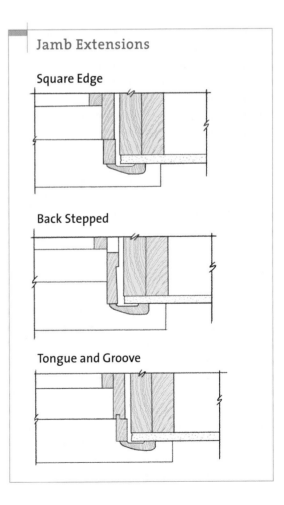

Jamb Extensions

Square Edge

Back Stepped

Tongue and Groove

Preassembled Jamb Extensions

Securing jamb extensions can be a challenge. For this job, remodeler Chuck Green rips his own jamb extensions, preassembling the two sides and top extension jambs into a single unit, which he pins to the rough framing rather than to the window unit. In the example shown, he installed vinyl-clad windows that have a sleeve on their jamb edges to receive the extension jambs. Once the jambs are in position, he shoots a few squirts of low-expansion foam insulation into the cracks to hold the jambs firmly in place.

1 Measure the depth of the opening and then rip the jamb stock to the required width.

2 Fasten the pieces together at the corners, predrilling pilot holes and driving two trim-head screws per corner.

3 Set the assembly in place, where it slides into a sleeve provided in the vinyl-clad window units.

4 Nail through the jamb into the framing with pneumatically driven trim nails, using a small pry bar to hold the jamb steady against the force of the gun nails. (Be careful not to hit the pry bar with the nails.) With the jambs pinned in place, check each one against a straightedge to make sure it's right, prying or tapping them gently into place if not.

5 Shoot a few dabs of low-expansion foam insulation into the crack to hold the jambs firmly in place.

Use a tape measure to establish the rough length for the extension jambs.

marks, which would otherwise be seen along the reveal.

There's nothing wrong with attaching jamb extensions to the rough framing around the window (see the sidebar on the facing page), but it's more typical to attach extensions to the window unit by "through-nailing" from the front of the extension into the front of the jamb. For accuracy, the surest method is to drill pilot holes and drive trim-head screws, as shown in the photos above. That's easy enough for jamb extensions 1 in. or 2 in. wide, but for wider extensions, the best method is to mill a back-shelf, or step, on one face of the extension pieces. This allows the installer to place screws through the backside of the jamb extension into the edge of the main window jamb. Alternatively, a pocket-screw boring jig to mill screw pockets into the back of the jamb accomplishes the same thing.

Hold the jambs in place to mark them for a final cut to length.

Once the pieces are cut to fit, drill pilot holes and then "through-screw" the side jambs to the window frame with square-drive trim-head screws. Then screw the head jambs.

Pin the head jamb to the side jamb at the top corners with another pilot hole and trim screw set at an angle.

Installing Window Casings

With the jamb extensions secured, you're ready for the casings. The simplest profile is a plain, flat 1x4 or 1x6; typically, basic flat casings are installed with a butt joint where the side casings meet the head casing. Profiled casings are usually installed with a miter joint at the corners, so the profiles match up. A third option is a built-up casing that starts with square, flat stock butt-joined at the corners, and then adds a smaller cap molding at the edge, installed with miter joints.

When it comes to style, of course, that's just the beginning—window moldings are limited only by the trim carpenter's imagination.

Older homes from the Georgian or Victorian era are like living museums of complicated window trim details, involving built-up head casing, side casing, sill and apron assemblies. Most carpenters won't see that kind of time consuming and delicate task very often, though. By and large, you'll be installing two side casings and a head casing—with either a miter or a square joint at each corner—and moving on.

Marking the reveal

Window casings are usually installed with a slight "reveal"—an offset of about ⅛ in. to ¼ in.—where the casings meet the jambs.

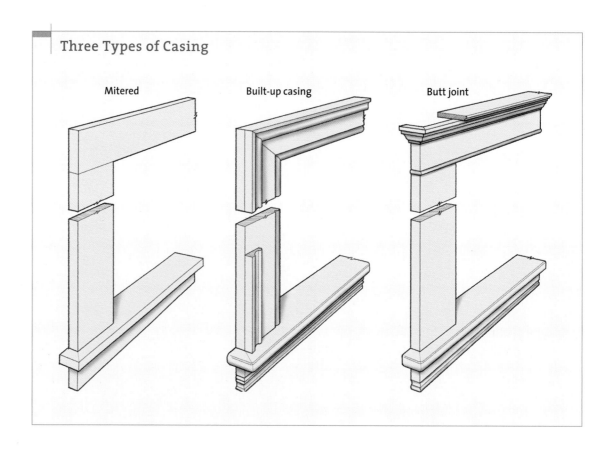

Three Types of Casing

Mitered

Built-up casing

Butt joint

Traditional Head Styles

Miter joints for window casing have some drawbacks: Not only does the window opening have to be perfectly square, but miters also tend to open up easily if the wood shrinks (see Appendix A on pp. 215–238). To avoid problematic miters, carpenters have devised a number of ways to join casing and these methods have developed into distinctive styles that have both aesthetic and practical functions.

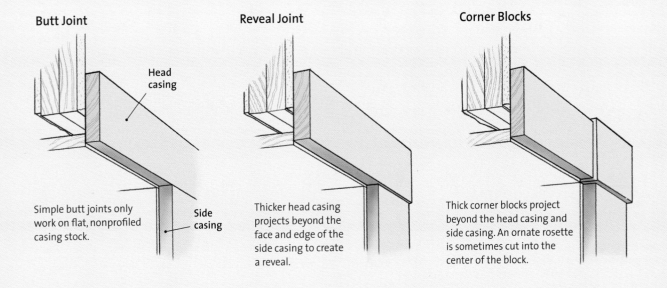

Butt Joint

Head casing

Side casing

Simple butt joints only work on flat, nonprofiled casing stock.

Reveal Joint

Thicker head casing projects beyond the face and edge of the side casing to create a reveal.

Corner Blocks

Thick corner blocks project beyond the head casing and side casing. An ornate rosette is sometimes cut into the center of the block.

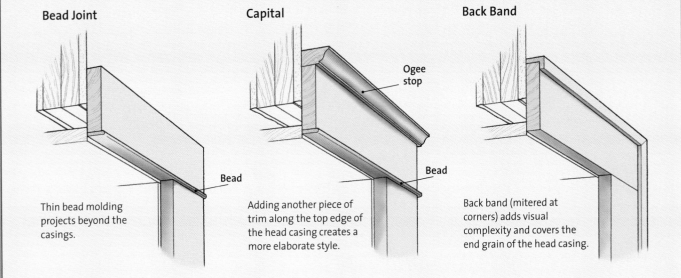

Bead Joint

Bead

Thin bead molding projects beyond the casings.

Capital

Ogee stop

Bead

Adding another piece of trim along the top edge of the head casing creates a more elaborate style.

Back Band

Back band (mitered at corners) adds visual complexity and covers the end grain of the head casing.

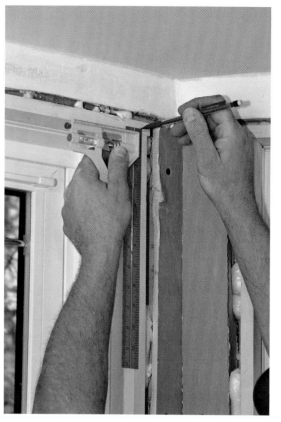

A tri-square set to the desired depth serves as a simple jig for marking a consistent reveal on the window jamb.

Before you start to nail on casings, mark the location of fasteners you've used to attach the jamb extensions. That way you won't shoot in your nails on top of screw heads.

This creates a step, adding an extra shadow line that contributes to the visual complexity of the trim. But a reveal also serves a practical purpose, fooling the eye and hiding any slight misalignments between the casing and the jamb if one or the other isn't perfectly square. Your eye can easily see when two corners don't meet, but it is unlikely to notice minor differences in the width of a reveal line.

You can mark the reveal quickly with a small tri-square or with a simple "reveal block" (see the sidebar on p. 63).

Order of installation

There's a running debate among trim carpenters about in what order to install casings. Some carpenters like to measure, cut, and install the two side casings first, then cut the head casing to fit. Others like to put up the head casing first, then cut and install two side casings.

It's really a matter of personal preference. However, depending on the situation, there's logic on both sides. For a narrow window, it's easy to cut a miter on one end of the head casing, hold the short point to the reveal you've marked, mark the other short point, and make the second cut. Once the head casing's nailed up, it's easy to hold each side casing beside it, mark those for length, and cut them. (See "Casing a Window" on p. 86.)

Large windows are a different story. If you're handling a 7-ft. or 8-ft. casing for a big double window, you can't really hold one end where it goes and mark the other end without a helper—but it is possible for one person to nail up both side casings, rest a piece of material across their tops, and mark the long point of the miter on each end of the head casing. If you give yourself an extra ⅛ in. to play with, you can fine-tune the joint at both ends before nailing the head in place between its mates. It's like anything else in carpentry: Experience counts and a carpenter will eventually recognize which technique will be the simplest and quickest in each particular case.

Fastener choices

On the outside edge of the casing, the nails have to make it through ¾ in. of casing and ½ in. of drywall before they hit the trimmer. An 8d nail (2½ in. long) is standard here. For large moldings with a nice, fat edge, that same nail works to fasten the inside edge of the casing to the window jamb. But, when you go with lighter moldings, 6d or even 4d nails are better for pinning to the jamb. Nailing the slender inside edge of clam shell molding to the window jamb can be a real pain, because the material sometimes splits and splinters. A pneumatic brad nailer firing a 1-in. pin works best.

Installing the Apron

The apron under the stool serves both visual and structural purposes. It masks the rough opening beneath the stool, but it also helps support the stool.

Usually, the apron is made of the same material used for the casings. Cut the piece to match the full width of the cased window,

To hold glued joints tight while they set up, cut some thin strips of pine into springs and wedge them between the trim pieces and the walls or ceiling. Just like clamping a glued joint, the pressure will help form a strong bond.

Casing a Window

1 Hold the head piece across the window and mark the short points directly off your reveal marks.

2 After cutting the 45° cuts on each end, nail the piece in place.

3 Find the length of the side casing.

4 Cut the piece long, and check the miter, re-cutting as needed until the fit is perfect.

5 Flip the piece upside down, resting the long point on the sill, and mark the square end for length in place.

6 Make the square cut to length and glue the face of the miter cut.

7 Nail the side casing in place and repeat for the other side.

Installing the Apron

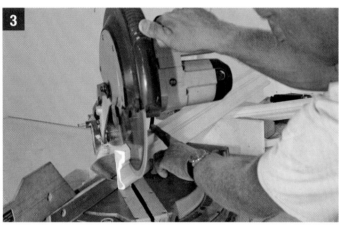

1 Mark the casing stock for the apron by holding a piece in place and making a tick mark at the left edge of the casing, the right edge of the casing, and the window center.

2 Using a Speed Square, extend the center mark underneath the window so that it will be clearly visible for setting the apron.

3 Take the piece to the chop saw and cut a 45° angle on each end, with the long points on the outside face.

4 Align the center mark on the apron to the center mark on the window and attach the apron with gun nails into the rough window framing. Also nail through the sill into the apron from above.

For the mitered returns, cut a 45° angle on a piece of apron stock and square-cut the small return piece. Apply glue to the return and hold in place with a couple of light-gauge fasteners.

and center it under the sill, using the line transferred from the window to the wall, as described earlier. Properly centered, the apron ends will line up directly under the outside edges of the side casings.

Flat casing looks fine with simple square ends, but for profiled moldings, you'll need to cut mitered returns at the ends of the apron. Cut a matching 45° angle on the end of a long piece of stock, and snip the small return piece off with a square cut. Ordinarily, glue is enough to keep this small piece in place, but send in a couple of light-gauge fasteners to hold it while the glue sets.

The finished apron, with miter return in place.

Instead of making a mitered return on a simple apron, you can just round the end in place with a sanding head on the Fein® MultiMaster™ tool.

Hanging and Trimming Doors

Trimming doors is often a relatively simple task: It's similar to casing out a window, except that there is no sill or apron to contend with. Nail two side casings and a head casing to each side of the doorjamb assembly, and you're done. (See "Casing a Door" on pp. 125–127.) You can get more elaborate, but for most trim jobs, you won't have to fuss with many compound angles.

Yet the trim carpenter is often called on to install the doors, not just to trim them out. And that's a bigger topic. Slapping a factory-built split-jamb door into a framed opening in a production house can be done relatively quickly (see the sidebar on p. 108); but even an untrimmed prehung door calls for a little savvy. There's also a whole complex series of operations required to fit and hang a replacement door in an existing jamb as part of a custom remodeling job.

Doors don't just have to look good—they also have to work well. Success requires fitting the door neatly into its opening, lining up the hinges plumb and straight, placing the strike correctly, and installing the latch hardware so that it operates as it should. Door hanging is a specialty of its own, and whole books have been written on the subject. We won't turn this chapter into a book,

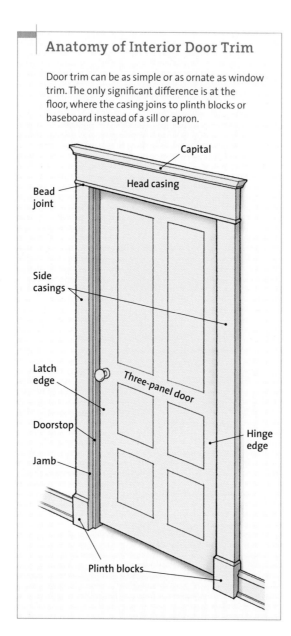

Anatomy of Interior Door Trim

Door trim can be as simple or as ornate as window trim. The only significant difference is at the floor, where the casing joins to plinth blocks or baseboard instead of a sill or apron.

Capital

Head casing

Bead joint

Side casings

Latch edge

Three-panel door

Doorstop

Jamb

Hinge edge

Plinth blocks

When ordering a door to be retrofit into an existing, out-of-square opening, be sure it's big enough. It can be scribed and cut down to fit.

but we will give you the information you need to handle most of the door work you're likely to run into on the job.

Ordering Doors

When ordering a door, the convention for specifying the size is to indicate the width first followed by height. Typically, this is done in both feet and inches. The usual nomenclature uses hyphens as in 2-6 x 6-8 (for a door that's 30 in. wide by 80 in. high). Be careful when you read 3-0 (for a 36-in.-wide door) that you don't misread this as 30 in. wide.

One of the pitfalls of ordering doors is specifying the swing. The traditional terminology refers to the "hand" of the door. We know it like this: If the hinges are on the left side when you walk through a door, it is a *left-hand* door. If the hinges are on the right side when you walk through it, it is a *right-hand* door. But, to make life complicated for carpenters, there is no common industry standard for how "left-handed" and "right-handed" are defined. Doors, of course, have two sides; if the knob is on your right when you look at the door from one side, it's on your left when you look at it from the other side.

To be safe, and to avoid miscommunication, simply tell your supplier which side you want the knob to be on when walking through the door (opening away from you). From that simple directive, the supplier can determine which "hand" to order from a given manufacturer.

Door Hanger's Toolkit

While a couple of power tools are useful for hanging doors, most of the essential tools are hand tools and jigs.

Door jack

Full-time door hanger's like to use a "door bench" with a carpet-lined cradle for holding the door on edge and a waist-level bench top where you can lay out your tools and not constantly have to bend over for them. But for most trim carpenters doing a few doors at a time, this is a lot of jig to cart around. A simple door jack made from a 6-ft.-long 2x4 will do. Lay out your door jack with a 2-in.-wide slot to hold the door. This works for a standard 1¾-in.-thick exterior door. For a thinner interior door blank, the uprights can be spaced closer together.

Door level

While a standard 4-ft. level will do just fine, a 66-in. or 72-in. door hanger's level is worth the investment if you hang many doors. Having an extra long straightedge makes aligning the hinges easier when shimming the jambs and it's important to get them in a perfectly straight line. A bow in the jamb will cause the hinges to bind.

Shoot board

A "shoot board" is a must-have item for undercutting doors. To make your board, start with

A door jack holds the door on edge, while a couple of shims provide a snug fit so the door can't wobble.

A door hanger's level comes in handy for checking that the hinges are dead plumb and the jambs get shimmed straight.

To make a shoot board, screw the base and straightedge together first, leaving the base wider than you need. Then take a pass with the saw you will be using to cut the base to the exact width of the saw shoe.

two straight boards—one that we'll call the straightedge about 2½ in. wide by at least 4 ft. long, and the other we'll call the base the same length and about 3 in. wider than the shoe of your circular saw. Laminate the pieces with glue and screws, leaving the bottom piece wider than you need. Next, using the straight-edge as a guide for your saw (and with a new, sharp blade in the saw), cut the bottom piece to width. The edge of the shoot board's base is now as straight as the straightedge and the exact width of the saw shoe. This jig does more than make a straight cut, however. It also holds down the grain, so the blade doesn't tear out on cross grain or on veneer.

If you do a lot of door work (or have frequent need for making long accurate cuts with a circular saw), you may want to invest in the Festool's TS 55 EQ Circular Plunge-Cut Saw—a high-quality circular saw mounted in a machined guide track that is ideal for trimming doors.

In use, the wide base of the shoot board supports the saw shoe and the narrow straightedge provides a fence to guide the saw.

Making a Door Jack

To make a simple door jack, **start by screwing two short lengths of 2x to a cross piece of the same material. Space the uprights about 1³/₄ in. to 2 in. apart, so the door can slip between them easily. Screw on a pair of diagonals to support the uprights. A pair of shims slipped between the door and the two uprights will snug the door into the jack.**

Door hook

This simple jig for holding a door blank in place consists of two bent hooks, one for the door and one for the frame, joined by an elastic material such as surgical tubing or a piece of bicycle inner tube. To make your own, you can start with any suitable found metal. A cheap over-the-door hanger hook is a good option for the door side, and small metal framing clips will provide stock for the jamb hook. Bend these in a vise and drill a hole in each through which to tie the elastic band. In use, you hook one end over the door and the other end to the casing or the jamb. Rest the door on shims at the bottom and pull it tight at the top with your elastic hook, and your hands are free to scribe the door.

A shop-made door hook is a simple tensioning device that hooks over the top of the door and on the edge of the jamb. It's not a precision instrument, and can be made with a couple of found pieces of metal and a stout rubber band.

Hinge-mortising template

Commercially made hinge-mortising templates are not essential, but they can speed up the job if you're installing a number of new door blanks. It takes a relatively long time to set up one of these jigs, which makes them impractical for fitting just one door. But if you're doing a number of doors, they can be a real time saver because the hinge layout is automatic once the jig is set up. If you do doors regularly, screw the setup to a 1x4. This makes for a long, but transportable package, which is efficient to use for even one door.

Hinge-mortising bit

When using a router to mortise a hinge, freehand or with a template, a hinge-mortising bit

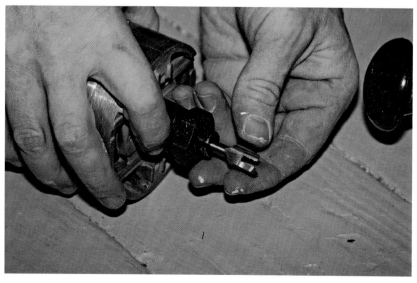

A hinge-mortising bit is designed to cut a flat-bottomed mortise. The gullet between each cutting edge helps clear chips out of the way, which helps you see where you are cutting.

makes quick work of cutting a flat-bottomed mortise. The particular style shown in the photo above has a positive hook angle and an open gullet—features that make for fast and efficient chip clearance.

Power plane

A good power plane is essential for trueing the edge of a door. Most of these come with a simple removable fence. The typical fence is fixed at 90°, but, with practice, it can be used to bevel the door edge.

If you hang many doors, it's worth investing in the Porter-Cable® 126 Porta-Plane®. This tool is specifically designed to plane doors. It's not very versatile, but for door work it can't be beat. The base is 2¼ in. wide and 16 in. long—the narrowest and longest base of any power plane on the market, which makes it ideal for straightening the edge of a door. The fence tilts, making it easy to cut the required 3° bevel on the strike side of the door. This plane uses a spiral cutter head that cuts at an angle to the edge of the door, producing a

The Porter-Cable 126 Porta-Plane is specially made for door work. The adjustable fence can be set to the angle of the bevel. The first pass of the plane knocks down the high point, and a second pass completes the bevel.

smooth cut even in squirrelly edge grain. The depth of cut is changed using a lever at the front of the tool, which can be adjusted as you take a pass when following a scribe line.

Chisels

While routers have made many chiseling jobs faster, the chisel is far from obsolete. You don't have to be a connoisseur of the perfect chisel: Most professional-grade tools available on the market will work just fine. The trick is keeping them sharp (see Appendix B on pp. 239–241). A dull chisel will crush, rather than cut, the wood fibers, making a mess of any attempt to mortise a hinge or door latch.

Lock-boring jig

Door blanks usually ship already predrilled for a cylindrical lockset. But you may occasionally have to drill doors to accept this hardware. You can make the holes freehand with a 1-in. drill bit and a 2¼-in. hole saw, but it's faster and more accurate to use a lock-boring jig, such as the Porter-Cable 511 or the Classic Engineering 10800 Boring Jig Kit (see "Drilling and Boring for Locksets" on p. 123). The advantage is that the jig automatically establishes the backset (either 2⅜ or 2¾ in. depending on the door hardware you are installing), and it guides the drill exactly perpendicular to the face of the door. Without one, you have to hold the drill so the shaft of the hole saw stays at a perfect right angle to the door, otherwise the latch set may be slightly cocked and may bind when operating it.

Installing a Prehung Door

These days, most doors for new construction ship "prehung." This means the manufacturer supplies the door with hinges, installed in its jamb. Some prehung units also have factory-installed casing, and a split jamb, to make the installer's job even easier (see "Split-Jamb Doors" on p. 108). But the majority of prehung door units require the carpenter to set the whole assembly securely into the rough-framed door opening, and then apply the casing. Both installing the unit and the casing typically happen after the drywall is up.

Checking the opening

The primary concern at the outset of a door-hanging job is whether the rough opening is the right size. With a prehung unit, the rough opening should be at least ½ in. wider than the prehung unit, measured outside of jamb to outside of jamb (measure across the unit near the top hinge). Ideally, you want about a ¼-in. gap on either side of the prehung unit. If the gap gets much more than this, you'll have to use additional shims, which can be awkward. But better too wide than too tight.

Figuring the height can be a little trickier. In general, you want the door to open at least ½ in. above the *finish floor*, and you want the rough opening to be ¼ in. above the ears on the head jamb. Note that most prehung units have the head jamb dadoed into the side jambs, which leaves a bit of wood—the "ear"—sticking above the top of the head jamb on each side. This ear needs to be only about ½-in. long to stabilize the joint, but they often come an inch or two long and need to be trimmed back.

For example, if you have a standard 6 ft. 8 in. x 2 ft. 6 in., the width of the rough opening needs to be 32 in., assuming 1x jamb stock, which typically measures out at 1¹⁄₁₆ in.). The height of the rough opening would be 83 in., assuming 1½ in. from the top of the door to the top of the "ears" and ¾-in.-thick hardwood flooring (see the drawing on p. 98).

To be on the safe side, try to get a sample of the finish flooring before you hang the door. If it's going to be tile, check with the tile installer to verify the thickness of the finish flooring, including whatever underlayment and adhesive, or mortar bed system, may be used. Also note that prehung units are sometimes sold with the legs of the side jambs 1 in. longer than the bottom of the door. Check this measurement. If they are only 1 in. long and your finish flooring is ¾ in. thick or more, you may need to cut a couple of shims from ¼-in. or

Sizing the Rough Opening

Rough openings should be framed 2 in. wider than the door, leaving room for 3/4-in.-thick jambs on each side, plus a little room (but not too much) for shims. Header heights must account for the "ears" on a prehung unit as well as the undercut on the door and the thickness of the finish floor.

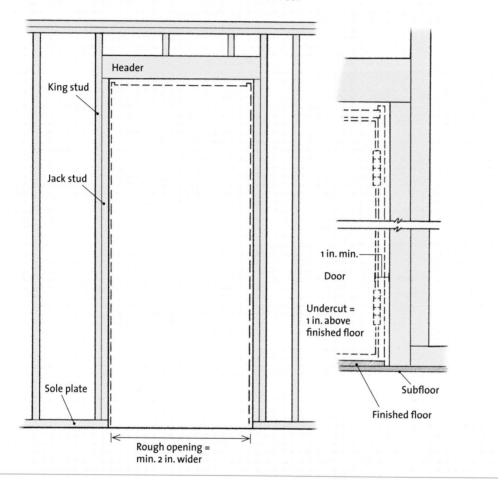

Header

King stud

Jack stud

Sole plate

Rough opening =
min. 2 in. wider

1 in. min.

Door

Undercut =
1 in. above
finished floor

Subfloor

Finished floor

Accommodating Ventilation

Heating, cooling, and ventilation concerns may add a twist to how much you undercut a door. Houses with central air handlers have "supply ducts" and "return ducts"—typically, air is blown into individual rooms through supply ducts to each room but has to find its own way back to a centrally located return in a hallway or common area. The builder may want to "undercut" the doors (allow a 1-in. air space at the bottom when closed), so that air can flow freely when the doors are closed and allow the cooling or heating system to do its job. If the rough openings leave room at the top, the doors can be installed at the proper height; otherwise, each door will have to be cut off at the bottom.

Rough Opening Heights

It's not uncommon for a home to have several different finish flooring materials. If you have any say in the framing, aim to set all the head heights at the same level, and plan on undercutting the bottom of the doors by different amounts to accommodate the flooring.

In most houses, it's safe to allow 3/4 in. for hardwood flooring, plus another 3/4 in. for the top jamb, and 1/2 in. for play. So, in most cases, you'll add 2 in. to the door size in height as well as width: 6 ft. 10 in. for a "six-eight" door, 7 ft. for a "six-ten" door, and so on. Any doors that go into rooms with thicker flooring, such as tile, will end up being cut off just a little at the bottom.

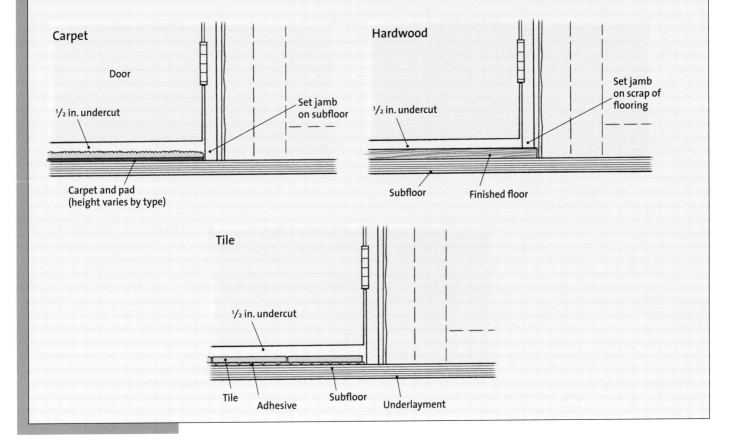

Carpet

Door

1/2 in. undercut

Set jamb on subfloor

Carpet and pad (height varies by type)

Hardwood

1/2 in. undercut

Set jamb on scrap of flooring

Subfloor   Finished floor

Tile

1/2 in. undercut

Tile   Adhesive   Subfloor   Underlayment

1/2-in. plywood when installing the unit over the subfloor (assuming you have the head room in your rough opening). Otherwise, you'll have to undercut the door. A 1/4-in. undercut is too little to allow good air circulation between rooms and, if the floor isn't perfectly level, may not allow enough room to open the door without it running into a rise in the floor.

Once you are certain the rough opening is the correct size, check the corners for square and the jambs for plumb (both ways). Then check to make sure everything is in the same plane by cross stringing the opening. If the

Cross-Stringing an Opening

To cross-string the opening, set drywall screws in the two upper corners and in one lower corner. Hook a mason's line or chalk line on the lower corner screw, pull it across the door opening on the diagonal, loop around as shown to run the line straight across the opening to the other upper screw, then go diagonally across the door opening again.

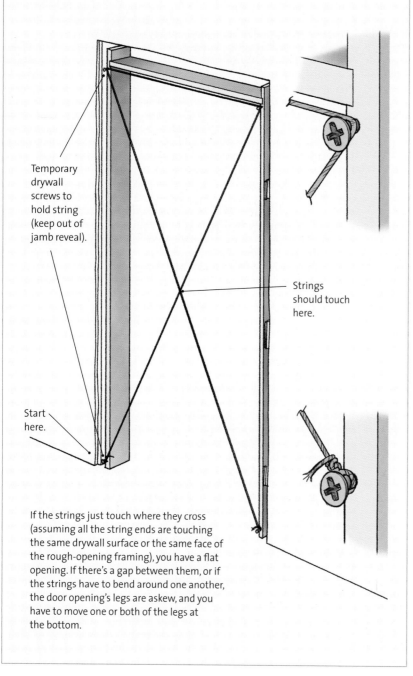

Temporary drywall screws to hold string (keep out of jamb reveal).

Strings should touch here.

Start here.

If the strings just touch where they cross (assuming all the string ends are touching the same drywall surface or the same face of the rough-opening framing), you have a flat opening. If there's a gap between them, or if the strings have to bend around one another, the door opening's legs are askew, and you have to move one or both of the legs at the bottom.

legs of the rough opening are askew, it will be nearly impossible to make the door hang properly and you'll have to correct the framing.

The string will tell you which way the legs have to move. In theory, if both legs are plumb, they should also be parallel and the opening will be flat; if only one leg is out of plumb, then that is the one to move. Assuming there's no finish floor in place (only a plywood subfloor), you ought to be able to get a reciprocating saw blade under the wall plate and cut through the nails, then persuade the wall over to where you need it to be. Use some long screws at an angle to fasten the plate down again.

If this sounds like a hassle, it is. If you're following a good framer, you'll seldom need to do this kind of thing.

Preparing the door

Prehung doors come with various types of packaging, from shrink-wrap plastic to simple stabilizer pieces tacked to the jamb. You need to pull all that stuff off before you set the door, and if the ears are too long, this is the time to trim them back. A sharp handsaw works well for this. Leave the door hanging in the jamb.

Placing the unit

It's important to set interior doors at a consistent height, to maintain visual continuity. A level layout line marked next to the door opening establishes the height of the door, and provides a reference line to help level the door head. Now tilt up the door in its frame and slide it into the opening. Shims set between the jamb and the rough opening will hold the door roughly in place but still allow the jambs to be pried up or down as you fine-tune the height of the door.

Before installing the door, remove any packaging material and pull off the stabilizing strips that may be tacked to the jamb.

The head jamb usually lets into the side jambs to form a dado joint (left). If the upper end of the jamb is too long to fit the opening, trim off the excess with a sharp handsaw (right).

Level layout marks help keep all the doors at a consistent height and help with leveling the head jamb.

Setting the hinge side

To pin the door in place, start on the hinge side. The hinges have to line up plumb in both dimensions, so that the door won't swing open or closed on its own. As you work, check frequently with a 6-ft. level to make sure you're keeping that hinge line plumb and straight.

You can gently tap the jamb one way or the other with your hammer and a block of wood, or the heel of your hand, to get it lined up perfectly. Use a Speed Square to make sure the doorjamb is flush with the drywall, but when you have to choose, make the hinges plumb—you want the door to operate properly, and

Setting a Prehung Door

1 | Set the jamb and door in the opening.

2 | Wedge the head jamb in place using shim shingles.

3 | The shims keep the door unit from falling out, but allow you to raise or lower either side using a pry bar.

4 | With the head jamb wedged in place, gently tap the jamb from side to side as needed to flush up the jamb with the drywall.

Set the jamb plumb using a 6-ft. level (left), **making sure to check that the hinges are plumb and aligned (right).**

you can fix any other problems when you trim it out.

The hinges offer a handy attachment point for the jamb. Pull the center screw from each hinge and replace it with a longer wood screw that will reach all the way through the jamb and penetrate the jack stud (typically, a 2½-in. screw works best for this). Set a pair of shims at each hinge location, pushing them in or pulling them out as needed to move the jamb in or out and make it plumb. When everything

looks right, send the long screws home to hold the jamb in place. You'll come back and add nails in a little while, after the rest of the door is set.

Leveling the head

If the hinges are plumb and the door is square, the top of the door should be level. Setting a consistent gap between the door and the top jamb should ensure that the jamb is also level. The eye is a reliable enough measure of that

To secure the hinge side of the door, pull one screw from each hinge. Using shims to stabilize the jamb and hold it plumb, replace the original hinge screws with screws long enough to reach the framing behind the jamb.

With the hinge side of the jamb pinned, you can level the head jamb by eye, prying it up or down with a pry bar.

The metal extension of a folding ruler makes a handy gauge for setting the gap between the door and jamb.

gap, but you may want to cut a thin wood shim or use a metal gauge to check it.

Setting the strike side

Set the "strike side" of the doorjamb the same way you did the head jamb: by maintaining a consistent reveal where the door meets the jamb. With the door closed, you can push or pull on your pairs of shims to get the jamb where you want it. When it's right, send some long finish nails home to pin it in place. If you need to, you can still pry the jamb back with a pry bar to tighten the gap. Be sure to locate some shims directly behind the spot where the strike plate will be—this area will take a daily beating from the door latch as the door opens and closes in use.

With the strike-side jamb set, you can go back and firm up the attachment of the hinge side with more shims and more nails. Finally, cut off your shims with a drywall knife, and you're ready to case it out.

When the head jamb aligns to your liking, pin the top corner of the strike-side jamb to hold it there. Add more shims and nails at the bottom and center, checking the space between the door and the jamb to maintain a straight line and a consistent reveal.

With the strike-side jamb shimmed and nailed, the final step is to add some shims and nails to the hinge side.

Finish up by cutting off the shims with a utility knife, and the door is ready for casing.

Hanging New Doors in Existing Jambs

The real test of a door-hanger's skill (short of building your own doors, or installing complex French doors or pocket doors) is hanging a new door in an existing jamb. It's the kind of work that remodelers run in to a lot. Whether it's giving the whole house a trim makeover, trying to make some existing rooms match the style of a new addition, or repairing a century or two's worth of wear and tear, installing new wood doors is a common upgrade for an old house.

Off-the-shelf doors from any lumberyard may suit the purpose, but if not, the world is full of door makers who can supply you with door blanks in any style you like, from any wood you choose. In most cases, the existing openings will be a typical standard size (6 ft. 8 in. or 6 ft. 10 in. high, for instance, and 2 ft. 6 in. or 2 ft. 8 in. wide). And with any luck, all your openings will be close enough to plumb and square that you can get away with using a standard-size door.

Don't take the opening size or shape for granted, though. Old houses move—in fact,

Split-Jamb Doors

Split-jamb doors go a step beyond prehung doors: They not only have the jamb assembled and the door attached, but they also have the door casing applied to the jamb. The jamb itself, as the term implies, is made in two pieces, one with the door attached and both with the casing applied. The jambs match up with a tongue-and-groove joint, and you install the door by sleeving the two halves of the unit together in the opening, one from each side.

There are pros and cons to using split-jamb doors. On the one hand, split-jambs eliminate a lot of labor time. And there's enough play in the tongue-and-groove joint to let you get the casing snug to the wall with ease, even if the wall is a little fatter or a little thinner than you figured. On the other hand, you're limited to the off-the-shelf trim choices that suppliers provide. If you want custom trim, you may not find split-jambs in styles that match existing trim or made of materials that live up to your expectations.

The typical tract-home installer sets the door side of the unit with a couple of nails in the casing, and then slips the jamb-only side into place. The installer operates the door to make sure it opens and closes, checks the reveal, then puts some more nails into the casing to hold the assembly tight and moves on. What's missing? Shims behind the hinges, shims behind the strike plate, and fasteners through the jamb into the door jacks. This door is held in place by just the casings. For a lightweight, hollow-core door, that's enough. But any solid door will need solid backing.

For solid doors, use precut (not tapered) shims cut from different thickness material (1/2-in. plywood, 1/4-in. lauan, and 1/8-in. hardboard) and use a door level (or a 4-ft. level taped to a straight 2x4) to define a plumb plane on the hinge side of the rough opening. Tack the shims in place to the rough opening jambs, and then mount the door-hung side of the jamb. It's fussy, but it works.

Before installing the other side of the split jamb, infill the latch side with solid backing and finish the job by securing the jamb with long screws and long finish nails that reach into the door framing, as shown in the drawings (below).

Hinge Side

Initially, tack the door side of the split jamb in place with a few finish nails through the casing. Once the jamb-only side is installed, securely nail off the tongue-and-groove joint with a 2 1/2-in. nail that penetrates the framing. Additionally, replace one screw in the hinge with one that's long enough to reach deep into the jack stud.

Latch Side

Along the sleeved joint (which doubles as the door stop), drive 2 1/2-in. finish nails every 16 in. on both sides of the door, squeezing the jamb together for a snug fit on the wall. After securely anchoring the door, nail off the casing consistently.

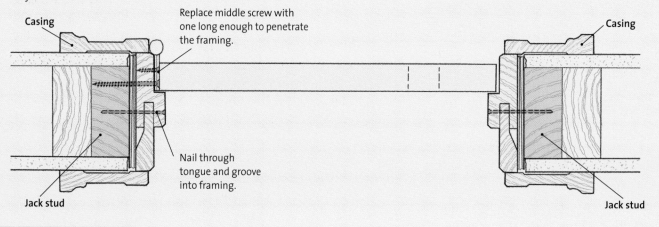

Casing

Replace middle screw with one long enough to penetrate the framing.

Nail through tongue and groove into framing.

Jack stud

Casing

Jack stud

new houses move, and door openings change. Check the heights and widths (all sides) with your tape, check the corners with a square, and check the cross dimensions. If something's screwy, order an extra-wide and extra-tall blank so that you can scribe and cut it to fit.

Cleaning up the jambs

It's possible that you have the original hinges for the existing door and want to save and reuse them. More likely, however, you'll have to prepare the existing jamb and the new door to receive new hinges. Any existing mortises in the old jamb have to be patched first, to create a new, smooth surface on the jamb; then you'll have to lay out and cut new mortises into the jamb for the new hinges.

Start by using a small fixed-base router to clean up and enlarge the existing mortises, then cut a patch piece of fresh wood (called a "Dutchman") to fill the void (see "Patching Mortises in a Doorjamb" on pp. 110–111). With practice, cutting a Dutchman can be done almost as quickly as filling the old hinge mortises with epoxy wood filler. On paint-grade work, an epoxy-like Minwax® High Performance Wood Filler is sufficient but takes several coats and lots of fussing with a sander and chisel to build up and shape a satisfactory patch. A Dutchman provides a more consistent and predictable solution.

Cutting the blank to height

With the jamb in "like new" condition, it's time to turn your attention to the door blank. The first task is to fit the blank to the opening. Start by measuring the height of the opening and cutting the bottom of the door if needed (allowing for finish flooring, if that is not yet installed, for the threshold if there's going to

Old houses settle, and the sag is often reflected at the head of door openings. A quick check with a framing square reveals the degree of the problem. In this case, a difference of more than $1/4$ in. over 1 ft. will require an oversized door blank that must be scribed to fit.

The first step in hanging a new door in an existing jamb is often to remove the existing doorstop.

Take Note • When removing old woodwork, such as a doorstop, use a utility knife to score the paint or finish in the corner between the stop and the jamb before you take a flat bar to the doorstop. This will prevent large flakes of paint from tearing out and speed up the prep work you need to do before refinishing the jambs after replacing the stop.

Patching Mortises in a Doorjamb

1 To fill the mortises from an old set of hinges or door latch, start by marking out an area larger than the mortise.

2 Use a tri-square to measure the depth of the old mortise. This will establish the thickness you need to rip a piece of wood for the "Dutchmen" patches.

3 Use a sharp utility knife guided by your square to slide through the cross grain on your top and bottom marks. This will prevent an errant piece of grain from tearing out, particularly at the outside corners.

4 Use a piece of the stock you have ripped for the Dutchmen to set the depth of the router.

5 Rout the new mortise, taking care not to go over the layout lines. A light, fixed-base router will provide more control when working on a vertical surface than a heavier plunge router.

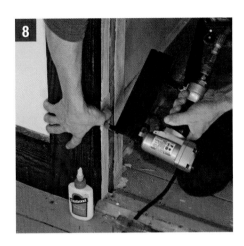

6 Clean up the mortise with a chisel. The cuts you made with a utility knife will have given you a head start, and make it quick to find the exact edge with the point of your chisel.

7 Keep your tape measure in your belt and measure the length of the Dutchmen off the mortise itself.

8 Glue the back of the Dutchman and nail it in place. If you will be cutting new hinge mortises over the Dutchmen, drive the nails below the depth of the new mortise after the glue dries so you don't ruin your router bit or a chisel when cutting the new mortise.

9 Sand out the patch with 80-grit paper to knock down the height, followed by 120-grit paper to smooth it out.

10 In theory, the Dutchman can be ripped to the exact width of the mortise, but the author prefers to rip it about $\frac{1}{16}$ in. wider; then as a final step, clear up the edge with a hand plane. This knocks off the saw marks on the side of the Dutchman and creates a crisp edge along the jamb reveal.

The best way to cut a door blank to length is to use a saw guide or a shop-made shoot board. Clamp the shoot board to the cut line, with the finished edge of the board aligned perfectly with the cut marks (inset).

be one, and for the specified gap under the door). Check and double-check your measurements before you pick up your saw—if you take too much off, there's no way to put it back on.

Be extra careful as you cut, too. For solid wood frame-and-panel doors, you'll be cutting across the grain on the vertical stiles, and with the grain on the bottom rail. Mark the line carefully and score the wood with a sharp knife before you make the cut. For best results, use a saw guide or "shoot board" (see p. 93).

Either the off-the-shelf guide-mounted saw or the job-made shoot board is particularly helpful when you're trimming the ends of lightweight hollow-core doors. Without the

solid guide, those doors tend to splinter when you cut them. Hollow-core units are made with a thin skin of wood veneer, tropical hardwood plywood, or a formed synthetic such as vinyl or melamine over an inner core of honeycomb cardboard, with softwood structural frames at the edges under the skin. Cutting the thin skins with a circular saw can be a nightmare: The saw tends to chip out the synthetic or blow apart the wood grain of the plywood or veneer, leaving your cut edge looking like a coconut that just tangled with a lawnmower. To prevent this, clamp your straightedge to the piece and score along the marked line repeatedly with a very sharp drywall knife. Then be sure that your saw does not stray across that scored line—when in doubt, stay on the waste side of the line. The shoot board not only helps keep your saw from straying, but it also holds down any splintering fibers, helping to prevent that "frayed" look at the edge.

Before cutting the bottom of the door, make sure the depth of cut is deep enough to cut through the door when the saw is riding on the shoot board.

But cutting off the bottom of hollow-core doors is always a pain, however you do it. For one thing, your blade is likely to hit metal fasteners (staples or nails). Then if you cut too much off the bottom of a hollow-core door, the entire softwood reinforcing stick at the bottom edge may be in the off-cut piece (that stick of solid lumber is often only 1½ in. to 2 in. thick). In that case, you'll have to tear apart the off-cut scrap and glue and nail the reinforcing piece back into the hollow edge you've created, or else rip your own new reinforcing stick out of fresh lumber and install that. This is one of those times when the cost savings of using a hollow-core door may be outweighed by the extra labor involved in making the unit fit (and with a compromise on quality to boot). You may end up wishing you had opted for solid doors to begin with.

Scribing the door edges

In service, a door should fit comfortably—not too tight, and not too loose, with an even gap on all sides (slightly less than ⅛ in. is good). If the openings are square and you've ordered doors that fit perfectly, you won't need to

Make the cut by running the saw along the fence on the shoot board. As long as the shoot board is clamped down firmly, the cut can be made quickly without a lot of fuss, and the shoot board will prevent the cross grain on the stiles from tearing out.

scribe or plane the doors. "Perfect" is a relative term in carpentry; your customer may be willing to live with a slight variation in order to save time or meet a budget. But if you're dealing with openings that are ¼ in. or more out of square, or that are just narrower than the standard door width, you'll probably have to make the doors fit. To achieve that involves holding

Scribing a Door Blank

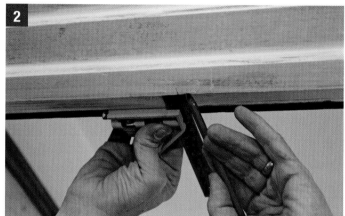

1 To scribe a door to fit an uneven opening, start with a blank that's slightly larger than the opening. Since the sides of the finished door are unknown, work off the centerline of the door by measuring across the width and marking the center on the top and bottom rails.

2 Measure the width of the opening and mark the centerline at the head and on the threshold.

3 Use a door hook to hold the door against the opening, and position the door blank on the centerline marks.

4 Use a couple of shims at the bottom to wedge the door blank upward to hold it steady.

5 Once the door is positioned securely, trace the outline of the door. Here, the doorstops have been removed on the side jambs, and the pencil is being guided at an angle by the author's fingers held against the jamb to provide a consistent ⅛-in. gap between the door and the jambs.

6 This opening is so out-of-square that the door blank overlaps the casing at the head. The author uses a square to place a mark on the door that accurately reflects the height of the head jamb.

7 Use a compass to scribe the bottom of the door. The scribe line should run parallel to the bottom of the opening, even if the floor is out of level.

To mark the depth of the bevel on one side of the door, hold a pencil about 3/16 in. below the corner. Brace your third and fourth finger against the top edge of the door to hold a consistent angle and run your hand down the length of the door. When planing you want to leave the pencil mark, knocking off about 1/8 in. from the corner.

Take Note • Whatever power planer you choose to use to bevel the door, be sure to keep an extra set of knives on hand so you can send a knife out for sharpening when it needs it, and still keep working. The blades dull fast on dense hardwoods (or instantly if you hit a nail), and you want to keep a nice, crisp edge on your tool when you're working on doors.

Planing the door

To plane the edge of a door, you need to stand the door on edge in a door jack (see p. 93). With practice, you can efficiently plane a door bevel even without a specialized door plane with an adjustable fence. Guiding a power plane with a fixed fence takes a steady hand and practice. If in doubt, clamp a piece of straight wood to the door, lined up with your scribe line. This guide board isn't a physical guide; rather, it's a good visual reference as you're planing. It's hard to tell sometimes how close you're getting to your scribe line, but with a fat wood edge to look at, you can easily see what you're doing. And it's important not to pause, hesitate, or waver while you're planing, especially on your first pass, or you'll get a wavy line that will show up against the jamb when the door is closed. By the same token, as you take your first cut with the power planer, be sure you know where the door jack is on the floor so that it doesn't trip you up and spoil your nice, clean cut.

If you have to do a lot of doors, you'll be glad to have a specialized power planer designed just for door work, like the Porter-Cable® 126 Porta-Plane (see the photo on p. 96). On the other hand, the Porter-Cable's

the oversize blank in the opening and scribing all the edges, and then planing them to the line. Try to get a door blank sized a bit larger than the opening between the jambs, but small enough to fit inside the casing.

If you don't have a helper to hold the door blank in the opening for you as you scribe the edges, you can make yourself a door hook for holding blanks in place (see p. 95). Before scribing, make sure to center the door in the opening. To do this, mark a centerline on the door and a centerline on the jamb, then line up the two marks. The side rails on the door should measure roughly equal widths when you're done scribing and planing.

To plane the bevel, cock the shoe and the fence to one side about ⅛ in. Here the author steadies the tool by holding the fence, and keeps an eye on the gap between the top of the fence and the face of the door. As long as that gap remains even at about ⅛ in., the plane will be running at the correct angle. The first pass simply knocks off the corner, and subsequent passes bring the bevel to the pencil line.

2-in.-wide base doesn't suit it for much else besides planing doors, and it's an expensive tool when you consider how specialized it is. A lower-priced all-purpose power planer will also do a good job.

Plane the long edges of the door (the hinge side and the strike side) to about a 3° bevel. The short side of the bevel will rest against the stop when the door is closed. That way, the door closes easily but still shows a small edge gap against the jamb. You can set that 3° bevel on the Porter-Cable's fence, but getting the same result with a standard power plane takes a certain knack. Start by planing down just the inside edge of the door, where you'll be removing the most material, and then sneak up on

the line on the outside edge on your later passes. Use a fixed 90° fence on the planer, but only rest the bottom edge on that fence on the face of the door. At the top of the fence, you want about a ⅛-in. gap. If you maintain this gap as you run the plane down the edge of the door, the plane will stay at the correct angle. With practice, you'll develop a touch for getting a nice, smooth, consistent bevel.

Hinge layout

Hinge location and spacing should be consistent throughout the house. In fact, it's more or less consistent throughout the country, but not completely so. A widely accepted rule of thumb in the eastern U.S. is to locate the top

After planing the bevel, take a hand plane and ease the corner over, rounding it slightly to match the "soft" factory corners of the unplanned edges.

of the top hinge 5 in. down from the top of the door, and the bottom of the bottom hinge 10 in. up from the bottom of the door. The third hinge, if there is one, centers between the other two. Note: Not everyone follows this rule. In some western states, the typical practice is to set the top hinge 7 in. down from the top, and the bottom hinge 11 in. up from the bottom. There's no code or law governing any of this, so you can really put the hinges wherever you want; the conservative thing to do is to check the other doors in the house and follow suit. Failing that opportunity, check the

prehung doors on the rack at your local home center. Most likely, you'll see the 5-in. and 10-in. placement.

More important than vertical placement is the offset of the hinges horizontally on the door and jamb. You need to leave enough "meat" between the door edge and the hinge leaf to maintain the strength of the connection and the integrity of the door's edge.

Several companies supply hinge-mortising jigs that can more or less automate this whole process. Two units that come highly recommended are the Porter-Cable 59381 Hinge

Why Bevel the Edge of the Door?

The latch side of a door must be beveled about 3° to prevent the far corner (the one against the doorstop) from knocking the edge of the jamb as the door swings open. A 3° bevel on a 1½-in. door equals about ⅛ in. on the stop side of the door. It's good practice to bevel the hinge side about the same amount to prevent the hinges from binding if the jamb is turned inward, or if a screw head in the hinges doesn't seat properly.

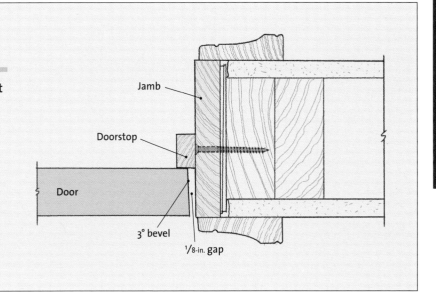

Butt Template Kit and the Bosch 83038 Deluxe Door and Jamb Hinge Template Kit. Both units work on the same principle: Several router templates, sized to cut out a standard hinge size when using the appropriate router bit, are mounted on a guide bar. You can move the individual hinge mortise templates up and down the guide track to the desired locations, and then lock them down in place. To match an existing jamb, you simply hold the track against the jamb and align the templates to the existing mortises; then you can attach the whole jig to the door blank and rout out all three mortises on the door at once.

Using a jig has advantages over cutting mortises by hand with a chisel. It's considerably faster once you get going, so if you're doing many doors, you'll save a lot of time. In addition to making sure the jamb matches the door, the jig also lines the hinge mortises with one another, so that everything matches up readily when it's time to set the door in place.

It takes a little practice to get the hang of using the mortising template, though—when you first start using it, you might want to practice on some scrap lumber or on an old discarded door.

Mortising with a chisel

For those times when you have to hang only one or two doors, it's convenient to know how to cut mortises with a chisel, the way the old-timers used to do it. It's really not hard. You start by tracing the outline of the hinge onto the door or the jamb. (Give yourself a straight layout line first to use as a reference, leaving ¼ in. or so of "meat" on the door—and be sure to space the hinges the same on the jamb as you do on the door.) With the hinge as a guide, draw a line on the face of the door at the corner to indicate the depth of the mortise. Very carefully, cut the outline of the hinge mortise using a utility knife. Then, tapping your chisel gently with your hammer, make a series

Laying Out the Hinges

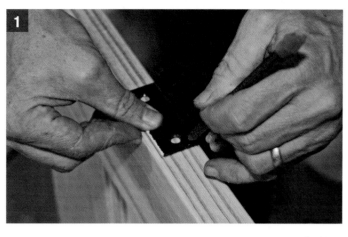

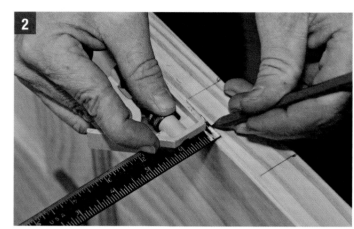

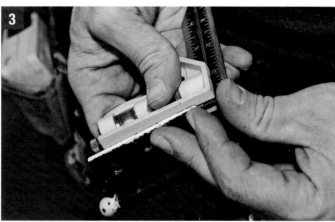

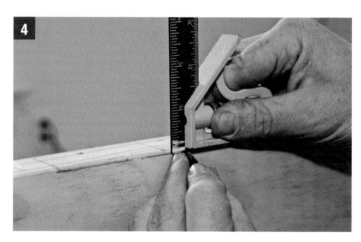

1 | Position the hinge on the door, and trace the outline.

2 | Use the tri-square as a guide to mark the hinge offset on the edge of the door.

3 | Measure off the hinge itself to set the depth of the mortise.

4 | Mark the depth of the mortise on the door, using the tri-square to guide your pencil.

Whether freehand routing or chiseling out hinge mortises, start by slicing the cross grain at the ends of the mortise to prevent any tear out. Use a small square as a straightedge so you can press hard without worrying about miscutting. It will take several passes with a new blade in the utility knife.

Measure off the hinge itself to set the depth of cut on the router.

of closely spaced chisel cuts at a slight angle across the grain of the door stile, until you have "hatched" the entire area of the mortise with shallow cuts. (You can also remove most of the mortise by freehand routing and then finish up with a chisel, as shown in the photos on p. 122.)

Next, bring your chisel gently across the face of the mortise, chipping out the little sections of wood between your hatch cuts (the chips will readily come loose). The key to mortising well is to control the depth of these hatch cuts precisely and space them closely (less than ⅛ in. apart) so you don't tear a lot of grain when you chip them out. Finally, clean up the bottom of the mortise with a few pushes of the chisel, and you're done.

Once you get good at this technique, you'll find that for the occasional individual door, it's not worth setting up your templates and router just to cut one set of hinge mortises. Just keep a sharp chisel on hand, and you can do a fine job.

To safeguard against tear out at the corners, push the router into the mortise at both ends, rather than pushing in at one end and pulling out at the other. Without a template it's almost impossible to get a crisp, straight line with the router alone, so don't even try to finish the mortise with the router. Just get close to your layout lines.

Routing approximately to 1/16 in. will take out enough meat to allow you to clean up the mortise with a chisel, creating perfectly straight edges on the mortise.

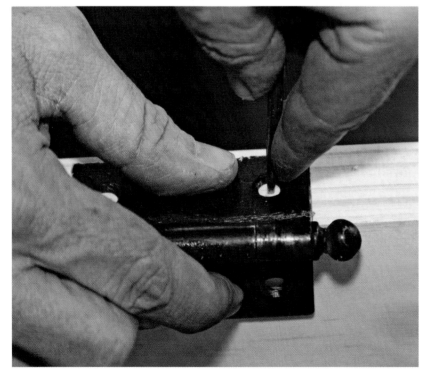

Once the mortise is cut, it's time to predrill pilot holes and secure the hinges with screws. A self-centering bit provides a fast, one-step way to drill perfect pilot holes but it can be done by first marking the centers of the holes as shown here.

Once the centers are marked, you can drill a pilot hole for the screws. The hinge is removed here to keep it from falling out as you chuck up the drill.

Mortising by Hand

Mortising a hinge by hand with a chisel takes a little practice, but once you get the hang of it, it can be done quite efficiently. The trick is to make a series of evenly spaced cuts, taking care to sink the chisel to an exact depth. Use your layout lines as a gauge. After filling the mortise area with these parallel cuts, reverse the chisel and come back at it from the other direction. Finish off by cleaning up the bottom and corners of the mortise.

Drilling and Boring for Locksets

If the door blank you are working with is not predrilled for a cylindrical lockset (most doors are), the best way to drill the holes is with a lock-boring jig.

Typically, doorknobs are located in the center of the lock stile, about 36 in. up from the bottom of the door (measuring to the center of the knob). The backset (the distance the hole is set back from the edge of the door) depends on the door manufacturer. Some latch sets require a 2⅜-in. backset, while others require 2¾ in. There's usually a paper template included with the latch set's instructions. Use this to lay out your borehole location if you're not using a jig.

Bore the face of the door first, and then bore the edge for the latch assembly. On the face bore, stop before you go all the way through, back out, and drill the rest of the hole from the other face. This will prevent you from punching through and tearing out grain on either face of the door.

A lock-boring jig like the Porter-Cable 511 takes the anxiety out of boring the lockset on an expensive door blank. The jig clamps to the edge of a door and perfectly guides the drill for both the face bore and the latch bore.

Locating a Lockset

The lockset is typically located in the center of the lock rail at 36 in. from the finish floor. However, the backset (the distance the hole is set back from the edge of the door) depends on the lockset. Some require a $2^3/8$-in. backset, others require $2^3/4$ in.

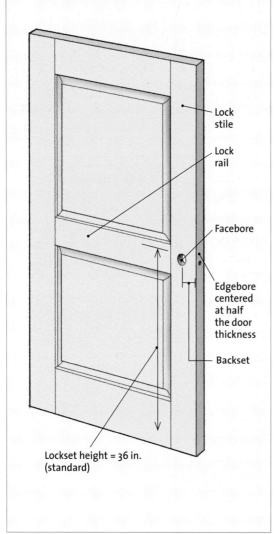

Lock stile

Lock rail

Facebore

Edgebore centered at half the door thickness

Backset

Lockset height = 36 in. (standard)

The Latch Assembly

When laying out the facebore and latchbore for a lockset, use a square so you can pinpoint the exact centerlines. There is not a lot of room for error: The latchbore, in particular, must be bored straight, keeping the hole parallel to the face of the door and lined up along the centerline of the facebore.

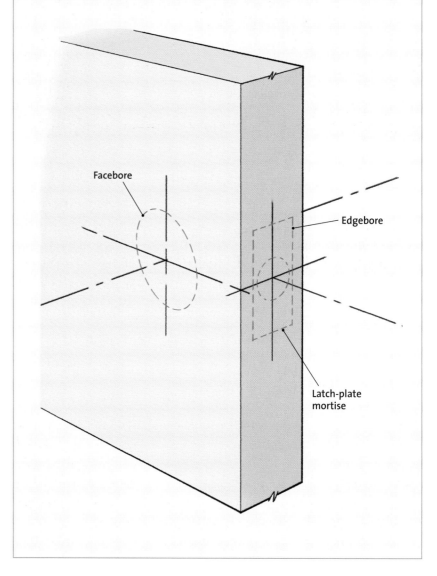

Facebore

Edgebore

Latch-plate mortise

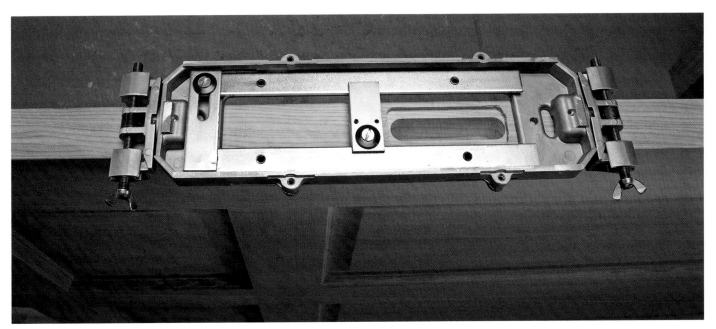

Once the latch is bored, you can insert the latch assembly and trace around the outline of the latch plate. The latch plate should be mortised into the edge of the door and into the jamb. It helps to do the door first, install the latch set, and then hold the strike plate for the jamb in position and align it with latch itself.

A simple latch set usually requires a 1-in. bore in the edge of a door, but a full-mortise lockset typical in many old houses requires a mortise from 2¼ in. to as much as 4 in. deep. It's possible to make a mortise like that by drilling a series of 1-in. holes and cleaning it up with a stout mortising chisel, but it's time consuming and very nerve racking (on a 2-in.-thick exterior door that leaves only ½ in. on either side of the mortise; on an interior door that shrinks to just ¼-in.) But by far the best way to accomplish this harrowing deed is with a mortising template like the Porter-Cable 517.

Casing a Door

Installing door casing is similar to installing window casing, without the sill or apron. Instead, the casings land on the finish floor, or

on plinth blocks. If the finish flooring hasn't yet been installed, make sure to leave room for the floorboards or tiles to slide neatly under your door casings. Cut a couple of spacer blocks and set them on the floor next to the jambs; when you hold your casing stock in place to mark it, the bottom of the casing will rest on the blocks where it should be.

As with a window, you'll probably find things go more smoothly if you install the head casing first, and then fit the side casings to it. But for a double door, where it may be hard to get an accurate measurement for the head casing without a helper to hold one end of your tape (or one end of your material), it can be simpler to install the side casings first, then rest the head casing on them and mark it in place.

Doors, like windows, sometimes get an "upgrade" on the head casing: you can add a reveal joint, corner blocks, a bead joint, a capital, or just a back band for added depth. For more on these details, see "Traditional Head Styles," on p. 83.

Casing an Exterior Door

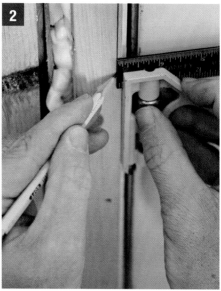

1 Before casing an exterior door, trim the squeeze-out from any foam sealant used to weatherize the opening. A handsaw makes quick work of this.

2 Mark out the reveal line all the way around the door.

3 Measure the height of the side casing to the top reveal line.

4 Beaded casing requires a "jack miter" (the bead is mitered and the flat part of the casing butts together). To cut the side casing to length, start by nipping the bead off at a 45° angle for the mitered part of the cut.

5 Use a tri-square to measure the base of the bead, and add this amount to the length of each side casing.

6 To cut the head casing, begin by marking the width of the side casing on the end of the head casing.

7 Use a compound miter saw to cut the miter on the bead of the head casing. Use the depth stop on the saw to precisely control the depth of cut.

8 The jack miter can be finished off with a jigsaw. You can start the cut with a tablesaw and finish off the last ½ in. with the jigsaw, or clamp a block to the casing to serve as a fence to guide the shoe of the jigsaw, as shown here.

9 Nail off the casing with 2½-in.-long finish nails.

Crown Molding

Crown molding is one of the hallmarks of a well-appointed room, the final touch that truly "crowns" the room's finish work. Bridging the angle between the walls and ceiling, crown molding adds interest to the wall-to-ceiling transition while it visually balances the baseboard's floor-level weight and heft. Stylistically, crown moldings tend to echo the classic forms of column capitals, enhancing our perception that the ceiling is resting on a substantial support, while adding a sense of stability and completeness to the room's form.

Aesthetics aside, crown molding's basic function is to cover up cracks or crooked lines at the wall-to-ceiling intersection. Here again, the finish carpenter may be called upon to "fix" what framers or drywallers have left behind, or what gravity and decades of seasonal change have bestowed on an older home.

Compared to baseboard or even door and window casing, crown molding can be a much fussier medium in which to work. Springing at an angle from the wall to the ceiling, crown molding requires compound-angle joinery at every corner (a special challenge when corners are not as square as they should be). A compound angle means that each end-cut is cut with both a miter and a bevel, which adds complexity to measuring and fastening

Crown molding trims out the corner between the wall and the ceiling. Because it rides on two surfaces, joints must be cut at compound angles.

as well as cutting. And because its traditional curved profile provides only a narrow flat portion at the top and bottom edges that contact the ceiling and the wall, crown molding is not as readily scribed as a simple flat baseboard. To accommodate any dips in the ceiling or curves in the wall and ceiling of an old house, carpenters often have to employ a subtle combination of fudging, shimming, scribing, and spackling. Add to all that the problem of fastening—especially in creatively framed old houses where the location of solid wood within the walls is a matter of mystery—and installing crown molding becomes a significant challenge.

Spring Angle

Two main characteristics define crown molding: its profile and its spring angle. The classic crown molding profile is a standard ogee, but another famous look is a dramatic, wide, swooping cove.

A compound angle includes both a miter and a bevel. With crown molding at the outside corner, the long point of an outside miter is along the top edge. For an inside corner, the long point for a coped joint is on the bottom edge.

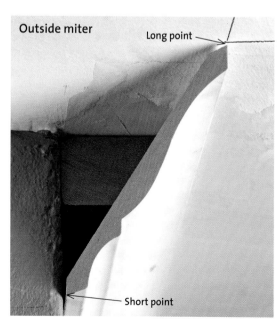

Outside miter

Long point

Short point

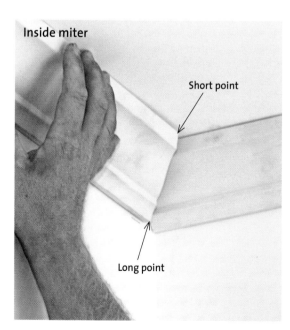

Inside miter

Short point

Long point

Standard Crown Profiles

Standard "Cyma" Crown

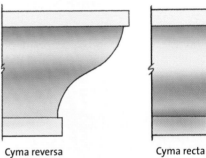

Standard crown has a "cyma recta" curve (the reverse of an ogee, which is also called cyma reversa) combined with a small cove, along the bottom edge.

Cyma reversa   Cyma recta

Cove Molding

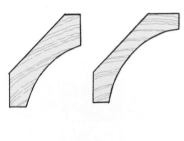

Any crown molding with a concave profile is called a cove molding. Coped inside corners are a must— the long sweeping curve is sure to open up a large void if a simple miter shrinks at all.

Bed Molding

Bed moldings are typically less than 2 in. wide, and are traditionally used as an exterior molding between the frieze board and the soffit. But they can also be used inside as a small crown or as one element of a built-up cornice.

Band Molding

Ceiling trim doesn't need to be elaborate to be effective. A flat band molding (baseboard profiles turned upside down) applied to the top of the wall can go a long way to dressing up a room.

Spring Angle

Just like a set of stairs, crown molding has a "rise" and a "run." Its "rise" is actually the vertical drop from the ceiling (measured on the wall) while the "run" is the distance that the crown projects out from the wall (measured on the ceiling.)

Sometimes the spring angle will be part of the molding description when you buy it, typically specified with its complement. For example, "52/38 crown" is a crown with a spring angle of 38°; "45/45" is crown with a spring angle of 45°.

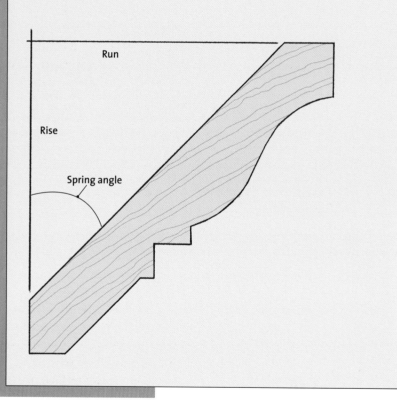

For a standard 38° crown, the saw settings are 31.6 for the miter (top) and 33.9 for the bevel (above). Most compound-miter saws have detents at these odd angle settings.

Regardless of its profile, every crown molding has a specific "spring angle"—the angle between the crown's beveled backside and the wall where it rests. This angle will affect the molding's appearance, its nailing characteristics, and how it lies against the wall and ceiling, but, most important, it determines the cut angles required to join it.

The least demanding spring angle is 45° (common to most cove moldings), but more common is 38° crown (for a steeper face common to most ogee crown). It's unusual to find anything else in the average home center. In fact, a 38° crown is so common that almost all compound sliding miter saws now come equipped with detents—small divots in the miter and bevel adjustments that hold the saw at the correct miter and bevel angles.

But, in restoration work, it's not uncommon to find a wide range of moldings with different spring angles.

The spring angle is the key concept for joining crown. The term will pop up again later in this chapter when we talk about cutting, joining, and fastening.

Crown Toolkit

Running crown doesn't take that many tools: a miter saw, a coping saw, and some kind of nailer are the only must-haves. But a few extras can help make the job run smoother.

Miter saws

The type of saw you have will affect how you can cut crown. A regular miter saw will work just fine with an auxiliary fence, but may limit the size of crown you can cut. The largest of these saws—the DeWalt 12-in. and the Hitachi 15-in. miter saws—will cut crown with a rise up to 6 in., but for anything larger, you will have to cut the crown flat (see "Cutting on the flat" on pp. 149–150). For this, a sliding compound miter saw is usually the most versatile option.

Crown stops

Some large miter saws come with an accessory stop that holds the top edge of the crown in the right place against the table. This comes in handy when positioning the crown "upside down and backward" on the saw—a technique that doesn't require figuring out the miter and bevel angles for the compound miter (see "Upside down and backward" on pp. 148–149). While these stops are very convenient, you can save yourself the $25 and make an auxiliary table that will hold the crown in the same way on the miter saw.

A 12-in. compound miter saw accommodates crown molding up to 6⅝ in.

For anything larger, a sliding compound miter saw will do the trick, but the material has to be cut flat.

For efficiency and accuracy when cutting "upside down and backward," it's best to have a positive stop on the miter-saw table to hold the edges of the molding in an exact position on the saw. This can be done with accessory stops, or with an auxiliary plywood table, as shown here.

Auxiliary Crown Fence

An auxiliary fence made of plywood will hold crown in a similar position as it will be when installed, which simplifies the angle cuts. When using a jig like this it's important to secure the miter saw and the support legs to the workbench, then secure the auxiliary table to the support legs. The whole assembly should not slide around at all.

In the assembly shown here, both fence and table are made from 3/8-in. plywood. The tricky part is determining the height of the fence. It needs to be tall enough to support the crown but will need a cutout to accommodate the blade housing. If the fence is too high in the center where the blade comes down, it will prevent the blade from descending deep enough to cut all the way across a piece of crown molding.

1 Secure the saw to the bench. The jig will also be secured to the benchtop, so it's important that the saw not be allowed to move independent of the auxiliary fence.

2 Build two L-brackets out of ¾-in. plywood. The length of the brackets is not critical, but the height of the vertical leg should be the exact height of the saw table. Screw the L-brackets to the benchtop so it is as secure as the saw.

3 Screw the auxiliary fence to an auxiliary table, and then screw the entire assembly to the L-brackets on both sides of the saw.

4 Use a piece of crown molding to set the position of the front stop.

Without a hose to drag around, a cordless nailer comes into its own nailing off crown molding.

Use a large 2-ft. framing square to check outside corners.

Take Note • Use a Speed Square to check inside corners for square. The buildup of drywall mud in the corner can throw the angle off 90°. By looking at how the walls compare to the square, you can get a sense for the discrepancy. If it's significant, back cut the copes to fix the problem.

Nailers

Using a pneumatic nailer is not only faster than hand nailing, but the air tool also allows you to create a better joint. Banging on the joint with a hammer and a nail will push the pieces out of alignment, especially if the pieces have been glued first. An air nailer punches the fastener in without moving anything.

A cordless nailer shines for nailing crown molding because you aren't trying to lift the weight of the hose over your head with each fastener you drive. The Paslode Trim Pulse is especially nice here because it will drive a nail as small as ¾ in. This size comes in handy for closing outside miters. Otherwise, a brad nailer is a close second for this task.

Square

Any square will work to check inside corners but a large, 2-ft. framing square will be useful for checking outside corners and for drawing a full-scale section of the crown assembly to find the "rise" of the angle.

Bevel square and protractor

A siding bevel square is useful for finding a variety of unknown angles, but it's often useless without a protractor to read the angle. For this, a simple, clear-plastic "grade-school" protractor works just fine, but not all of them are accurate. Check before you buy by taking a sliding bevel with you to the store: First, set the bevel square to 90° using the protractor, as shown in the top photos on p. 136. Then flip

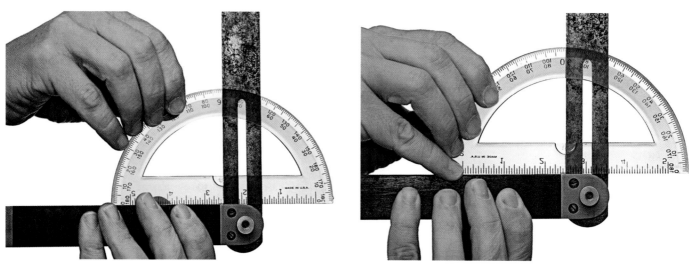

To check the accuracy of a protractor with a bevel square, set the square to 90° using one side of the protractor. Then holding the bevel setting, flip the protractor and see how the other side reads. If both sides read the same, the protractor is accurate.

If you're installing a lot of crown, a Bosch MiterFinder will become almost as indispensable as a miter saw. It's a digital bevel square that not only reads the exact angle of a wall or the spring angle of a particular piece of molding but also performs the calculation to find the exact miter and bevel settings for the saw.

the bevel square to read the complementary 90°. They should be the same.

Bosch MiterFinder

Bosch makes a unique electronic tool that has become a must-have item for many professional trim carpenters. It's essentially a large folding bevel square with an onboard computer and an LED screen that can measure any angle to within $1/10$ of a degree as the legs are opened between two surfaces. The computer calculates the miter and bevel required to cut the crown on the flat for any angle and crown molding (see "Digital bevel square" on p. 151). The precision afforded by this tool renders most other methods for finding compound angles mere stabs in the dark.

Starrett® "5-in-1" Protractor

L. S. Starrett (www.starrett.com) offers a viable alternative to the Bosch electronic protractor that's a lot easier to carry in your tool belt. This tool has two 2½-in.-wide blades that pivot and

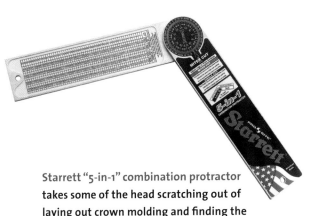

Starrett "5-in-1" combination protractor takes some of the head scratching out of laying out crown molding and finding the compound cuts for crown miters. This of this as a low-tech version of the Bosch MiterFinder that's a lot easier to carry in your tool belt.

a simple protractor gauge on the "back" side of the tool. This protractor displays both the angle and its supplement (180° – the angle). On the "front" side of the tool, a precision dial indicates the angle of both the miter cut and the "straight cut" (the complement of the miter cut). From the miter cut, it's possible to find the saw settings for a compound angle reading off a simple table printed on the tool. It's low-tech, but it works well.

Stepladder

In most houses, carpenters will need some way to step up to reach the ceiling. Since it needs to be maneuverable, there's a tendency to choose the lightest equipment available, but this is not something you want to skimp on. A good work platform needs to be rugged enough to support the weight of anyone who might climb on it. Drywall benches are a nice alternative for low ceilings, but most carpenters like to get right up on the work, so a stepladder is usually in order. Don't skimp on buying a stepladder: Use a Type 1 or 1A. Anything less will probably not hold up to frequent use.

Take Note • For ceilings higher than 9 ft., consider renting or buying a rolling ladder-frame staging system (sometimes called Baker staging).

Portable tablesaw

Unless the job requires only a very small bed or cove molding in the corner between the wall and the ceiling, access to a tablesaw is essential for ripping blocking. (Any standard 3½-in. or larger single-piece crown should be attached to blocking. See "Where's the nailing?" p. 139.) Forget trying to find the ceiling joists; they usually won't be there on two sides of the room anyway.

Prepping Crown Jobs

Before you start laying out crown, take a few minutes to evaluate the room's lines and angles. Old houses frequently show sags in the ceilings and frequent bumps from patched plaster. In new homes, ceilings may be close to level, but walls may have bows or curves. In either case, you just have to play along with the house's existing quirks. As a rule, aim for running crown molding parallel to the ceiling, rather than strictly level. In most cases, window heads and ceilings often settle in the same direction, so the tilt is not always noticeable. But these discrepancies will throw the corner angles off, so you'll want to proceed carefully at the corners and expect to test your cuts with scrap material before committing to finish cuts on long runs.

Also, take note of any small features in the room that you'll need to work around, such as box-outs for chimneys or plumbing chases.

olling Ceiling Cracks

Seasonal movement of roof trusses can cause gaps at the intersection of the wall and ceiling. This phenomenon, known as "truss uplift," occurs when the lower truss cords above the ceiling dry out and shrink during the heating season while the top cords against the roof tend to gain moisture and expand. This causes the whole truss to curve, much like a board tends to cup when exposed to differential moisture (see Appendix A on pp. 215–238).

The ceiling movement can cause drywall to crack at the intersection of interior walls and ceiling. Some builders allow for this natural seasonal movement by fastening interior walls to the trusses with clips that allow for some movement. Others allow the corner to "float" by holding the ceiling drywall fasteners back about 16 in. from the corner, hoping the drywall will stay in place even if the truss bows upward. Remodeling contractor Chuck Green of Westborough, MA, solves the problem with a built-up crown detail that's designed to ride up and down with the ceiling. Green attaches his nailer backing only to the ceiling, and installs a flat trim foundation to the wall. He purposefully doesn't fasten the crown assembly to the wall foundation, so it can slide up and down with seasonal changes.

Truss Uplift

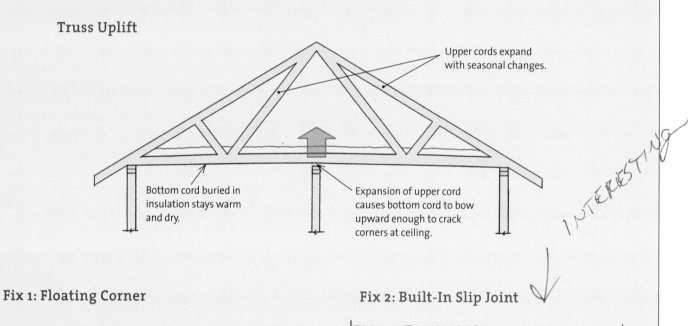

Upper cords expand with seasonal changes.

Bottom cord buried in insulation stays warm and dry.

Expansion of upper cord causes bottom cord to bow upward enough to crack corners at ceiling.

INTERESTING

Fix 1: Floating Corner

1x6

Bottom cord of truss

Top plate

16 in.

Hold back fasteners in ceiling to allow drywall to flex.

Fix 2: Built-In Slip Joint

Bottom cord of truss

Blocking and crown attached to ceiling

Foundation (base stock) attached to wall

It's best to box out any exposed plumbing pipes and heating ducts before undertaking the trim work. But once these are enclosed, these smaller box-outs are often a good place to begin.

Before committing to that starting point, however, scope out the entire run. Figure out which direction people are most likely to come into the room from: That's where they're most likely to see the crown and where you want to make sure it looks right.

Where's the nailing?

Crown molding is harder to fasten than flat molding such as baseboard because only a small part of the molding actually contacts the wall and ceiling. Finding the nailing under the wall and ceiling surface can be tricky: Studs may not be on center, and joists may not line up with studs. Joists, of course, only cross the wall at two ends of the room; on two sides of the room the ceiling framing runs parallel to the walls, and there's unlikely to be solid wood at all where the crown's ceiling edge falls.

Stud finders and magnets are helpful, but they're inconsistent, and on old plaster and lath walls stud finders are more or less useless. Overall, the time spent with these is not worth the aggravation. Unless you're building on a soffit designed for the crown, or running a small bed molding or cove that can be supported solely by the wall's top plates, the most practical way to provide nailing for one-piece crown is to run solid blocking in the corners.

Running angled blocking Find the spring angle of the crown, and rip 2x stock to that angle. You can get two pieces of blocking for 3½-in. crown molding out of one 2x6. (It will take a second, straight rip on the second piece

Solid blocking ripped from a 2x4 provides a secure base for crown molding that will bridge any imperfection in the ceiling or wall. Be sure to cut the blocking narrower than the space behind the molding. The blocking doesn't have to touch the back of the crown to provide good support.

Long screws secure the blocking to whatever available framing exists behind the walls and ceiling. It doesn't have to look pretty as it will be covered by the crown.

to make it fit.) Rip the blocking a touch undersize, so that when it fits tight into the corner it leaves a little space behind the crown molding for play.

Fasten the blocking into the corner with long drywall screws. The blocking doesn't have to run continuous, and it's easier to work with

Ripping Blocking for Crown

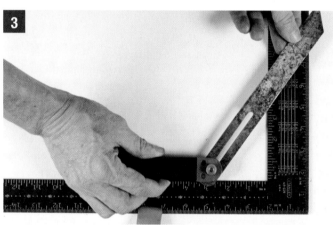

1 | To find the dimensions for ripping the blocking, draw a section of the crown on a clean piece of paper or plywood, using a framing square and a scrap of crown molding.

2 | Trace the line of the backside of the crown, as well as the angle of the framing square.

3 | Use a bevel square to determine the angle to set the saw.

4 | Rip the blocking.

short pieces if you're working alone. On the other hand, it's faster to run long pieces.

If you're fastening the blocking into a double top plate that runs continuously around the room, 1-ft.-long blocks secured with a couple of screws every 2-ft. on-center will provide sufficient nailing. But you're going to drive twice as many screws this way than if you put up 8-footers secured with one screw every 2 ft. on-center. In an old house that is balloon framed, however, the blocking will have to be secured to the studs, so the blocking pieces need to be long enough to pick up nailing on at least two studs.

Running 2-ft. to 4-ft. lengths is often the best compromise. Keep in mind that this blocking doesn't have to look pretty and crown's not structural, so you don't have to pick up every stud.

Once the blocking is in place, you can nail crown near the center area and hit the nailing strips. Because of the crown molding's geometry, a single nail in the center of the profile pulls both its edges tight to the wall and ceiling. This way, you don't have to worry about nailing through the molding's edges into joists and studs that may or may not be there.

Layout

The edges of most crown molding are very thin, and it's not always clear to the carpenter installing the molding when it is seated exactly right. In fact, most crown molding is milled so the meeting edges on the back face are slightly beveled, ensuring that the outside edges fit tight to the wall and ceiling.

For this reason, it's helpful to have a line on the wall to work from. In a new house, you can simply hold a piece of the molding in place and mark the wall. If the ceiling is relatively

Nailing Crown to Blocking

If the blocking is slightly recessed from the back of the crown, a single nail in the center of the crown molding's profile pulls both edges tight to the wall and ceiling.

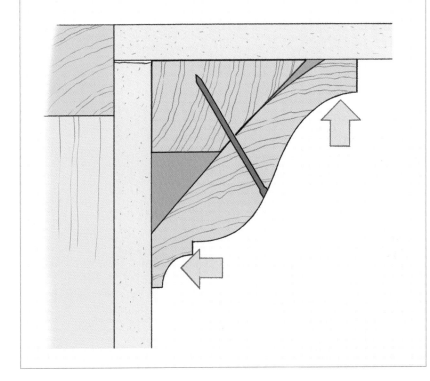

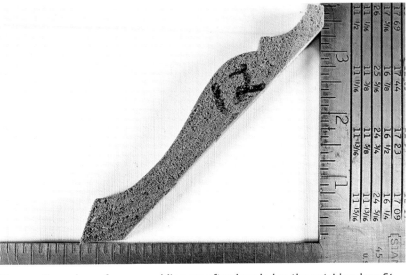

The meeting edges of crown molding are often beveled so the outside edges fit tight to the wall and ceiling. While this provides some leeway to accommodate irregularities in the ceiling surfaces, it also means it can be difficult to seat the molding on the wall without a predetermined reference line.

flat, an elevation mark in each corner and a couple near the center of a run is often sufficient. It's not necessary to snap a chalk line all the way across the wall. However, if you are setting blocks to support a cornice, a continuous chalk line is a convenient reference.

Fitting to a crooked ceiling

In old houses, where walls and ceilings aren't usually smooth or flat, plan on "mapping" the planes with a level and string to find the low points, and using a framing square to evaluate the angle between the wall and the ceiling at various points. Ceilings are typically the worst. Most old houses have some kind of sag, usually a gentle curve toward the center of the room. Sometimes it can be ignored; long lengths of crown are surprisingly flexible and will sometimes "wrap" around shallow dips. But sometimes more attention is required.

In theory, the top edge can be scribed for the occasional ceiling bump, but this fix is to be avoided, if possible. What makes crown distinctive is the shadow lines created by its contoured faces. The eye easily picks out any departure from parallel in these lines. So major ceiling problems must be dealt with in other ways.

Build the ceiling down If headroom allows, consider putting up a new ceiling over strapping, and shimming the strapping level. This is a time-consuming job, but the most gratifying solution for a severely sagging ceiling. Another option is to build a small soffit that visually becomes part of the crown assembly. If the soffit's front reveal is deep enough, the sag in the ceiling virtually disappears.

In new construction, layout is quick: Hold a piece of the molding in place and mark where the bottom edge of the crown falls on the wall.

Ceilings aren't always flat and smooth. If caulking, paint, or joint compound won't make up the difference, you may have to furr and shim.

Working with Mockups

Trim specialist Ken O'Brien of Troy, Michigan, has built a business for himself that focuses on trimming out modern homes with historic trim (ineedcrown.com). When he meets with the client, he brings a range of samples that he can hold up on the wall to help sell the job. A client can immediately see what they are getting, overcoming what is arguably the hardest part for many homeowners—visualizing the change that new trim will have on a room. By demonstrating a number of different crown assemblies, O'Brien can discuss the design aspects of his work much more effectively with people who might not otherwise have the design vocabulary to describe what they want. But these mockups also have a utilitarian function once he lands the job. By holding the mockup in a corner, he can automatically measure how far down the wall it comes, and how far out on the ceiling.

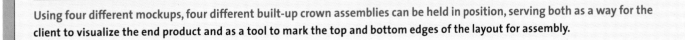

Using four different mockups, four different built-up crown assemblies can be held in position, serving both as a way for the client to visualize the end product and as a tool to mark the top and bottom edges of the layout for assembly.

Soffit Cornice

To hide an extreme belly in a ceiling, consider building a soffit from ¼-in. plywood. The soffit can be secured to a nailer that's shimmed flat, and the top edge of the soffit can be trimmed out with a flexible molding. The more extreme the sag in the ceiling, the deeper the front face of the soffit should be to "hide" the discrepancy between the flexible molding that hugs the ceiling sag and the straight leading edge of the soffit.

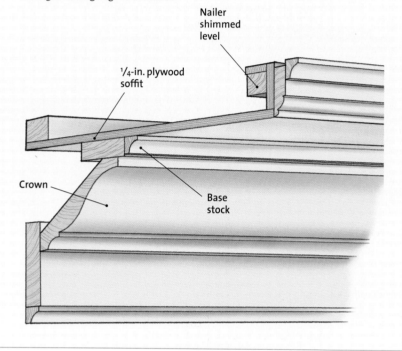

Nailer shimmed level

¼-in. plywood soffit

Base stock

Crown

Carpenter David Frane developed this notched **screed for floating a ceiling or wall: It's nothing more than a scrap of molding that "keys" to the front lip on the crown. The screed rides along the molding, filling the gap at the edge with mud while the other end of the screed feathers the mud to "zero" (no depth).**

Plan for a gap If the sag is slight, but still more than the crown molding can tolerate flexing to, the best solution is often to shim the blocking that supports the crown level and affix the crown so the top edge hits the low point of the sag. Set the crown to a level line on the wall. If the gap where the crown molding's edge meets the ceiling is not too great, it can be caulked and painted.

"Float" the ceiling (or wall) If the gaps are greater than caulk will allow, they can often be filled by skim-coating the ceiling. Carpenter David Frane developed a nice notched screed that keys to the front lip on the crown, while the other end skims the surface of the ceiling, feathering the mud to "zero" toward the center of the room. This notched screed effectively controls the depth of the mud at the crown edge. Use a dry-mix curing joint compound, such as Durabond® 90, which will bond better and won't create shrinkage cracks the way a drying mud will when a thick buildup

Order of Installation

It doesn't really matter where you begin or which way you work around the room, but having a predefined installation order helps keep the job organized and eliminates the head scratching when you begin. A common strategy is to start on the wall opposite the primary entrance to a room. To streamline the job, keep all the coped joints running in the same direction, so you don't waste time adjusting the saw.

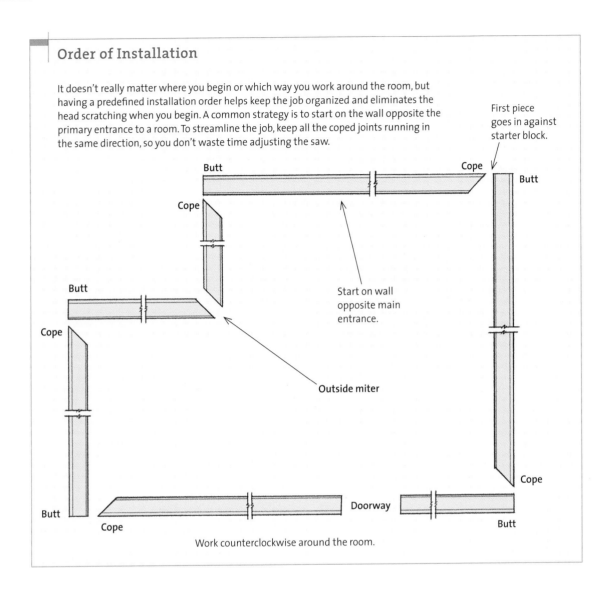

First piece goes in against starter block.

Butt

Cope

Butt

Cope

Butt

Start on wall opposite main entrance.

Cope

Outside miter

Butt

Cope

Butt

Cope

Doorway

Butt

Work counterclockwise around the room.

dries. Be sure to repair any loose plaster before skim-coating.

Avoid one-piece crown Built-up crown assemblies offer more leeway for fudging. If the ceiling sags or slants, you can run the multiple pieces at slight angles, effectively splitting the difference between true parallel and whatever variation in the planes to which you are installing it. Once the whole assembly is finished, it will look like a single piece of molding applied flat and straight on the wall. Rather than drawing attention to crooked spots along a scribed cut, this method can actually fool

the eye into thinking the walls and ceiling are straighter than they really are. (For more on this, see "Built-Up Crown" on pp. 163–166.)

Installation order

It's almost time to start chopping up the molding, but first take a moment to define the installation order. For efficiency, you want to eliminate the time and fuss of resetting the saw for each cut. The goal is to set up all the cuts pointing in the same direction.

If possible, start with the trim on the longest wall opposite the door, with one coped end and the other end butted square into the

Consistency is the key to efficiency: Chop all the square cuts with a sharp handsaw and leave the saw set for the back bevel of the inside cope. This will be faster than readjusting the miter saw.

When running all of the crown cuts in the same direction, install the first piece of crown against a temporary starter block (left). The cope on the first piece butts this block (right).

corner. You can "butt-left" and "cope-right" (as right-handed people seem to prefer) or the other way (as lefties like). It doesn't matter, but consistency is the key so you don't continually have to reset the angle on your saw. Keep the saw set for the back bevel of the coped inside corners and cut the square cuts with a handsaw.

Using a starter block If you set up all the cuts in the same direction, the first piece of molding will have a butt on one end and a cope on the other. This means that the first cope must be installed against a temporary block—a scrap piece of crown, about 1 ft. long, square cut to fit in the corner and temporarily screwed in place. Be sure to hold the nails away from this

When measuring crown, butt the tape against the wall, not the molding (left). In the case of this inside corner, the true zero point will be the long point of the cope.

starter block: nail the first piece of crown near the center of the run and toward the butt end only. This provides enough support to hold up the entire length of crown but leaves the coped end free so the starter block can be removed and the piece of crown slipped into place.

Measuring crown lengths Measure the length for crown along the bottom (wall) edge, and keep track of the short points (on an end with an outside miter) and long points (for inside corner copes) along that edge. Because of the mud build-up in corners, it's often hard to get an exact reading by bending a tape measure into an inside corner. Even the most practiced carpenter can misjudge exactly where that bottom edge of the cope joint will land. On long lengths, aim for a measurement that is $\frac{1}{16}$ in. to $\frac{1}{8}$ in. long, with a slight backcut on the square-cut end. The piece can then be bent slightly to get it in place. If it's slightly long, it will snap into place, and the knife edge of the cope will bite slightly into the adjoining piece.

Pinch Sticks

For measuring short lengths of crown molding **enclosed by walls (inside an alcove, for example), use a set of "pinch sticks."** By holding the two narrow sticks together and sliding them until one end of each hits the wall, you can get a more accurate representation of the length at both the top and bottom edge. Once you have the distance, mark the sticks with two lines for positive realignment and use a spring clamp to hold them together while you transfer the length to the molding.

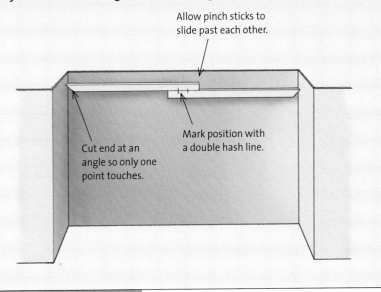

Allow pinch sticks to slide past each other.

Cut end at an angle so only one point touches.

Mark position with a double hash line.

Crown molding can be cut flat with a compound miter saw, but the miter and bevel settings are not obvious. These angles vary depending on the spring angle.

The auxiliary table both extends the height of the fence and provides a secure stop that holds the crown in an exact position. Cutting this way, the top edge of the crown is on the table and the bottom edge is on the fence.

Testing a Miter Saw for Accuracy

A good test for an accurate miter saw is the "octagon test" taught to us by master craftsman David Crosby. Cut an octagon made of equal-length segments. The sixteen 22° miter cuts required to complete an octagon will magnify any slight error in each angle, and the final cut will tell you all you need to know about the accuracy of a saw. This can be done first with 1x stock to check the miter accuracy, and again, keeping the material flat but with the blade flopped to 22°, to check the bevel accuracy.

Corner Joints

The trickiest part of crown molding work for most carpenters is the joinery—especially inside and outside corners. Here's the place where an investment in tools can really help: Cutting large crown is much easier with a well-built, accurate compound miter saw.

Upside down and backward

There are two ways to cut miters in crown molding. You can set the piece on your miter saw flat against the table, or you can set it at an angle, with one edge resting on the table and the other on the fence. Carpenters typically call the latter, angled method "upside down and backward" to describe how the molding is positioned in the saw relative to how it goes on the wall. It's "upside down" because the bottom edge of the crown (the edge that will go on the wall) rests on the saw's fence, and the top edge (the edge that goes on the ceiling) rests on the miter table.

It's "backward" because the piece will have to be flipped end for end, as well as turned upside down, as it's moved from the workbench to the wall. This means you have to be able to keep track of which direction the cut goes. This can get confusing to even the most seasoned carpenter, so it's helpful to make yourself a couple of pattern blocks to keep track of the direction of the short and long points.

The big advantage of cutting crown this way is you don't have to concern yourself with

Visualize this: When positioning crown at an angle on the saw, the table represents the ceiling and the fence represents the wall. With this orientation, you are cutting the crown as it will be installed, but "upside down" and the miters point in a "backward" direction.

Working with Pattern Blocks

A set of pattern blocks provides a visual reference of the correct angle that can help take some of the head scratching out of cutting crown. Label the blocks for each type of cut: "left outside" (for left-hand side of an outside miter), "right outside," "left inside," and "right inside." To help stay oriented, remind yourself that when you cut an inside corner using the auxiliary fence, the long point is always up on the fence. For an outside corner, the long point is down on the table.

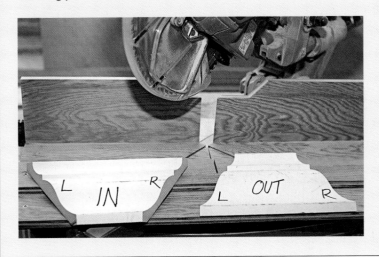

figuring out separate (and unusual) miter and bevel angles. You simply set the miter table to bisect the wall corner. (For example, set the miter table at 45° for a typical 90° corner.) The blade, representing a plane that bisects the angle of the intersecting walls, automatically creates the proper bevel on the crown as it slices through the angled molding. In actual practice, however, the wall corner may be a little out of square, so the faces of the cut may need to be back-beveled with a few strokes of a block plane, or you may have to adjust the saw's miter angle a touch.

Cutting on the flat

If a piece of crown molding is too large to fit on the miter saw in its angled position, you have to cut it "on the flat" using a compound miter saw. Buying the saw is the easy part, though. The tough part is figuring the exact miter and bevel angles.

The saw settings to use depend on (a) the angle of the wall corner and (b) the spring angle of the molding. Calculating these angles requires a fair amount of complex math—more than these authors care to tackle on each job. When in doubt, we rely on a couple of tables, instead (see the tables on p. 150). One

Cutting Crown Flat: Settings for Joining Two Crown Pieces at a Right Angle

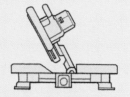

Type of Crown (spring angle)	Miter (angle on table)	Bevel (tilt of blade)
30°	27°	38°
35°	30.5°	35°
38°	31.6°	33.9°
40°	33°	33°
45°	35.3°	30°
52°	38°	26°

Cutting Crown Flat: Settings for Joining Three Crown Pieces at a Right Angle

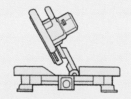

Type of Crown (spring angle)	Miter (angle on table)	Bevel (tilt of blade)
30°	11.7°	19.4°
35°	13.4°	18.3°
38°	14.3°	17.5°
40°	14.9°	17°
45°	16.3°	15.7°
52°	18.1°	13.6°

Note: While it is very difficult to set the decimal degrees on most miter saws, the degree of accuracy provided in these charts gives you a running start at determining which side of the line to favor on your miter or bevel gauge. Any more than 1/10th of a degree, however, is pointless; it's impossible to read on any miter saw.

Take Note • Measuring spring angles and calculating miter and bevel cuts will get you close, but not perfect. Inevitably, you will have to fine-tune the cuts. With paint-grade crown, plan on adjusting your saw by 1/2° increments to sneak up on the cut. For stain-grade work, work to 1/4°.

table provides the miter and bevel settings for crown wrapping around a 90° wall. The other table is for figuring the miter and bevel setting for joining the three pieces that wrap a bull-nose corner (see the sidebar on "Wrapping a Bullnose" on pp. 156–157). This second table can also be used for figuring the crown cuts in an octagonal room.

For spring angles not shown on these charts, you will have to interpolate—make a reasoned estimate based on the numbers that fall between those provided.

Finding exact angles

Finding the perfect miter and bevel settings depends on knowing the exact wall angles. Most corners in a house are not perfect right angles, so some degree of fudging is required.

Test fit At the very least, use the charts to make a few sample cuts on a couple of pieces of scrap crown, and hold these in place. If the joint is open on one side or the other, you can adjust the cut as needed. This trial-and-error approach is often sufficient for approximating an inside corner that will be coped.

At the start of a large job, cut a couple of test blocks and use them to check each inside corner. By holding the blocks in the corner, you can get an idea of how you might need to cut the back bevel, before cutting the cope on a full-length piece of stock.

Bisect the corner Outside miters aren't as forgiving as a coped joint. If you're cutting "upside down and backward," it's easy to find the exact miter angle to use by laying it out on the ceiling, as shown in the photo series on pp. 152–153.

Digital bevel square These days, many professional trim carpenters don't ever bother with charts and fudging. Instead they measure each angle precisely with the Bosch MiterFinder, then let this tool calculate the miter and bevel angles required for cutting crown flat on the saw.

Aligning joints The shorter the pieces you are joining, the more precise your cut will have to be. The longer the pieces are, the more latitude you have to twist the molding to bring the joint into alignment. By twisting it, you are simply changing its spring angle slightly. If the

Bisecting an Outside Angle

Wall corners aren't always perfect right angles, but you can find the exact miter for the corner geometrically:

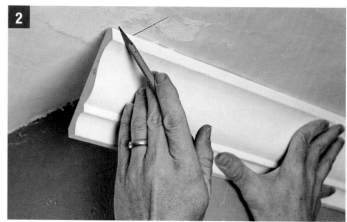

1 | Hold a scrap piece of crown in place where the molding will rest and trace the top edge on the ceiling.

2 | Do the same on the opposite side of the angle.

3 | Hold a bevel square on the corner, with the blade extending through the "X" made where the layout lines intersect. The angle between the top layout line and the blade of the bevel square defines the miter angle you need.

4 | Read the angle on a protractor (137°).

5 Subtract 90° from this number (137° – 90° = 47°).

6 Set the miter angle on the saw.

7 Position the molding against the auxiliary fence and cut.

8 The assembled outside miter.

Calculating Miter and Bevel Settings

The Bosch MiterFinder will calculate the exact miter and bevel settings for any crown on any corner, as follows:

1
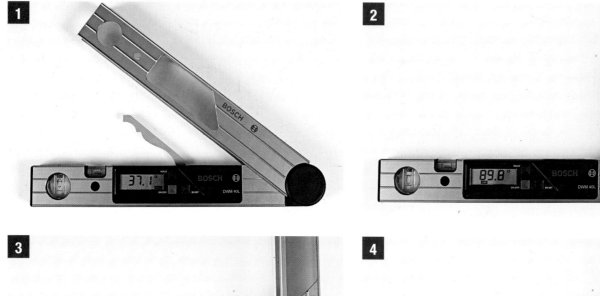

2

3

4

1 Spread the arms on the MiterFinder to the spring angle of the crown (in this case 37.1°), then press the BV/MT button to enter it into the memory. "SP" will appear in a black box at the lower left corner of the display.

2 Place the MiterFinder in the corner of the walls and open it until both arms are flat against each wall. Press the Bevel/Miter button again. "CNR" will appear on the display.

3 To find the miter angle, press the BV/MT button again. "MTR" will appear on the display.

4 To find the bevel angle, press the BV/MT button one last time. "BVL" will appear on the display.

simply changing its spring angle slightly. If the piece of crown isn't long enough to allow you to twist it by hand, you can sometimes force it off its spring angle by driving a shim at the top or the bottom, which may have the same effect of bringing the bevels together. Or if the joint's tight at the back and gaps open a bit toward the front, you can shave a little off the back of the bevel with a sharp block plane and push the pieces back toward the wall at the top to bring things together.

That same kind of fine-tuning of the bevel can also be done on the saw, of course. Professional-quality miter saws are finely adjustable and can home in on the perfect cut. Plan on shaving the faces of both sides of the miter—playing too much with just one side will alter the profile curve so it doesn't mate up with its partner.

All of these adjustments are subtle. They won't buy you a full ⅛ in. but they might buy you a ¹⁄₁₆ in.—enough to draw the joint tight.

Coping inside corners

A coped joint is a marriage of complete opposites: One length of molding is cut square and butts tight to the wall. The second piece—the coped end—"keys" perfectly to the profile of the butted piece at a right angle. Inside copes on crown molding aren't as challenging as they're often made out to be. In fact, they are rather forgiving and that's their beauty.

The procedure for coping crown is similar to coping one-piece baseboard or any other profiled molding (see "Cutting coped joints" in Chapter 2, on p. 44). But with crown, nothing's straight or flat about the profile, so you have a lot more meat to cope out.

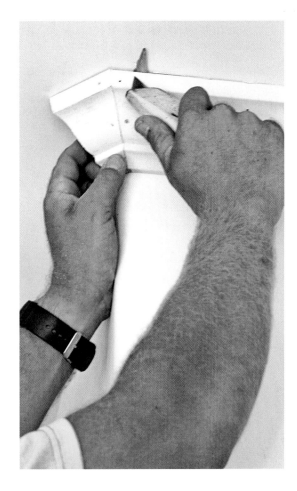

Close a miter that is slightly open at the bottom by driving a shim under the top edge, as shown. Similarly, fix a miter that is open at the top with a shim forced under the bottom edge.

To Cope or Not to Cope?

Coping creates a nearly perfect joint visually. But it will take time to perfect the technique, and typically takes longer to cut than an inside miter. The precision afforded by the Bosch MiterFinder and a top-of-the-line miter saw, combined with the stability afforded by advanced adhesives and MDF stock, have given many professionals the confidence to use inside miters. But most carpenters still prefer coping all inside corners, simply because the joint proves more forgiving to the discrepancies found on jobsites. A coped joint will automatically adjust to an out-of-square corner, whereas the inconsistency of a corner angle with a miter usually involves a lot of back and forth to the saw.

Wrapping a Bullnose

Turning a bullnosed corner with crown is done much the same way as it's done with baseboard (see "Bullnose Corners" on p. 53). The corner is divided into three segments, which each take a 45° turn.

In the example shown here, Smokey Saduk starts by building a rough mockup of the corner using a standard crown with a 38° spring angle. He cuts the molding flat, at a textbook 14.3° miter and a 17.5° bevel to build a mockup of the corner that he can hold on the wall to test the fit.

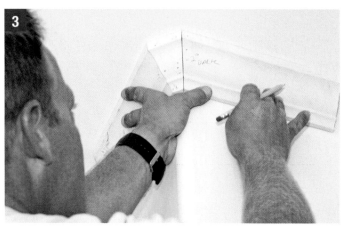

1 | Cut the molding for the mockup flat.

2 | Assemble the mockup.

3 | Hold the mockup on the corner to test the fit.

4 | After adjusting the mockup, use it to mark the length of the three pieces.

The joint is slightly open, so Smokey estimates in degrees how he needs to recut the joint, and marks this on his sample: "2° open." When the mockup has been recut to fit, Smokey uses it to make two marks on the wall that establish the lengths of all three pieces in this wraparound corner. Once the first two pieces have been cut and nailed in place, an exact measurement for the final piece can be taken, resulting in a perfect fit.

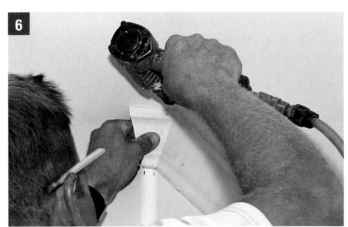

5 | Transfer the mark to the first piece.

6 | Install the first two pieces.

7 | Measure for the third piece.

8 | The finished bullnose corner.

Coping Crown

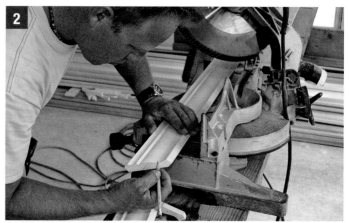

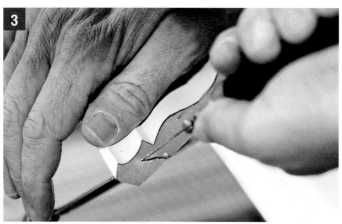

1 A coped joint starts with a reverse bevel that reveals the profile.

2 Rub the corner with a pencil lead to highlight this profile.

3 Follow the darkened line with a coping saw. To get into the corners, you'll have to come at the line from several directions.

4 To cut the delicate point on the bottom edge of the molding, start with the coping saw running parallel to the length of the crown.

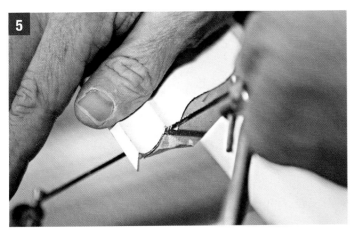

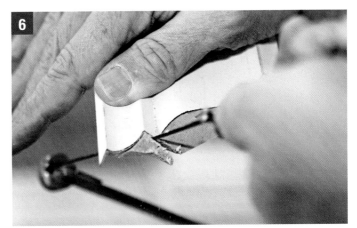

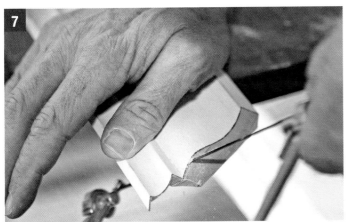

5 | Reverse again to cut the tight curve of the crown's bottom cove.

6 | Come at the corner from a new direction.

7 | The long sweeping curve of the reverse ogee can be cut in one pass.

8 | The finish cut usually needs to be cleaned up with a utility knife.

Coping is always a two-step process: first, a bevel cut reveals the outline of the profile, which is backcut with a coping saw. With practice, you can sail through a simple cope, particularly in MDF material, which cuts relatively fast with a coping saw. But if you've got big pieces of profiled hardwood, or if you have to make coped joints all day long, most carpenters are going to tire out with the coping saw—even if you have wrists like a professional baseball player.

Coping with a jigsaw Instead, experienced trim carpenters will often use a jigsaw. Some carpenters find it sufficient to support the saw on the narrow face of the reverse bevel, while others prefer to adjust the baseplate and cut from the backside of the molding, watching the blade along the front edge of the profile.

In either case, control is the issue. It's easy to slip and overcut, so a jigsaw with variable-speed control is a must. Invariably, the cut always seems to need a bit of adjustment, particularly in the tight corners of the profile. A grinder or rotary sander with a 60-grit wheel can be used to smooth the cut and ensure that enough material has been backed out of the cut for a clean fit.

Many carpenters who rely on a jigsaw prefer the control afforded by the Collins® Coping Foot (www.collinstool.com)—an accessory that replaces the standard flat plate on a contractor-grade jigsaw. The curved coping foot lets you support the saw near the blade, allowing you to cut from the back and easily trace the curve of the molding's profile. The coping foot takes a bit of practice but the learning curve is short. The trick is to keep two hands on the

Crown can be coped freeform with an ordinary jigsaw. In this case, the only support you have is the narrow face of the reverse miter cut on the end of the molding. This takes practice to execute well.

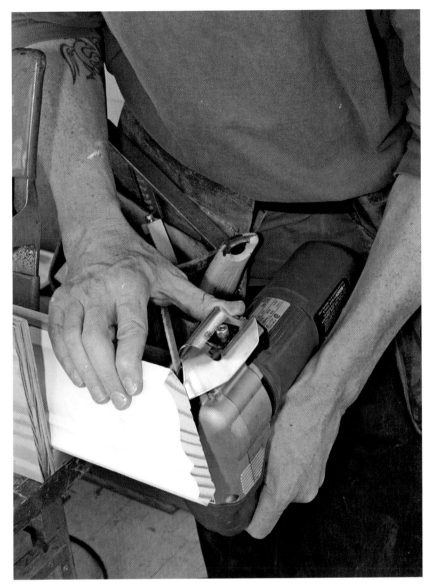

Start with a series of short nips with the saw blade plumb in both directions. The secret of using the Collins Coping Foot is to pivot the saw, rocking in and out of the cut. Don't expect to cut one long, sweeping cut or you're bound to overcut the line.

To use the Collins Coping Foot, clamp the crown in the simple jig recommended by the manufacturer. In this position, if the blade is kept plumb in both directions, it will be cutting in the same orientation as the opposing molding that meets the cope, so you can easily visualize the amount of back cut you need.

saw (though you may want to reach out a few fingers to steady the saw against the work) and rock the blade in and out of the cut, pivoting off the foot. You're not trying to cut a crisp line in one sweep, but instead are whittling away material from the line.

The most delicate part of any cope is the leading point at the bottom edge. To control this cut, pivot the blade into the edge, cutting parallel to the length of the crown. Keep two hands on the saw. Use the coping foot to support the saw on the crown and steady the blade.

You can attack the line from any direction, rocking the saw and chewing away at the cut. The manufacturer recommends Bosch T244D blades that have wideset teeth and deep gullets for nibbling away at the material.

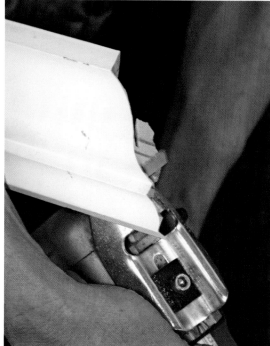

Test fit the finish cut against a corresponding piece of crown.

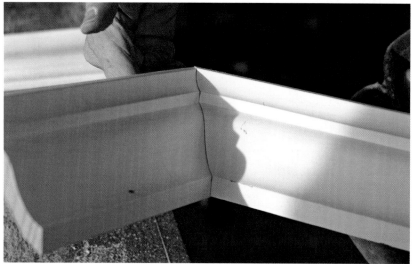

Scarf Joints

Crown molding usually comes in 12-ft. lengths, and seldom longer than 16 ft. If a wall is longer than the crown stock available, you'll need to "scarf" two lengths together.

A scarf joint is nothing more than a splice between two pieces, each with a compound cut on each side. Use something less than a 45°. A miter and a bevel both at 20° work well. Don't simply butt the pieces square. If it's stain-grade work, the difference in grain pattern will be easy to spot, and on paint-grade work, a cracked paint line will be much too noticeable.

In old houses, you may want to premanufacture long lengths of crown by making all the scarf joints first (there usually aren't too many). Wherever the ceilings and walls do not provide a perfectly flat base, the two opposing pieces in a scarf joint tend to come at one another from slightly different directions, making the joint difficult to align. Joining the pieces first and then nailing the crown up avoids this problem.

There are two ways to do this: One is to join them with cyanoacrylate-type glue, which is strong enough to hold the joint closed all by itself (see "Gluing joints" on pp. 174–176). The other is to cut a simple butt joint and join the pieces with a biscuit using a plate joiner. In this case, use a thin plywood or luaun splint on the back of the molding to stabilize the joint. Secure this splint with construction adhesive and use

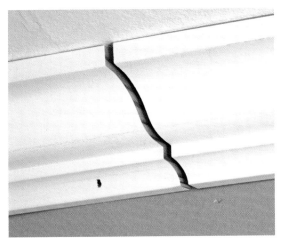

A scarf joint in crown works best when joined by both a miter and a bevel.

To make a simple scarf joint, begin by cutting a 20° bevel and a 20° miter (called a 20-20 compound cut) on both ends of the molding that will be joined. Cut an "open" bevel (with the cut end facing out) on one run.

Cut a closed bevel (with the cut end facing the wall) on the other run.

Nail up the piece with the open bevel first, then close the bevel by applying the second piece.

½-in. T50 staples until the adhesive sets up. (If you're using blocking behind your crown, remember to hold the blocking away from the scarf joint to make room for this splint.)

Built-Up Crown

When you start to get into larger crown molding and more elaborate blocking, it's time to consider using a built-up crown molding assembly. Large crown treatments are normally done by building up assemblies using multiple smaller moldings and foundation pieces. This method lets you skip the step of cutting and installing nailer blocking—the foundation pieces, although they're part of the finished surface, also serve as nailing for the crown.

When multiple pieces are built up into a complex shape, any shrinkage is spread over multiple joints, so that a large crack won't appear at any one seam. In fact, complex crown details were traditionally built up from smaller pieces, even back in the days when old-growth lumber was plentiful. Even given an abundant supply of clear wood with tight,

Installing Built-Up Crown

Small rooms with low ceilings may do best with a simple one-piece or two-piece crown, but larger rooms with higher ceilings will benefit from a more elaborate built-up treatment (especially rooms that have a formal status or function, like formal dining rooms or libraries).

A relatively simple built-up crown assembly starts with a "wall foundation" made of a profiled baseboard. This molding is applied upside down on the wall so the profiled edge runs along the bottom. Start with a full-scale drawing of the crown assembly from which you can pull dimensions.

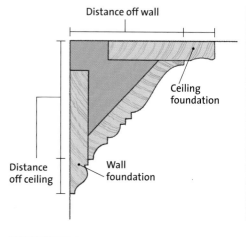

1 Measure down from the ceiling to establish the bottom edge of the wall foundation.

2 Use a tri-square to pull a line that establishes the location of the crown molding on the wall foundation.

3 Cut and install the wall foundation. When cutting an outside miter on the wall foundation, use a Speed Square to ensure the base molding is perfectly square to the saw table.

4 Measure off the wall to establish the outside edge of the ceiling foundation.

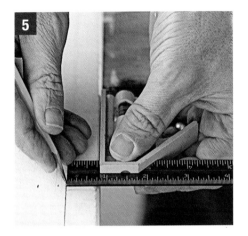

5   Use a tri-square again to pull a line that defines that location of the crown on the ceiling foundation.

6   To establish an outside miter, mark out the corner on the ceiling, first drawing one side . . .

7   . . . and then the other. These lines define the length measurements for the ceiling foundation, as well as the corner angle, which may not be a perfect right angle.

8   With the ceiling foundation attached, the assembly is ready for crown. Note how these foundation pieces can bridge a lot of the waviness in the walls and ceiling of an old house.

9   Install the crown molding between the foundation pieces. Once primed and painted, this assembly has the visual weight and depth of a larger molding, but at a more affordable cost. And in the process of applying the three elements, you get three separate opportunities to adjust to any irregularities in the wall or ceiling.

To fit tightly against a sloped ceiling, bevel the back edge of the crown back at a steeper angle. Hold a scrap of the crown molding on the ceiling and scribe the correct bevel that would allow the molding to lay flat against the ceiling.

Use a tri-square to transfer the line to the back of the crown molding and then knock down the bevel to the correct angle with several passes of a power plane.

straight grain, large moldings were expensive to manufacture and prone to movement 150 years ago, just as they are today; and with old, mature lumber increasingly scarce, large wood moldings have lost in quality what they've gained in price.

If there's an exception, it would be large cove molding. With its serene, swooping curve and deep shadows, a 6-in. or 8-in. piece of coved crown is one of the most impressive profiles around, and you really can't build that effect with multiple pieces. In that case, a wide MDF molding may fill the bill, at least for paint-grade work: it will be as stable as any wood molding, and more reasonably priced.

Cathedral Ceilings

Running crown around the perimeter of a flat ceiling is a snap once you've had to run it in a home with a complex ceiling plane. The most challenging by far is where a level wall line meets a sloped (cathedral) ceiling at an inside corner.

Two problems must be solved here, the first is relatively easy to fix: The top bevel on the back face of the crown is designed to meet a horizontal ceiling, not a sloped ceiling. The back edge of the horizontal run must be beveled to a steeper bevel, as shown at left. The second problem is more difficult to solve: The molding running down the rake won't match the molding running along the horizontal.

Two common attempts to resolve the problem include running two different size moldings—for example, a 2½-in. crown up the rake and a 3½-in. crown along the horizontal. This works better with some moldings than others, but inevitably some artful carving is

required in the corner to get the profile lines to match—an awkward solution at best and extremely time-consuming to pull off well. And in the end the rake crown always looks a bit diminutive. Another fix that's tempting to try is to alter the spring angles, running the rake molding at a shallower spring angle (closer to parallel with the ceiling) and running the horizontal crown at a steeper spring angle (closer to parallel with the wall). In theory, this would work if the slope of the ceiling wasn't too steep (less than 3:12), but we've never seen this situation in the field.

Instead, we recommend trying one of the following ways to handle this a little more elegantly.

Pendants

Perhaps the best way is also the easiest: terminate each run into a pendant. The pendant can be made with scrap 1x. How elaborate it gets depends on how much attention you want to draw to these corners. (If there are architects on the project, and they have not addressed this problem in the design, present it and let them design the pendant. That way, you won't have to rip it out when they reject your solution.) The photo series on p. 168 shows one design option—the box-out capped by a couple of small pieces of crown.

Soffits

If you're lucky, the house designer will have made the transition to a sloped ceiling with a step-up for a clearstory or with a soffit along the perimeter. In this case, the crown on the

Installing a Corner Pendant

A pendant at the corner of a sloped ceiling starts with a two-sided box made of 1x. The trickiest part is nailing it into the corner.

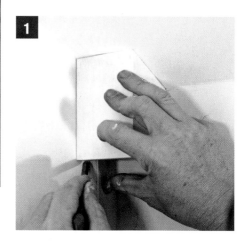

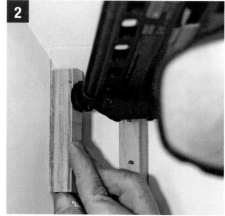

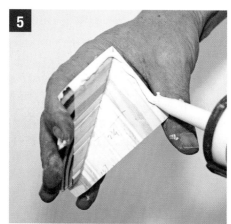

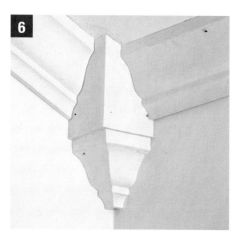

1 Hold the box in place and mark the length of two 1x1 nailers.

2 Cut the nailers to length and secure them to the wall.

3 Apply a bead of adhesive caulk to the top edge of the box.

4 Nail the box home.

5 Cap the end of the box-out with an "ice-cream cone" fashioned from two triangular pieces of crown stock.

6 The completed pendant. Note that the length of the box-out must be long enough to pick up the longer crown angle on the rake side, but the difference is not as pronounced as it would be if the rake crown extended all the way into the corner.

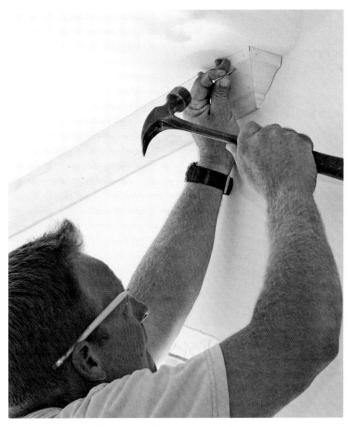

Handle a step-up in the ceiling plane with a 90° return to the wall. Visually, it works best if the end of this horizontal run isn't returned right at the corner. In this case, carpenter Smokey Saduk chose to hold it back 1 in. from the bullnose.

horizontal run gets a hard return to the wall, and the crown on the rake dies into the fascia on the soffit. If there's not a soffit already, you might suggest to the customers boxing out the corner. It may be a more elaborate project than they had in mind, but it will likely be more satisfying in the end, especially if the soffit includes recessed lighting.

Transition patch

Long Island remodeling contractor Mike Sloggatt deserves credit for developing this solution, and master carpenter Gary Katz for perfecting it. It involves cutting a pie-shaped patch to affect the transition between a horizontal run and a sloped run of crown, not unlike the process used to wrap crown around a bullnosed wall corner (see "Cathedral Ceiling Transition," on pp. 170–172). Be forewarned: This detail will take considerable time the first couple of times you do it. It's not a slam-dunk by any means. Besides the frustration involved in learning to perfect it, we also feel it's a viable solution only on a shallow sloped ceiling. The steeper the ceiling pitch becomes, the more disjointed and awkward this corner treatment looks.

Fastening Crown

Securing the crown molding to the wall and ceiling is greatly simplified if you've installed good blocking, or if you are building up a multipiece crown on a foundation of flat stock. The blocking, or the foundation pieces, can be attached to the wall with screws, which will be hidden behind the finish molding.

Cathedral Ceiling Transition

A horizontal run of crown can be "stepped" around the corner to meet a sloped piece of crown. In essence, you are first turning the crown horizontally around the corner and then mitering this piece to meet the sloped crown on the rake. The result is a little pie-shaped piece of crown we affectionately call a "mangled knuckle joint." The lower the slope of the ceiling, the better this option will look.

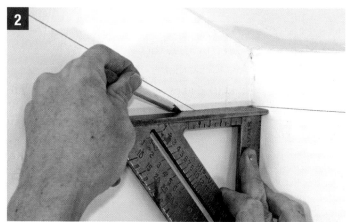

1 To establish your bearings on this joint, first mark the bottom edges of crown on each wall.

2 Use a square to continue the horizontal run on the rake wall.

3 The transition between the horizontal run of crown and the rake crown is a continuation of the horizontal run, so cut the end of the horizontal run as a simple inside miter.

4 Use a Bosch MiterFinder to find the angle for the rake crown: First measure the slope of the ceiling (in this case, it's 113.6). Then subtract 90° (to get to the angle from the horizontal) and divide by two (since the miter between the rake crown and the transition patch bisects the angle): $(113.6 - 90)/2 = 11.8$.

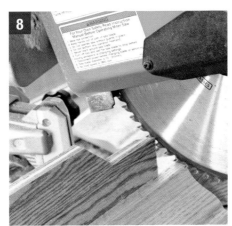

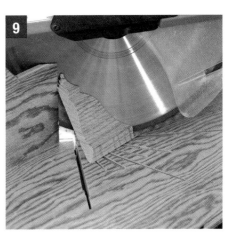

5 It helps to visualize what you are doing, so we've drawn this out on the ceiling, as follows: Start with the short point of the miter for the horizontal run, since this is where the joint pivots to turn up the ceiling. Mark this point on the ceiling as shown.

6 Transfer this point onto your rake crown to define the cut on that end: Here's the long point of the rake cut.

7 And here's the short point of the rake cut.

8 You could cut this angle by sneaking up on these long- and short-point measurements, but it's faster and more precise to use the angle you calculated with the MiterFinder. The important thing to remember is that this angle must be cut with the crown sitting right side up in the saw.

9 To cut the transition patch, first cut an ordinary inside miter to match the horizontal run (cutting upside down and backward in the saw).

Continued on p. 172.

Cathedral Ceiling Transition (continued)

10 Hold this piece in place and mark the length on the bottom edge: This mark serves only as a check while cutting the rake angle. It's helpful to know that the long point of the rake cut will fall exactly where you want it, while cutting the angle.

11 Cut the rake angle (in this case at 11.8°), remembering to cut right side up in the saw.

12 Once the transition patch is cut, use a CA-type glue to secure it to the end of the rake crown.

13 Nail the assembly in place.

Shoot the crown molding to the backer, or to the underlying trim piece, with a 15-gauge finish gun nail. A 2-in.- to 2½-in.-long (8d) nail driven through the thick "meat" in the center of an ogee crown will hold standard 3½-in. crown to blocking. A 1-in. to 1½-in. nail will fasten the thin edges of crown into flat foundation pieces.

If you are not using blocking or a foundation piece, spend a few moments before you start nailing off the crown to verify where your nailing is. Walls that run parallel to the ceiling joists usually have some kind of nailing for the ceiling drywall, but it may be nearer the corner than the outside edge of the molding, and therefore will require a longer nail. Many truss roofs are strapped to even out the ceiling and tend to have good nailing around the room perimeter.

Outside miter joints often get cross-nailed across the bevel, as well as glued. This is where a nailer comes into its own: pinning the joint with a brad nailer, or better yet, a 23-guage pin nailer, is not just faster than hand nailing, it's also a better joint than you'll get with hand-driven nails.

You do have to be careful how you place your nails. The nail has to go into a fat section of the molding, and it has to be parallel with the piece it's going into. Get the angle wrong, and the nail will pop out the face—it's better to

Take Note • If you're not using blocking behind the crown, use an awl to verify that you have solid nailing, then pick a nail length that can reach it.

A 2-in. to 2¹/₂-in. nail is suitable to hold most crown molding in the "field" and at inside corners.

On long runs, nail from the center of the run **and work your way to the ends.**

Cross nail and glue an outside miter. Use a brad nailer for this to avoid the chance of a blowout.

err toward the back side than toward the front face. And, of course, it's better to err on the small side for fasteners at that location.

The grain on wood moldings can cause problems when nailing near the ends. Sometimes the fastener will try to follow the wood grain and bend around toward the face of the material. A hand nail may work better in such cases, but you must predrill into the pieces before tapping the nail gently home.

Gluing joints

Most carpenters glue their crown joints to hold them closed over time, relying on yellow carpenter's glue, either an aliphatic resin or a Type II glue, or even construction adhesive.

Trim carpenter Ken O'Brien likes to use glue as well as nails for all his molding assemblies, applying a polyurethane-based construction

Cross Nailing an Outside Corner

A pair of brads through the meatiest section of the crown profile will help draw a miter closed.

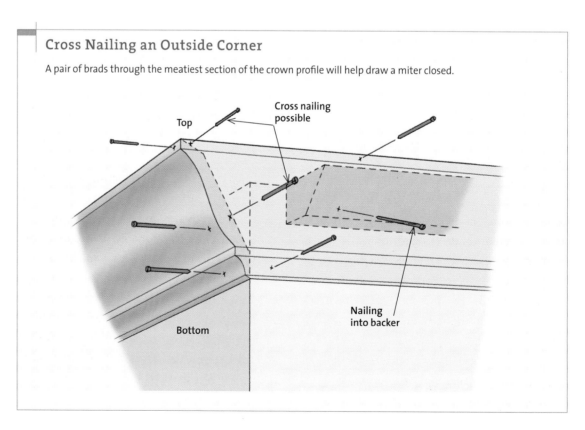

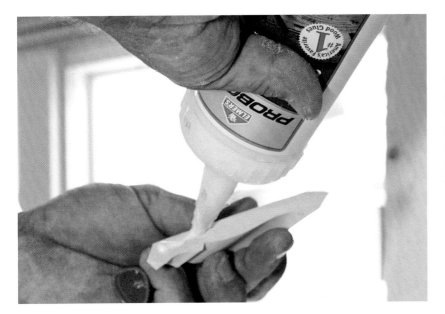

Carpenter's glue, or aliphatic resin, is stronger than white glue and more heat resistant, so it's less likely to melt if the wood heats up when sanded and gum up the paper.

or panel adhesive such as Liquid Nails™ or PL-400™ to every contact surface. He prefers it because it's viscous, not runny, but not so thick that it creates a gap between the meeting pieces. This type of adhesive will take a couple days to cure fully, but once it does, O'Brien claims that it's stronger than the material itself: If you try to break that joint, the bond stays intact and the material around it breaks apart.

CA glue

The development of cyanoacrylate, or CA, glue has had a big impact on trim carpentry. Most people know these adhesives by the brand names Super Glue™ and Krazy Glue®, but a wide range of CA glues are available that have a profound impact on lots of industries. CA glue is used regularly in manufacturing industries as a retention dressing for nuts and bolts and for assembling electronics. CA glue also makes an effective adhesive for wood joinery. The bond is stronger than nails and sets up fast enough that the joint doesn't need to be clamped.

The CA product that currently has the widest appeal among finish carpenters is FastCap®'s 2P-10. It is by far the best option

Take Note • A Type II carpenter's glue that claims to be "weatherproof," meaning it's water *resistant*. It's a good choice for all sorts of interior climate conditions, but should not be relied on as a substitute for a construction adhesive or epoxy in exterior applications.

for preassembling small miter returns, as well as preassembling short outside corners or wrap-around crown assemblies at the top of doors or windows.

2P-10 comes in a "kit" that includes several different viscosities of the adhesive, the activator and a deactivator, in case you do actually bond yourself to the work. Be sure to practice with 2P-10 to get a feel for how quickly it bonds and what you have to do to keep the edges aligned. Experiment with applying the adhesive to one side of a joint and the activator on the opposing piece, or a little on both. You can speed up the set time this way, which is convenient when you don't want to have to clamp the pieces.

Gluing a Miter Joint

Cyanoacrylate, or CA, glue like FastCap's 2P-10, is strong enough to hold a miter closed without nails. It's applied in two parts. First, the adhesive is squeezed onto the joint. Then an aerosol "activator" is sprayed on the opposite piece. Do not spray the activator directly onto the gel adhesive or it will set immediately before you have a chance to bond the pieces together. Even so, once the activator hits the adhesive, you only have about 30 seconds of working time, so you have to act fast.

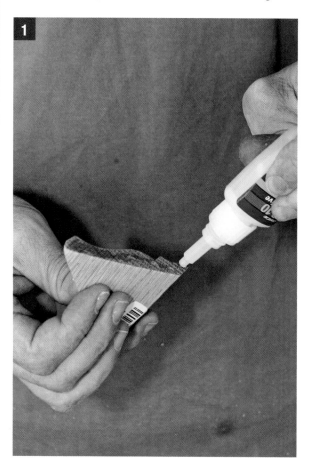

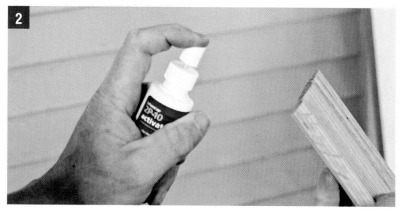

1 Squeeze the adhesive onto one piece.

2 Spray the activator onto the mating piece.

3 Align the pieces carefully, keeping your fingers away from the glue.

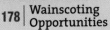

Wainscoting

The tradition of wainscoting, or wood wall paneling, goes back at least as far as the Middle Ages in Europe. In the U.S., wainscoting was a common feature in homes built in the 1700s and 1800s, during the Georgian, Colonial, Federal, and Victorian eras. And it's still found as a design element in contemporary homes, especially those that echo an earlier period style.

Traditionally, wainscoting is a multipiece raised-panel assembly with a bottom and top rail, side stiles, and center stiles (called "muntins"). A cap molding (or "chair rail") finishes the top, and the bottom may get an additional baseboard, a shoe molding, or both.

Traditional full wainscot is far less common today than in the past, however. These days, a builder trying to add interest to a wall is likely to opt for a simple applied wall frame (or "plant-on")— just the suggestion of paneling, created by attaching moldings to the drywall—or, at most, a simple beadboard panel wainscoting, rather than a traditional raised panel wainscoting assembly. Even these minimal treatments aren't that common; in most houses, what you're likely to find is a bare wall.

Raised-panel wain-scoting **can add an extra touch of class to foyers, halls, stairways, and formal rooms.**

Traditional Wainscoting

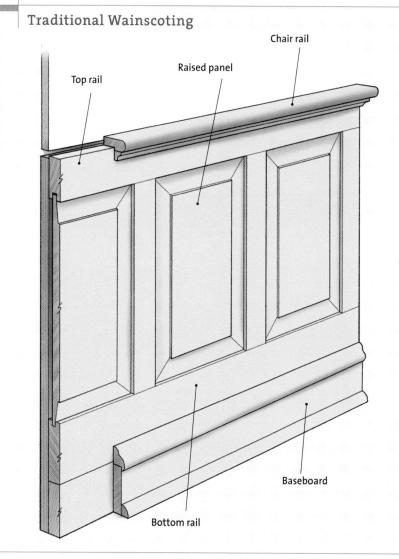

Top rail

Raised panel

Chair rail

Baseboard

Bottom rail

Wainscoting Opportunities

That leaves wainscoting as a great dress-up extra for the remodeler or the custom finish carpenter—something to offer customers who own a plain, recently built home. Wainscoting can also help custom builders set themselves apart from their less imaginative competition. There are plenty of places where a little wainscoting can make a big difference: everything from simple, paint-grade beadboard on the lower part of the wall in the entry hall or mudroom of a cottage near the beach, to a paint-grade raised-panel treatment in a new suburban living room and dining room, all the way to full floor-to-ceiling walnut or cherry paneling in an upscale formal library room or an attorney's downtown office.

In recent years, traditional frame-and-panel wainscoting has been making a comeback, propelled by advances in technology. Supplied with a measured drawing of the wall, a modern woodshop can easily create an entire raised-panel treatment out of inexpensive MDF sheet goods. When painted, the MDF wainscoting will be hard to tell apart from handcrafted work from the 1800s. You can also get generic MDF wainscoting kits with all the parts you need for the installation (although the installer may have to cut some panels to size and rout the raised-panel profiles on the panel edges).

And if a customer wants a stained, hardwood version, any cabinet shop that is equipped to make raised-panel wood doors can use the same shop techniques to assemble sections of wainscoting ready for the carpenter to nail up in the field (a section of wainscot is really no different than a series of five-piece raised-panel cabinet doors, built as a continuous unit). Growing numbers of national as well

Special order: This set of precut wainscot parts arrived neatly sorted, wrapped, and labeled. The materials, enough to dress up an entry foyer and a flight of stairs, took an experienced carpenter one day to install.

Beaded panel products let carpenters make quick work of simple wainscot treatments in an entryway or breakfast nook.

Install a corner piece to hide the beadboard edge.

as local companies now make custom raised-panel wainscoting part of their stock in trade, and any carpenter who knows how to take the measurements and do the field installation can now order components manufactured to fit. This lets a good trim carpenter compete with a fully equipped cabinetmaker for that kind of work.

Carpenters who have the skills and equipment can still make their own raised-panel wainscoting, machining the floating panels, rails, and stiles from either MDF or solid wood.

But we won't cover those shop techniques in this book, because for most finish carpenters, it is more practical to order the parts from a well-equipped shop and stick to the field installation side of things. Site measurement and layout are critical tasks but without good numbers to work from, the shop can't give you components that will fit.

Wainscoting Design

Whether it's a field-applied MDF raised panel or a stain-grade frame-and-panel assembly built off-site in a cabinet shop, the design and layout issues are pretty much the same. The trick is to divide the wall area up into sections with pleasing, well-proportioned dimensions.

Height

There's no hard-and-fast rule for the height of wainscoting; it typically covers the lower $\frac{2}{5}$ or $\frac{1}{3}$ of the wall. In a room with an 8-ft.-high or 9-ft.-high ceiling, wainscot might be 30 in. or 36 in. tall. For visual harmony, one good trick is to align the top rail with other features in the room. A typical countertop height, for instance, is 36 in. Bars are often 42 in. tall, while a standard desk or table height is 30 in. tall. Wainscoting works well visually at any of those heights; in rooms with very high ceilings, it can even look good at 60 in. tall.

Aligning the top rail of the wainscot with one of the other elements in the room (here, the window apron) creates visual harmony.

Panel width

For basic beadboard wainscot, the only width you're concerned about is the width of the individual tongue-and-groove boards. But with a traditional frame-and-panel system, the width of panels, rails, and stiles all become important. The basic element is the rectangle formed by each panel, and the design challenge is to maintain pleasing proportions for those rectangles in relation to the proportions of the room and its walls.

Keeping proportions in harmony is easiest if you match the width of wainscot stiles and rails to the room's window and door casings, and try to have panel proportions match or echo the proportions of other elements in the room (windows, doors, built-in cabinets, etc.). But your flexibility in playing with those proportions is limited by the need to adjust panel widths to divide wall areas evenly. (For more on this, see "Layout for Frame-and-Panel Wainscot" on p. 204.)

Chair rail

All by itself, chair rail can be enough to transform a room, simply by dividing the wall height into two unequal parts. Rooms with

Take Note • It helps to match the base of wainscot panels with the height of other baseboards in the house—especially if you can see the baseboard nearby, around corners or through doors. If you don't match the heights, at least consider how the different proportions will work together visually, and try to make any variation look like a conscious choice.

Chair Rail Options

Two-piece chair rail

Bead band

Bolection molding

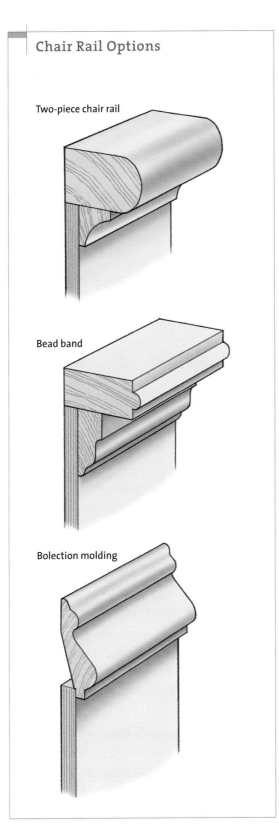

lots of windows and doors already have plenty of visual detail; where full wainscoting might make the room feel too "busy," a simple chair rail applied to the wall can be a good way to tie things together visually (and at considerably less cost than a full wainscot treatment). Painting the upper and lower portions of the wall in different (but complementary) shades can enhance this effect.

In a beadboard or frame-and-panel wainscot treatment, chair rail is a necessary element that caps off the wainscot. There's a range of typical looks, from a one-piece cap molding like the "bolection molding" (easy to install and effective at hiding the top edge of beadboard) to a two- or three-piece built-up treatment. Whether one piece or multiple pieces, the chair rail should be installed so it hides the expansion gap at the top of the wainscot assembly.

Chair rail design choices and molding profiles should harmonize with other trim in the house. A simple square band or bullnose, for instance, is suitable for homes with flat, plain window and door casing. A more elaborate built-up detail, such as the bullnose and bolection combination shown in this chapter, may be more appropriate in homes with complex window and door trim. You can also blend the top rail and chair rail of a wainscot assembly into the apron and sill of a room's window trim.

Where chair rail meets a window or door, you generally have to create one of two typical transitions. If the casing is heavy enough, the chair rail can simply butt to the edge of the casing. But if a wide chair rail meets a narrower door or window casing, the chair rail should lap over the casing and end in either a return or a suitable end cut.

A simple bullnose cap rail (right) tops off this beadboard wainscot treatment, while a small cove molding (far right) hides the joint where the chair rail meets the top ends of the boards.

This raised-panel wainscot treatment gets a similar bullnose cap rail, but a slightly more elaborate bolection molding underneath.

Where chair rail from a simple beadboard wainscot meets a plain door casing, both the bullnose and the cove lap over the casing and return.

For this raised-panel wainscot installation, the bullnose cap rail laps over the door casing and rounds over, but the bolection molding returns into the wainscot top rail with a mitered return.

Individual Board Wainscot

Vertical board wainscoting, commonly called "beadboard" for the beaded profile milled into the typical product, is easy to install and provides a nice, simple look. It's dressy, but not too dressy—like shirtsleeves and a tie, but not the full three-piece suit. Beadboard works beautifully in relatively informal settings like a kitchen or pantry, a half bath, a mudroom, or a hallway. In such locations, solid wood on the lower wall serves a functional purpose, too, protecting the wall from the bumps and dings of daily life and providing a good base for easy-to-clean enamel paint.

Materials

Traditional board wainscoting is produced as individual boards in narrow widths. Edges are profiled with a tongue on one side and a groove on the other (this allows boards to be nailed up through the tongue side, so the pieces can move freely without cracking, as seasonal humidity changes cause the wood to shrink or expand). Standard widths range from 2½ in. to 5 in.; boards may be ⅜ in., ½ in., ⅝ in., or ¾ in. thick. Pieces are usually milled with at least a beveled edge, to create a simple V-groove where the pieces butt together; more common, boards will have a beaded edge, and often an additional bead cut lengthwise along the center of each piece. (Historically, ordinary V-groove boards were mostly for porch ceilings, with beadboard preferred for wall wainscoting.)

Most beadboard installations are paint grade, so composite materials like MDF make an acceptable material. Depending on the grade, wood is sometimes cheaper than MDF, but if you do buy wood for a paint-grade install, watch out for knots and other imperfections—the money you save on lower-grade wood may not be worth the additional time and trouble of painting over the flaws.

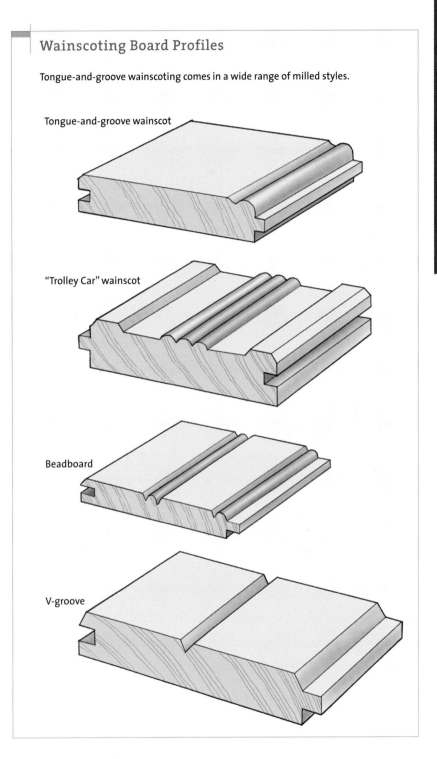

Wainscoting Board Profiles

Tongue-and-groove wainscoting comes in a wide range of milled styles.

Tongue-and-groove wainscot

"Trolley Car" wainscot

Beadboard

V-groove

Painting Individual Beadboard

Beadboard is a classic solution to the problem of wood movement: each board is free to slip back and forth at the tongue and groove joint. Held fast only on the tongue side, the pieces won't crack.

But if you install the boards first, then prime and paint, you may be in for a surprise a few months later. New homes typically have high humidity before all the building materials have fully dried out, and even older homes go through seasonal high humidity periods (moist indoor air is typical during the hot summer months in the North and during the damp winter months in the South when air-conditioning is not drying out the indoor air). If you paint beadboard during a damp period, the boards will

already be swelled up and tongue edges will be hidden in the grooves of the mating boards. When the dry season comes, unpainted wood will peek out at every joint.

Priming and painting the pieces before installation, or at least buying pre-primed material, will help prevent this seasonal peek-a-boo show. If you don't do that, expect a potential touch-up painting job in six months.

Knots are another problem. Small-dimension beadboard is a good use for cheap lumber that can't meet high grading rules at larger dimensions, but you sometimes get pieces with knots containing lots of pitch or sap. If you can't buy clear material, use a good stain-blocking primer like Zinsser's® shellac-based B-I-N® primer-sealer. Several coats are needed prior to top coating.

It's the painter's job to paint the wainscot, but the carpenter can help by pre-priming just the tongues so that the typical seasonal shrinking won't expose bare wood. It takes only a few minutes, using a cheap foam brush and a small can of white-pigmented shellac primer in a quick-drying alcohol solvent.

Nailing and blocking

Beadboard wainscot needs to be solidly nailed to wood in the wall, not just to the drywall or plaster wall covering. (Don't be tempted just to glue the individual pieces to drywall—that's a cheap solution prone to failure when the boards swell and shrink from season to season.) Studs alone won't supply nailing for boards that fall between the stud locations, so the wall needs to incorporate some sort of solid blocking or solid wood backing.

In new construction, the framers can simply install solid 2x4 blocks on the flat, between the studs, at a good height to catch the top, middle, and bottom of the wainscot boards. This is a good punch-list or "pick-up" item for whomever is installing cabinet blocking for the kitchen, blocking for closet rods or shelves, and the like. Alternatively, the builder can just install plywood instead of drywall on the lower portion of the wall where the beadboard is to go.

If the wall is already built without blocking, you need to retrofit some. The simplest way is just to tear off the existing drywall or plaster up to the height of the planned wainscot, and replace it with ½-in., ⅝-in., or ¾-in. plywood.

Take Note • If you install strips of backer instead of solid blocking, it's important to use material thick enough to stand slightly proud of the drywall or plaster above and below it on the wall. This way the boards can span neatly over the existing material, and any minor surface irregularities on the substrate won't keep the new beadboard from lying flat.

Removing the existing drywall or plaster and installing a continuous plywood backer is the simplest way to retrofit blocking for wainscoting.

Using strips instead of a whole sheet—that is, tearing out just enough plaster to attach narrow 4-in. or 6-in. strips of nailing material at top, bottom, and mid-height—will reduce the amount of demolition debris you create and the total cost of the added wood, but it is also more labor. That's a judgment call for the contractor.

Another option is to apply the backing nailers directly over the existing drywall or plaster. This may create complications, however: If the wainscot stands too far proud of the rest of the wall, you may have trouble blending it into other trim elements like door and window casing. But applying the nailing over the drywall has the advantage that it does not compromise the air-tightness of the existing wall (see the sidebar on p. 186).

Snapping level lines

When you need to remove wall material and install nailing for beadboard, layout comes before demolition. You're removing only part of the existing wall, and you have to define

Seal Up the Gaps!

When you cut into an existing wall and apply new nailers, either in a continuous sheet or in strips, you need to consider the air-leakage issue. Cracks in an exterior wall can allow cold drafts and a loss of heated air to the outdoors in winter, and the opposite problem in summer. In both seasons, there's a risk of moisture damage to a wall when the integrity of the interior surface is compromised, as well as the possibility of unsightly and allergenic mold growth. So whatever method you use to add nailers, be sure and seal the newly created crack with an effective sealant such as expanding foam in a can.

exactly which part that is. Start by snapping a level line with blue chalk that represents the top edge of the chair rail or other molding that will cap off your installation. (Don't use red chalk, because it does not wash off.)

If you're using nailing strips as the blocking, next mark the locations for the nailers. The top nailer has to catch the chair rail or cap molding, so you'll place it just slightly below the top layout line. The bottom nailer has to catch the bottom end of the wainscot boards; if you'll be installing new baseboard underneath the wainscot, you probably need

Mark the height of the chair rail's upper edge at wall ends and corners.

Snap a blue chalk line on the wall.

Deeply score the plaster (or drywall) with the point of a utility knife. Carry extra blades, because sandy, abrasive plaster quickly dulls tool edges.

Layout for Nailing Strips

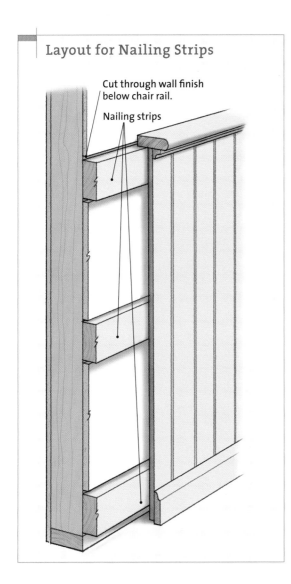

Cut through wall finish below chair rail.

Nailing strips

have to lay out. Use the pole to mark the important heights in every corner and next to each window or door, and then snap chalk lines to connect the points. This is quicker than using a tape measure, and it helps to avoid dumb mistakes (like making one mark at 16 in. and the next at 1 ft. 6 in.—duh!).

Demolition

Tearing out drywall or plaster is a fun job for a laborer, if you're gutting a whole room. But this case is different—you just want to delicately remove enough material to install the nailing, and you have to be careful. A drywall cutout tool like the Roto Zip® works well in these situations, but you can also simply score repeatedly along your layout lines with a utility knife until you've cut all the way through.

Old plaster actually scores more readily than drywall, but it also dulls the knives quickly, so make sure you have plenty of extra blades. Once you've scored your lines, you can break out the plaster with a hammer, and prize out the lath with a pry bar, cat's paw, or the straight claw of a framing hammer. If there's loose plaster above your cut line, you might want to re-secure it using plaster washers, and smooth over the washers and any rough spots using a cement-based plaster patching material such as Durabond.

For cutting out drywall, it's handy to have a drywall handsaw. The big, dull teeth won't do much to wood, but they saw quickly and neatly through gypsum board, and the hand-saw doesn't raise the dust (or make the racket) that a power tool will. Just be careful not to plunge the sharp point of the saw through the backside of the wall.

a nailer there as well. Top and bottom may be the only nailers you need for a short wainscot, but if your boards are 3 ft. or 4 ft. long, you probably want a center nailer as well. If you're just installing a plywood-sheet backer instead of nailing strips, of course, you only need the top line (one more reason to do it that way).

The quickest way to transfer your layout markings around the room is with a story pole—a narrow board with marks designating the heights of all the various elements you

Prepping for Wainscot Blocking

1 Old plaster pulls readily off the wall with a pry bar. Work carefully, so as not to damage areas you don't intend to remove.

2 Clean up frequently and thoroughly as you work. The sand and grit in old plaster can damage wood flooring and floor finishes, so you want to avoid grinding it underfoot.

3 Pry off strips of lath individually.

4 Use a chisel to chop off lath where the ends continue underneath existing trim that you plan to leave in place.

5 Some nails will pull through the lath; pull those with a flat bar or linesman's pliers.

6 Secure loose plaster that you don't want to remove using plaster washers. Replace large areas of loose plaster with drywall patches and blend in with plaster patching compound.

7 Use a plaster patching compound, such as the well-known "Durabond" brand, to patch rough plaster, cover plaster washers, and blend drywall patches into existing plaster.

Cut and fit plywood pieces in place of the old plaster and lath, to serve as nailer backing for the new beadboard. Secure the plywood to the existing studs with drywall screws or wood screws.

When you've removed all the old drywall or lath and plaster, check the stud faces carefully for old nails and screws. (If you don't get them all out, they'll get in the way when you try to make the new nailers lie down flat.) Then screw the nailing strips or sheet into the newly exposed studs. Add a new screw into the edge of the existing drywall at each stud next to the nailers, too, to button up the joint (your cut line may be some inches away from the nearest existing fastener).

Cutting boards to length

You'll set your new wainscoting to the level line you've already established around the room. This way, any sagging or slope that may exist in the floor won't get reflected up onto the wall. Measure the height from the floor to your layout line at a few points along each wall. If the lengths are all the same, you can cut all the boards at the same time. But if there's a floor sag to make up for, measure and cut each piece individually as you go.

Most of the time, you won't have to worry about carefully scribing the end cuts for a perfect joint. Molding below the chair rail will cover any ragged joints at the top, and

shoe molding will do the same at the bottom. But if you're butting the bottom of your boards right to a pre-installed base molding and don't plan on covering that joint with another molding, you'll have to take care to match your end cuts to the angle they'll be meeting.

One way or the other, it's wise to leave ⅛ in. to ¼ in. of room for the boards to expand lengthwise if they gain moisture (wood can swell somewhat even in the long dimension, and MDF material swells equally in all directions). A handy way to maintain this gap at the bottom is just to lay a strip of thin luaun paneling or similar material on the floor against the wall as a temporary shim, and rest your boards on that as you nail them up.

Nailing up the boards

The basic nailing pattern for tongue-and-groove wainscot is simple: Face-nail the first board in the center, locating the top and bottom nails where they'll be hidden by the small moldings added later. For subsequent boards, nail through the tongue at an angle.

Installing the boards "in the field"—in the center of runs—is simple enough. But the beginning and end of each run—at an

Pin each piece in three or four places, carefully nailing through the board at an angle next to the tongue.

inside or outside wall corner or at a door casing—create complications. Scribing, cutting, and fitting the pieces around window casings, sills, and aprons is also a head-scratcher. So before you start each section of wainscot, it's important to think a few steps ahead.

Start by measuring the full run of each wall section, and divide that number by the width of the individual pieces. Is the remainder close to a full-size board? If so, you can start with a full board and end with a board that has just a small amount ripped off its edge. But if the remainder is a small number, you have to end by nailing on a tiny strip. That's tricky to do, and won't look good. In that case, rip a piece in half and start with a half-width; then you can finish with another piece that is close to half-width as well.

At the same time, check to see how your joints will fall out at windows. If possible, you want to avoid having to rip and attach narrow widths next to the casings.

Starting at corners Whether you start a run at an inside corner or an outside corner, the tongue side of each piece must face away from the starting point. Rip the groove and beveled edge off each piece, and butt the pieces together; or, for the more finished look required with stain-grade work, rip each piece at the appropriate angle and miter the pieces together.

Sometimes it works best to join the two corner pieces together, and then attach the corner assembly to the wall as a unit. But dry-fit the pieces first to make sure the edges will be plumb on each side: whether you start with a single piece or with a preassembled corner, it's important to start out plumb. Continue checking for plumb as you work, to make sure you're not drifting out of kilter. Correct problems gradually over two or three boards, by pulling each joint slightly open at one end until you reach plumb. But as long as you're staying plumb, keep your joints tight by tapping each new piece snug against the last with light taps using a scrap block. Nail at an angle through the board into the backer, close to the tongue.

Also, as you approach the end of a run, check the corner you're coming to for plumb,

Miter at the Corner

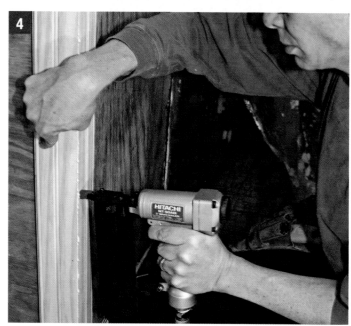

1 To start a run of beadboard at an outside corner, rip matching 45° angles on the groove side of two pieces, removing the groove and beveled edge.

2 Hold the two matching corner pieces in place to position them correctly.

3 Pin one side permanently and apply glue to the face of the bevel.

4 Nail the second side on, pinning the joint closed from both sides where the two pieces touch.

Using a scrap block, gently tap each new piece snug against the last.

and measure from the corner to the top and bottom of your current piece to see if the distances are equal. When your plumb wainscot has to meet an out-of-plumb corner, you don't want to make up the whole difference by ripping your last board out of parallel—the eye will catch the difference. Instead, gradually ease into it by widening the gap imperceptibly at the short point over a number of boards, or "feathering it in." Adjust a whole series of joints until the last board you place is parallel with the corner it will have to match.

In most cases, the last board you place will have to be ripped to fit the space. If you're butting to an existing piece of trim, take a few minutes to fine-tune the joint by back-beveling the new piece slightly (either on the tablesaw or with a block plane), and by scribing and planing it to fit tightly against the existing wood.

As you approach the end of a run, check measurements at top and bottom. If there's a difference, gradually "sneak up" on parallel by pulling the top or bottom of each new board closer into alignment with the edge you're moving toward.

Finishing the Run

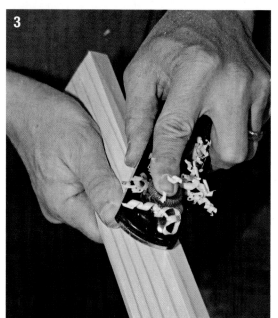

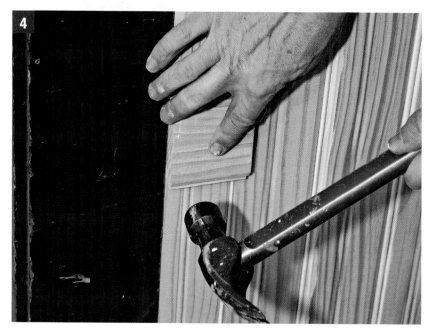

1 | Measure at the top and bottom for the thickness of your last piece. Rip your last piece to width.

2 | If you've adjusted carefully, the distances will be equal and you won't have to rip a tapered piece.

3 | Ease the back edge with a block plane.

4 | Tap the piece gently into place with a hammer and a scrap block.

Make a bullnose chair rail on-site by rounding over the edges and ends of a 1x board with a router and ripping the piece to width.

Lap the chair rail ends over square casing by marking in place and notching with a jigsaw.

Installing the chair rail

A simple bullnose chair rail is easy to make out of ¾-in. material: Simply round over the edge by running a router with a half-round round-over bit down the board, working from both faces. The ends of the board can also be rounded over, making it easy to create a lapped-over termination by simply notching out the end to fit.

Attach the chair rail by nailing into studs through the face, or at an angle from the top.

Underneath the chair rail, fasten a molding to hide the gap.

Beadboard Panels

Rather than nail up individual boards, there's a simpler way to achieve the look of beadboard: use profiled panels of MDF. This method takes a lot of the fussy labor out of the process. The measuring and cutting are simpler, and you don't need to worry so much about nailing and backing.

Nail off the chair rail at an angle from the top. It's good to catch studs, but the plywood backer for this assembly also provides good nailing.

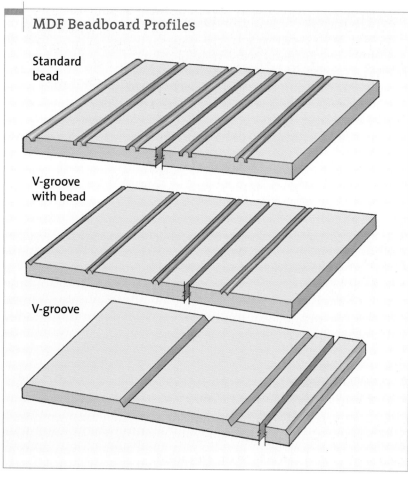

MDF Beadboard Profiles

Standard bead

V-groove with bead

V-groove

Material dimensions

Profiled MDF beadboard panels come in a range of thicknesses and stock sizes, and with various face profiles. The common thicknesses are ¼ in., ⅜ in., and ½ in. Some suppliers provide sheets 8 ft. long in common widths (30 in., 36 in., 42 in., and 48 in.), with beads and grooves running across the short dimension of the sheet. Other suppliers have 8-ft., 10-ft., 12-ft., and 16-ft. lengths, with the profiles running along the long dimension. There's usually a choice of typical profiles, too—simple bead, V-groove with bead, and simple V-groove are the most common. There's also a choice of spacing between the beads or grooves; 1⅝-in., 2-in., 2½-in., and 3-in. spacing simulate the look of narrow individual boards, while a wider 4-in., 6-in., or 8-in. space between grooves reproduces the appearance of wider boards.

MDF is rough on tools, too. If you expect to be cutting, routing, or planing a whole lot of it, be ready to change blades or bits frequently. But the material machines and cuts well: You can cut panels along the V-groove with just a utility knife, make sharp, clean rips in any direction with a circular saw or tablesaw, and smooth edges to close tolerances or plane to a scribed line using a block plane.

Design and layout

Whatever profile and size of MDF paneling you choose, when the material shows up at the site, you'll have to work with those stock dimensions to make the best use of material and achieve a pleasing appearance. At corners, it's nice to leave half the width or more of an individual "board," and it looks best if there's some symmetry of "board" widths where two walls meet. In complicated situations, it takes a little measuring, figuring, and head scratching

MDF is very heavy. One man can lift this 3/8-in.-thick, 3x8 MDF beadboard panel, but you'll probably need a helper for 1/2-in. thicknesses and 12-ft. lengths.

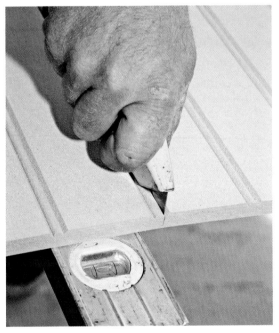

MDF beadboard cuts easily at the groove with a sharp utility knife. Score the piece repeatedly with the tip of the knife, and then snap the sections apart.

to determine a starting cut on your first piece that will make your layout look good on the other end of the wall.

As with individual board wainscot, typical beadboard-panel wainscot has a bottom rail and a top rail, but no end rails or stiles. The top rail can be a simple piece of cap molding

or a multipiece top rail with chair rail and cove molding. Ordinary baseboard usually serves as the bottom rail.

Some carpenters like to run the beadboard all the way to the floor and apply baseboard over it, but that leaves tiny holes where the beadboard's profiles run behind the baseboard.

Cutting Beveled Edges on MDF Beadboard

Where beadboard panels join at outside corners, you need a miter joint, which requires nice, clean, straight matching bevels on the two panel edges. Even at an inside corner, one piece has to be beveled where it overlaps the other piece. (Here's a measuring tip: For an accurate long point measurement, use a scrap to mark the point where panel surfaces intersect, and measure to that mark.)

Full panels are hard to handle on the tablesaw. It's easier to cut with a circular saw guided by a straightedge clamped to the panel. Setting the proper angle on your saw, measure from the edge of the saw foot to the blade, and set your straightedge guide that same distance back from your cutline. Now you can rest the foot of the saw against the straightedge for a wobble-free cut.

Pieces small enough to lift easily can be cut neatly on the tablesaw. But, for accurate dimensions, you must make sure to measure the distance from the saw fence to the blade at the correct point. Set a piece of paneling next to your saw blade to gauge accurately where the blade will cut the panel surface.

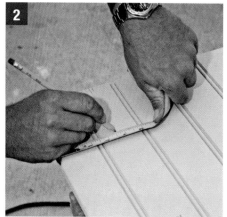
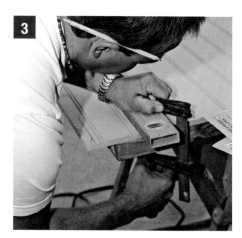

You can also bevel the edge on a tablesaw.

1 Measure the distance from the saw blade to the edge of the saw's foot, and set the straightedge guide that same distance back from the cutline.

2 Measure back from the cutline to set the location for the straightedge.

3 Clamp the straightedge to the panel (here, the carpenter uses a steel 4-ft. level as a straightedge).

4 Holding the saw's foot tight against the straightedge allows for a straight, accurate cut.

For a cleaner look, construct the assembly so that the beadboard butts down onto the top of the baseboard. (Depending on the panel's thickness, the baseboard may need to be "packed out" with a backer strip in order to stand sufficiently proud of the paneling.)

Installing the panels

Because the MDF panels are long enough to span the distance between studs, you don't need to provide special nailing for them—and you can apply them over drywall. Find the studs in the wall and mark their location before you start. For extra holding power, apply a nice bead of panel adhesive or all-purpose construction adhesive (subfloor adhesive also works well) to the drywall before you nail on the panels.

Beadboard Panel Wainscot

Cove molding   Chair rail

Let-in
plywood
backer

Beadboard

Baseboard

Ideally, the baseboard "bottom rail" of the wainscot assembly should stand out from the wall enough to create a small reveal where the panels butt to the baseboard, but not show a gap at the back where the profiled surface touches. In this example, two layers of 1/8-in. luaun plywood serve to shim out the baseboard.

To install the panels, first pinpoint the stud locations, and then extend a layout line up the wall with a level to mark the studs.

Apply a bead of construction adhesive at the stud locations and a zigzag pattern between studs.

Tip the panel into place and press it against the wall.

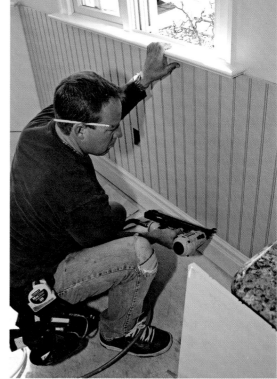

Use long finish nails to attach the panel to the studs. Adhesive supplies extra holding power, but do not rely upon it without nails.

In this application, the pre-primed MDF apron trim used beneath the windowsills serves as a continuous "top rail" for the MDF wainscot panels. Here, the carpenter uses a scrap piece of apron stock to check his cut angle for the miter joint.

Long finish nails through the trim and beadboard into the studs secure the entire assembly.

Installing the top rail and chair rail

Beadboard wainscot doesn't always get a top rail. Often, there's just a simple chair rail, with a small piece of scotia or similar light trim installed just below it to mask the joint. But a heavier rail assembly, more similar to the top rail of a raised-panel wainscot, can also work. In the example shown here, the same material used for the window aprons continues across the whole top of the beadboard, joining the windows and wainscot into a continuous visual element. The carpenter runs a simple, light piece of rounded over ½-in. stock as a chair-rail cap butting to the windowsills.

The apron goes on first, laying over the beadboard and mitered at the 45° corners in the room. For a long run between inside corners, it's helpful to tack up a temporary scrap block on one end for measuring and test-fitting the piece.

Next, the chair rail gets nailed down, on top of the heavier apron. In the example shown on p. 202, terminating the top of the wainscot just below the windows leads to complications: There is some fiddling needed to blend the chair rail into the already-installed windowsills. That's one reason it is more common to set wainscot height above the height of windowsills: that way, the top rail can simply butt to, or slightly overlap, the window side casings. (Where wainscot is set to the height of windowsills, another common

Take Note • When you need to hold a tape to the short point of a bevel cut, you can lay the piece on your chop saw with the bevel aligned to the edge of the saw's fence, then hook the tape to the fence.

A 1¹/₂-in.-wide strip of clear poplar, rounded over at the front edge, serves as the chair rail for this wainscot assembly.

treatment is to run both the apron and the windowsills long, as a continuous cap rail.)

Full Frame-and-Panel Wainscot

"Real" frame-and-panel wainscot is what you'll find in old historic homes. It isn't seen much these days, though it is making a comeback as new materials and new woodshop technology develop to support it. Today, there are many ways for a trim carpenter with good field technique to supply traditional-style wainscoting that will satisfy even a fussy customer.

A "floating" system

Classic raised-panel wainscoting design accommodates the normal expansion and shrinkage of wood and wood-composite products that takes place from season to season, as natural air humidity rises and falls.

Moisture-related movement happens a little differently for solid wood material than for panel materials. With sawn lumber, movement

is greatest across the grain of boards, and much less along the length of a board. The horizontal top and bottom rails of a wood wainscot system, therefore, shrink or grow mostly in the vertical dimension; the vertically installed stiles move mainly in the horizontal dimension. Panels glued up out of boards likewise move mostly in the cross-grain dimension (usually the short dimension of the panel).

MDF and plywood are different: They tend to shrink or grow equally in both dimensions. But the basic problem with panel products and sawn lumber is the same: how to allow the wood to move from season to season, but still stay put where it was installed.

Wainscoting solves this problem the same way frame-and-panel cabinet doors or house doors solve it. Fix the long horizontal elements of the assembly—its top and bottom rails—to the wall studs. The vertical stiles, captured by grooves in the top and bottom rails, are narrow enough that they can shrink or grow in width without overstressing the fasteners or adhesive where they join. And the rectangular panels that make up most of the system's square footage float freely within the frame formed by the rails and stiles—even though the narrow edge of each panel is captured by grooves in the edges of the stiles and rails, the panel can grow or shrink without tearing itself or its frame apart.

A modified version of this assembly is to profile the top and bottom rails with an edge rabbet, suitable for trapping the stiles and panels against the drywall or plaster behind them, instead of capturing the ends of vertical pieces entirely within the grooves on the rails. This system is a little simpler to machine and install, but it still works to let the panels move

Tight Fit for a Chair Rail

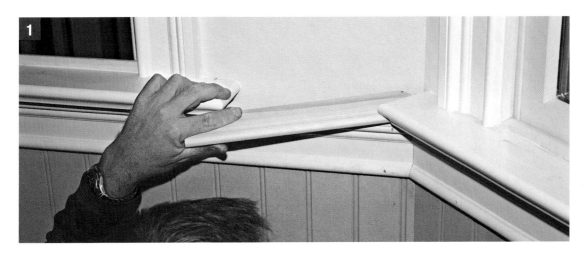

1 | The tight clearances and inside angles don't allow for chair rail to be installed easily between these two adjacent windowsills.

2 | To fit the tight quarters, the carpenter has to install this short section of chair rail in two pieces, connected with a scarf joint.

3 | Careful cutting, glue, and sanding help to blend the seam. Once painted, the joint will be invisible.

Layout for Frame-and-Panel Wainscot

Traditional frame-and-panel wainscot divides the lower wall area into a series of rectangles. The goal is to end up with equal-size panels and equal-size stiles across the width of each wall segment you're planning to trim. Sometimes you're forced to place an odd-size panel or stile in order to deal with an awkwardly placed corner or window; but you should strive for regular symmetry whenever possible, and in most cases you can achieve it.

The general process is simple, especially in the case of a clear wall with no interrupting doors or windows. First, measure the entire width of the wall you're laying out. (Measure as accurately as you can—precision is important in this case.) Let's say, in this case, we're laying out a 13-ft. wall.

Next estimate the number of panels you'll need—in other words, into how many segments you will divide the wall. Panels are usually between 1 ft. and 2 ft. wide; if you divide the total width by 2 ft., you'll be in the ballpark. For our 13-ft. wall, dividing by 2 ft. gives us 6.5 panels. But we don't want to use half panels, so we'll call it 7. (For some reason, an odd number of panels tend to look better than an even number.)

Now let's stop and think about the stiles. Because we're going to start and end with a stile, we have one more stile than we have panels: in this example, 7 panels and 8 stiles. The width of your stiles depends on the lumber you're using; let's suppose our stiles will be 3 in. wide in this case. So the total width of all the stiles, taken together, will be 24 in. (2 ft.). (By the way, even if panel widths vary between different walls, you generally should keep the stile widths consistent throughout the room, if not the whole house.)

Subtract the 2-ft. total for stiles from the 13-ft. wall width in our example, and that leaves 11 ft. total to occupy with panels. Divide 11 ft. by 7 panels, and we have the width of each individual panel: 1.57 ft., or 18.85 in. (about 18 7/8 in.).

Sometimes it's nice to see what your panel width would be if you used one more or one fewer panel. If we divide 11 ft. by 6 panels, for instance, we get exactly 22 in.—a width that leaves less waste if we're starting with 2-ft.-wide or 4-ft.-wide panel material (and with no fractions to boot!). But you might want to sketch out scale drawings of your various choices, or even trace them on the wall itself, just to see if the proportions seem pleasing to the eye.

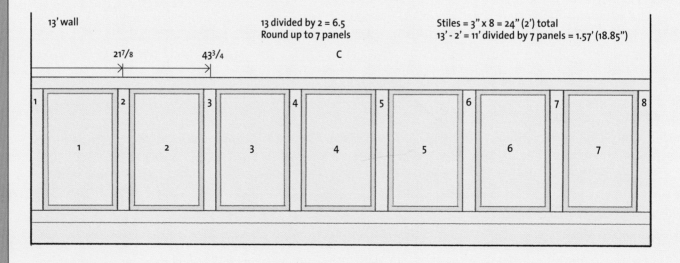

13' wall

13 divided by 2 = 6.5
Round up to 7 panels

Stiles = 3" x 8 = 24" (2') total
13' - 2' = 11' divided by 7 panels = 1.57' (18.85")

21 7/8   43 3/4   C

This partially assembled section of true raised-panel wainscoting in the corner of an entry foyer during a remodeling job illustrates the "floating" system. The rails and stiles of traditional wainscot are nailed to the walls and glued to each other, but the raised panels are allowed to float freely in order to accommodate seasonal movement caused by changing relative humidity.

within their frames without experiencing excessive stress.

Demolition and prep

When you install wainscot as a retrofit for an existing house, you typically have to remove existing baseboard. Work gently if you plan to reinstall any of the moldings. You may want to save the shoe moldings, for example; if so, pry them up carefully and pull the nails from the backside with curved pliers.

Assembling wainscot

Some carpenters like to preassemble entire sections of wainscot, then lift them into place and

nail them up as a unit. But if you've measured accurately and your pieces have been properly made, putting wainscot onto a wall piece by piece is relatively easy, and it relieves you of the joinery involved in preassembly. (For the sake of caution, though, it's a good idea to test-fit each run of wall as a set before you fasten any individual pieces permanently.)

Start by installing the bottom rail, using the same basic methods you would use to install baseboard (see Chapter 2). But unlike with simple baseboard, when you install the bottom rail of a full wainscot system it's important to get the baseboard level, even if that requires scribing it to an out-of-level floor. Most situations, however, will require only a minor tweaking. Generally, you can hold your top rail to a level layout, and cover any small gap at the bottom with shoe molding.

For short runs consisting of just a single panel, you can tack the bottom and side rails in place (first gluing the end joints), slide

Installing a Short Run of Wainscot

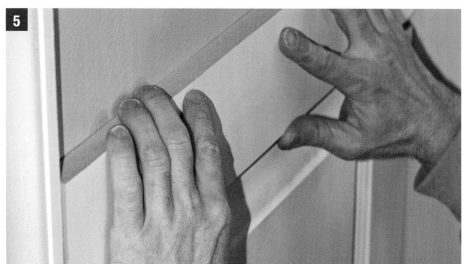

1 | Single-panel wainscot sections go together simply. First, tack the bottom rail in place.

2 | Then set the left and right end stiles.

3 | Slide the panel into its grooves in the stiles, and seat the bottom edge in the bottom rail groove.

4 | Apply glue to the end tenons of the stiles.

5 | Seat the top rail down over the stiles and panel.

6 Permanently nail off the stiles and rails anywhere that you have solid framing to attach to, but be sure to leave the panel free to float.

7 Even after tacking in place, fine-tune the location of wainscot sections with gentle prying or tapping.

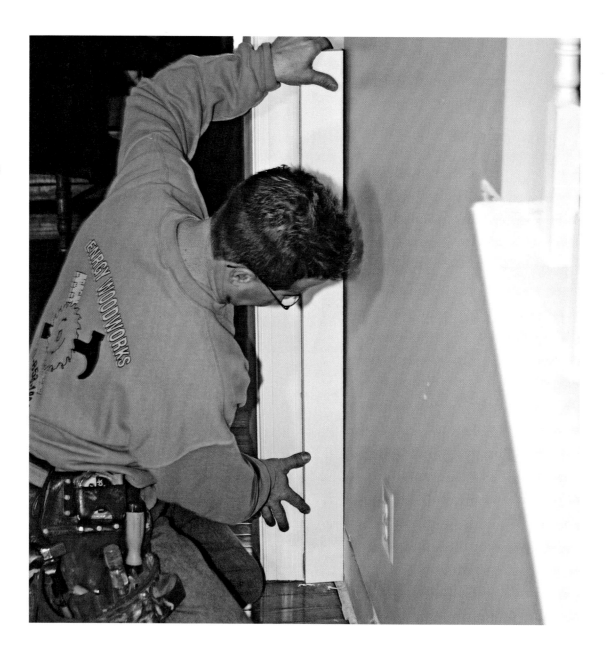

the panel into its space, then set the top rail.
Prying from the bottom with a flat bar and tapping at the top with a block helps you get the
whole frame and panel positioned and aligned.

For longer runs, you'll install the vertical
elements in series, working from one end to
the other. Set a stile, then a panel, then a stile,
then a panel, seating the tenoned end of the
stiles into the groove at the top of the bottom
rail, and slipping the narrow edge of the panels
into that groove, as well as the grooves in the

sides of the stiles. Stiles and panels will sit
temporarily in the bottom rail's groove while
you test-fit the whole assembly; when you're
satisfied with the fit, you can lift stiles up individually, apply glue to the joints, and seat the
stile end tenons back into their grooves. Then
you can glue the top tenons of the stiles, set
the top rail in place, and nail the whole works
to the wall.

With the panels and stiles in place, you
can now slip the top rail down over the whole

series. Glue the tongues of the vertical stiles into the grooves on the rails, but leave the large panels floating loose. Align the top rail carefully to its layout mark and nail it to the studs in the wall.

If your stiles and rails are machined with a back-rabbet instead of a groove, apply a small dab of adhesive caulking or construction adhesive to the back corners of the panels as well as the rails. Besides holding the panels to the walls long enough for you to install and secure the top rail, this serves as a soft shim to hold the panels forward against the back-rabbeted rail. This small amount of adhesive won't be enough to restrain the panel from moving as it adjusts to changing humidity in the room.

For long sections of wainscot, set the bottom rail first, and then place stiles and panels in series, moving from one end to the other.

Once you're happy with the test fit, slide the stiles up a few inches, apply glue to the joint (top), and snug the stiles back down into place for good (above).

Apply glue to the tenon end of each stile, and slip the top rail down over the stile tenon and the panel edge.

On a remodel, you may need to notch the chair rail to lap over the existing door casing.

The nails through the top and bottom rails into the wall studs do the main work of holding the whole system to the wall.

Installing the chair rail

The MDF chair rail for the wainscot assembly shown here came already bullnosed and primed. To round over the ends, the carpenter uses 80-grit sandpaper in a random orbital sander (see p. 212). As in the earlier example, he then marks the ends of the pieces against the existing door casing and notches out the ends to lap over the casing (see photo above). A small molding nailed underneath the cap, with the ends returned into the top rail of the wainscot panel (see p. 213), completes the assembly.

A Biscuit Joint for Long Runs

On long runs of bottom and top rail in a wainscot assembly, it's best to use a biscuit joint, rather than a beveled scarf joint, to piece together the boards. The biscuits hold the joint tight and serve to align the composite piece in plane, keeping the top surfaces flush and at the same time lining up the groove perfectly. That makes it easier to fit all the matching tongues and grooves together without fuss.

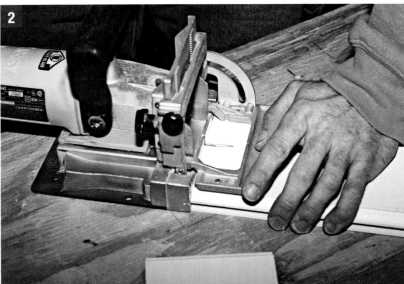

1 To make a biscuit scarf joint, hold the pieces in place and draw a "register mark" across the joint with a pencil.

2 Back at the bench, hold the biscuit slot cutter on the mark and cut the slot.

3 Connect the biscuit joint by squeezing glue into the slot, inserting the biscuit, and applying glue to the face of the joint and the slot in the mating piece.

4 Push the pieces together over the biscuit. The biscuit will swell slightly as it absorbs glue, forming a tight glue-line and holding the matching pieces in alignment.

MDF is easy to machine. To round over an end of the chair rail, first trim the corners on the chop saw, and then round off the curve with an orbital sander.

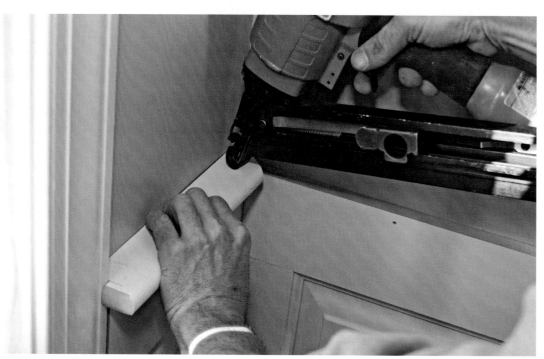

Nail the chair rail into the wainscot's top rail.

A Mitered Return for the Chair Rail Molding

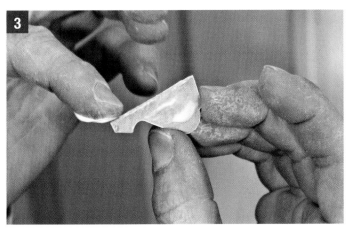

1 | For a mitered return on the molding beneath the chair rail, attach a piece ending in a closed-face 45° miter angle.

2 | Cut a wedge with the matching 45° bevel on one face and a square end on the other.

3 | Apply glue to both faces.

4 | Gently tap the piece into place.

"It is impossible to do anything intelligently to or with something you know nothing about."

—*Frank Lloyd Wright*

Appendix A: Selecting Trim Materials

Serious carpenters not only strive to master the tools of the trade but also to understand the nature of their materials. Our goal as carpenters is to become virtual wood scientists capable of predicting how a particular wood will behave when it's installed in a specific environment. Summarized here are some of the basics for understanding how to select the best wood for a job. For those interested in a more in-depth investigation, we highly recommend R. Bruce Hoadley's *Understanding Wood: A Craftsman's Guide to Wood Technology* (The Taunton Press, 2000). While Hoadley's work provides more information on wood science than any carpenter may need, it provides the extra knowledge a carpenter often seeks in becoming an expert in the field.

Dimensional Stability

Dimensional stability refers to a wood's resistance to its natural tendency to "move," or change shape. In solid woods, dimensional stability depends on characteristics inherent to that particular species, the part of a tree it came from, and how it was sawn, as well as the environmental conditions where the wood is installed.

Bow, Crook, Twist, Cup

Wood rarely dries evenly, and any imbalance of moisture content can cause it to "warp," or change shape unevenly. Because of the way wood cells function, wood tends to warp in specific ways:

Crook (or hook):
warp along the edge

Bow:
warp along the face

Twist:
warp along the width
and the depth

Cup:
curving of the face while the edges
remain roughly parallel (occurs when
one side of the board dries faster than
the other, causing one side to shrink
disproportionately)

Miter Gaps

Wood shrinks and swells more across the width of a board, than along the length. Since there is more wood to shrink at the heel, a miter will open at the short point as it dries out (below). If it swells, it will swell more at the heel, pushing open the miter at the long points (bottom).

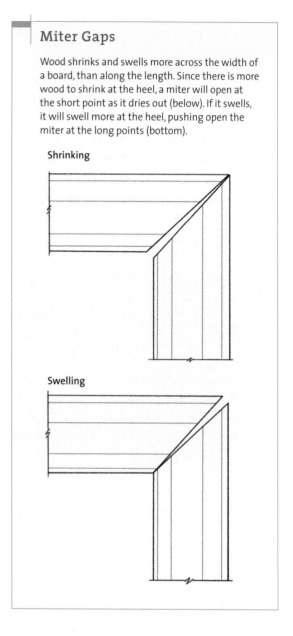

Shrinking

Swelling

When choosing trim stock, the goal is to select straight, flat, smooth stock that will stay that way. Because wood shrinks and swells with changes in temperature and humidity, a flat, square-edged board tends to grow, shrink, cup, twist, hook, or split as it absorbs water and then dries out. Although joints may seem to be fastened in place with glue and nails, they can still open and close as wood swells and shrinks.

Moisture content

The moisture content of a piece of wood not only affects the shape of that board but can also have an effect on the entire assembly you've built. If the wood is too wet when put into place, it will eventually dry to a moisture content approximating the conditions in the home, which can cause joints to open up. If wood is dried too far below the average moisture content in the home, swelling may cause wood to split, crack, or warp, fasteners to loosen, and glue lines to fail. A piece of wood need not be noticeably wet to have high moisture content. The only way to be sure is to use a moisture meter.

Moisture Meters

Every trim carpenter should invest in a decent moisture meter. There are two types of meters for measuring the moisture content in wood:

Dielectric meters send out a radio signal that passes through the wood. The meter reads the return signal and measures either the power loss or the capacitance (the measure of an electrical potential) of the signal—properties that vary depending on the amount of moisture in the wood. Dielectric meters tend to be expensive but they offer one distinct advantage: You need only pass the device over the surface, so you can measure moisture content without damaging finished materials. This is a great tool for home inspectors, but a less expensive resistance meter will work just fine for most carpenters.

Electric-resistance meters have two short, sharp metal prongs that you stick about 1/4 in. into the end or the back face of a board. The meter passes a low voltage electric current from one prong to another through the wood and measures the resistance. The wetter the board, the more easily current will flow through it. Ordinarily, electrical resistance is measured in ohms, but the meter translates ohms into percentage of moisture content. Readings vary slightly depending on the species of wood, but resistance changes little above 25% moisture content and tends toward infinity below 7%, so any resistance meter will only perform well between these limits.

Costs for resistance-type moisture meters vary widely. The more expensive models typically have external electrode prongs connected to the meter by a cord, which can be recalibrated for different species, and may automatically average multiple readings. A less expensive model with built-in prongs is typically fine for carpenters. Choose a model that includes a chart that will help you account for species and has an impact-resistant housing: It will get dropped.

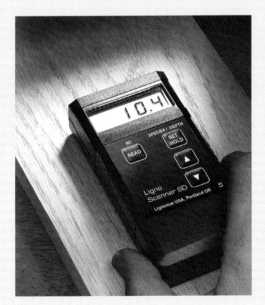

A dielectric meter can test the moisture content of building materials by sending radio signals through them. This is best for troubleshooting problems in existing installations.

Most carpenters will do well with a moisture meter that reads the resistance of a low-voltage electric current passing through the wood. To get a realistic measurement of the moisture content, test at least 10% of the stock required for the job and average all the readings.

Recommended Moisture Content

Use lumber that is dried to moisture content close to the midpoint between the high and low values the wood will see in service. The optimum moisture content will be midway between the extreme values that the wood is likely to reach. This optimum moisture content will vary by region.

6% avg. (30% R.H.)

8% avg. (40-45% R.H.)

11% avg. (58-63% R.H.)

11% avg. (58-63% R.H.)

(Source: USDA Forest Products Laboratory)

Acceptable moisture content Wood used for interior trim, cabinets, and flooring should be installed at a moisture content (MC) of no more than 8% to 12%. Ideally, it should be installed at the same conditions expected in a conditioned home, which will vary depending on local climate conditions. Shown in the map above is the average MC by region.

The best option is to use kiln-dried lumber for all interior woodwork. The heat of the kiln forces out the moisture in wood, and it's the only way to get material at 6% to 11% MC. In most parts of the country, the lowest moisture content expected from air-dried lumber is 12% to 15%.

Acclimating wood Buying wood at the right moisture content is only half the battle. Nice, straight lumber with acceptable moisture content won't stay that way unless you take care of it. If you store it in a damp basement or garage, or if the weather is especially humid, the boards will absorb water from the air and swell.

Bring the wood indoors where it will be installed, stack it with stickers between the boards, and let it acclimate to indoor humidity levels. If the wood must be stored on a slab, make certain to cover the floor area under the stickered pile with poly, so the wood does not absorb moisture from below. If the wood will be stored on-site for an extended period before it is used, cover the stickered pile with plywood and weigh it down with concrete blocks, toolboxes, or other equipment.

In humid or wet weather, you need to stabilize the indoor relative humidity level. Keep the house windows and doors closed and run house exhaust fans. It may be necessary to run a dehumidifier. You can also cover the stickered material with poly, leaving it open at both ends, and then direct a fan into one end of the stack so air is forced through the covered assembly. The moving air will have a drying effect and reduce the chance of the wood taking on too much moisture from the air.

Backpriming One of the best ways to control wood movement and prevent splitting, warping, and shrinking is to backprime it (coat the back surfaces with either primer paint or stain) before installation. In bathrooms, sunrooms, and pool areas—places where the woodwork will be exposed to extreme fluctuations in humidity and temperature—prime all surfaces, including the ends of any unglued joints, before installation and topcoat the material as soon after installation as possible.

Wood Characteristics

The strength and stability of any type of wood depends on the thickness of the growth layer in the tree, the thickness of individual cell walls, and the properties of the cells. These characteristics vary from species to species and depend on the site where the tree is growing and the weather during the growing season.

Growth rings

As a tree matures, wood cells form just below the bark during the spring and summer growing seasons. These cells are hollow tubular structures. During the spring and early summer, the number and size of these cells increases and the thickness of the cell walls decreases, allowing them to conduct water up the tree more easily. During the winter, the cell wall thickens and fewer cells are added. This change in growth from one growing season to the next produces the concentric growth rings we see in a cut log.

Woods Tendency to Warp

Most Stable	Intermediate	Least Stable
Cedars	Douglas Fir	Beech
Redwood	Southern pine	Cottonwood
Sugar pine	Maples	Elm
White pine	Oaks	
Birch		
Cherry		
Poplar		

(Source: U.S. Department of Agriculture Handbook No. 402. U.S. Forest Service: Forest Products Laboratory.)

Hardwoods have a more differentiated cell structure. Those that conduct water and nutrients are grouped in concentric rings in red oak, which leads to the pronounced grain variation and "open" quality of the grain.

In coniferous softwoods, the concentration of growth is one indicator of density. White pine (top) grows relatively quickly, producing widely spaced growth rings, and is considerably softer than the slower growing fir, which has very tight growth rings (bottom).

Heartwood vs. sapwood

The growth of a tree takes place in the outer areas of the trunk as new cells (called sapwood) develop beneath the bark. Toward the center of the tree, the older sapwood gradually changes to heartwood.

Typically, the outer sapwood region is lighter than the darker central heartwood. Both regions provide structural support to the living tree, but water and nutrients flow through the sapwood, as well as the inner bark. The heartwood consists of dead wood cells and the openings that once moved water and nutrients have closed, making the heartwood more resistant to water movement (and shrinkage) compared to sapwood.

Lumber dealers sometimes refer to all heartwood material as "brown" and material sorted for sapwood as "white," particularly with maple that is prized for its light tone. "Unselected" material has a mix of heartwood and sapwood.

Lumber Characteristics

Not all the wood coming from a single log will behave the same. A lot depends on how the lumber is cut from the log, which can be determined by examining the grain of a board.

Grain orientation and shrinkage

Because most boards are cut square from a tree that's growing circularly, the grain lies somewhere between a completely flat-grain board and vertical-grain (or quartersawn) board.

Think of the grain as a kind of architecture that provides stability to each board. Since this grain architecture varies depending on the cut of the lumber, each type of lumber cut from a log will respond differently when it dries and shrinks.

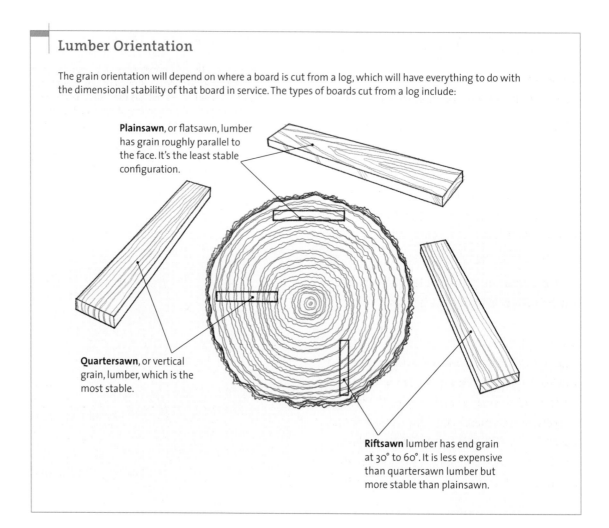

Lumber Orientation

The grain orientation will depend on where a board is cut from a log, which will have everything to do with the dimensional stability of that board in service. The types of boards cut from a log include:

Plainsawn, or flatsawn, lumber has grain roughly parallel to the face. It's the least stable configuration.

Quartersawn, or vertical grain, lumber, which is the most stable.

Riftsawn lumber has end grain at 30° to 60°. It is less expensive than quartersawn lumber but more stable than plainsawn.

Plainsawn vs. Quartersawn

Quartersawing produces more stable lumber than plainsawing but also yields fewer board feet per log and is necessarily more expensive.

Plainsawn log   Quartersawn log

Wood shrinkage occurs in three directions:

Longitudinal shrinkage. The least change takes place longitudinally (parallel to the grain).

Radial shrinkage. Moderate change will occur perpendicular to the growth rings (from the center of the tree outward).

Tangential shrinkage. The most change takes place along the line of the growth rings. At any point the change occurs along the tangent to the curve of the growth ring).

Understanding this can help you predict the behavior of a board as it dries.

Density

The terms *hardwood* and *softwood* can be misleading. We commonly refer to trees with needles, such as pine, fir, and hemlock, as softwoods, whereas deciduous trees with leaves, such as maple, oak, and cherry, we call hardwoods. However, some softwoods are actually harder than some hardwoods.

Tangential Shrinkage

The closer to the centerline of the log a board is cut the more even the shrinkage will be. In the examples illustrated below, board D has the best chance of maintaining straight edges, but has the most chance of cupping. B and C have the most chance of hooking as they dry. Board A is the least influenced by tangential shrinkage, so it will likely only shrink slightly in thickness.

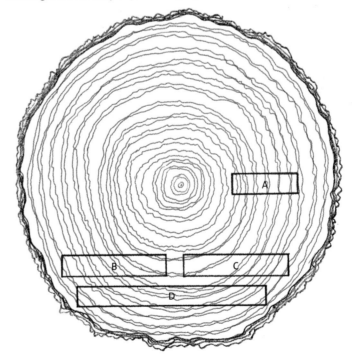

Reading a Board

The larger arrows below indicate tangential movement along the line of the growth rings, while the smaller arrows indicate radial shrinkage. Visualizing the movement of the wood along these lines helps to predict how it's likely to warp. In this case, most of the shrinkage will occur across the thickness of the board, but it may also hook.

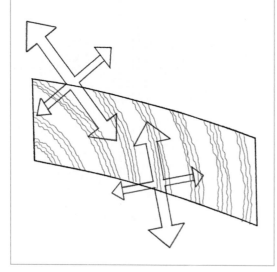

For example, southern yellow pine is denser than cherry, and tends to be more dimensionally stable, as well.

Hardness is an important quality of trim work that will get significant wear. Windowsills, baseboard, and chair rail are among the trim elements that actually take a beating. Generally, the hardness of a wood can be estimated by running your thumbnail across the surface. Softer woods like cedar and white pine are marked easily. Some poplar is about as hard as cherry, while some is noticeably softer. Maple and oak are considerably harder, and beech and hickory are nearly impossible to nick with a fingernail.

Specific Gravity of Selected Woods

Lignum Vitae	1.33–1.35
Ipe	1.06–1.09
Ebony	1.03–1.12
[Water	1.0]
Hickory	0.72
White Oak	0.68
Beech	0.64
Teak	0.63
Yellow Birch	0.62
Red Oak	0.56–0.63
Sugar Maple	0.56–0.59
Red Maple	0.54
Southern Yellow Pine	0.51–0.61
Honduras Mahogany	0.51
Black Cherry	0.50
Douglas Fir	0.46–0.51
Eastern Red Cedar	0.47
Western Hemlock	0.42–0.47
Yellow Poplar	0.42–0.51
Coast Redwood	0.40
Eastern Hemlock	0.38–0.40
Western White Pine	0.37
Sugar Pine	0.36
Eastern White Pine	0.35
Western Red Cedar	0.30–0.34

The best way to estimate the hardness and durability of a wood is to consider its density, which is usually expressed as specific gravity—the ratio of the density of a material to water. The denser the wood, the more resistant it is to dimensional changes. However, the lower the specific gravity, the easier the wood is to cut with sharp tools.

The hardness of a wood directly relates to its density. Dense woods are more difficult to cut, machine, and fasten but are generally less prone to shrinking and swelling.

Defects

Several characteristics of wood are especially undesirable in wood used for trim work. The most noticeable and prevalent are knots and wane, but even small defects like pitch pockets can have a big effect on the quality of the finish applied to the wood.

Knots Knots form where branches grow off the main trunk of a tree. Those formed by living branches are usually intergrown with the surrounding trunk, remaining an integral part of the wood. These are called *tight knots*. Knots from dead branches often become encased in later trunk growth and are usually found in the central portion of a large trunk. These knots (sometimes referred to as *black knots* are often loose when the trunk is sawn; if they fall out, they become knotholes.

All knots vary in size and shape, depending on the orientation of the boards cut from the trunk. When the board is flat sawn, knots appear as rounds or ovals and are called *round knots*. If they are smaller than ¼ in. in diameter, they are called *pin knots*.

A knot split lengthwise by the saw extends across the face of the board and is called a *spike knot*. Avoid boards with spike knots that extend across all or most of the face, as these boards will likely break at that point.

The form, size, and amount of knots on a given piece of lumber—and whether they are intergrown or loose—are all taken into account when lumber is graded.

Checks vs. Shake

Checks in lumber result from tangential shrinkage, and typically occur when lumber has dried too fast. Shake may look similar, but close inspection reveals that the separation occurs along the growth ring. This condition is caused by a bacteria, and the wood around the separations is soft usually (punky) and discolored.

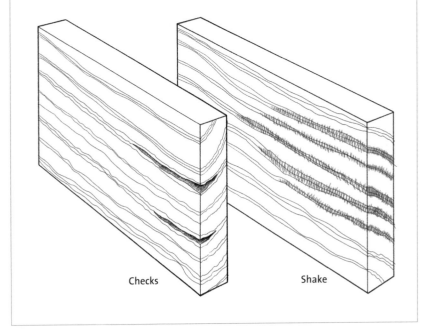

Checks   Shake

Shake and wane Shake and wane are rare in finished lumber since they are easily culled out in the grading process. Shake is a separation along the growth rings caused by a bacteria. The wood around the separations is dark and streaked, and it is often "punky," or soft. Wane is simply the remnants of bark, or the curved outer layer of the log exposed along the edge of the board.

Pitch pockets Pitch pockets are separations between the wood fibers that fill up with resin, often caused by insects. They're common in pine and cherry. The heat of kiln-dried lumber will "set" the pitch, turning it to a stable crystalline material. If the pitch is not set, how-

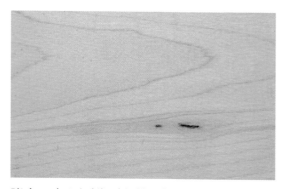

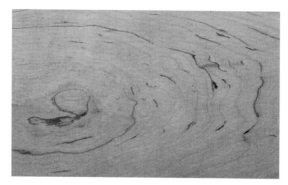

Pitch pockets in kiln-dried lumber are simply a blemish (left) and if filled do not pose any problem **for paint-grade work because the heat of the kiln will have "set" the pitch and prevent it from oozing. In some cases, pitch pockets that have set can provide interesting character to the figure of the wood (right).**

Harmless **blue stain. (Photo by Steve Easley)**

Potentially hazardous **black mold. (Photo by Steve Easley)**

ever, it will gum up sandpaper and can bleed through the finish.

Blue stain vs. mold Blue stain is a bluish or gray discoloration in softwoods caused by microscopic fungi that infect the sapwood, feeding off the sugars and starches of living trees. It has no effect on the strength of the wood and does not present any finish problems. Blue stain is often mistaken for surface mold, which is common on lumber allowed to get and remain wet during storage. Pigmented mold spores are a potential hazard and should be cleaned off the surface by scrubbing with water and detergent, followed by HEPA vacuuming the surface until dry. Bleach is not recommended, as it is a potential hazard in itself, and is not very effective at eliminating mold spores.

Lumber Grades

A single sawn log yields lumber of many different qualities. These lumber qualities are sorted, or graded, so buyers can select the type best suited to their needs. Grading is done by visually inspecting lumber at the sawmill. Woods used for trim work are graded differently than framing lumber. Structural grades select for strength characteristics, such as grain deviation, density, and growth rings per inch.

Common Trim Woods

Almost any select-grade wood can be used for trim work but the ones listed here are the most common hardwoods and softwoods used for finishing out a home.

The photographs are good representations, but grain patterns and texture vary widely so these do not fully represent the range of diversity in all species that are available.

Eastern white pine

Sugar pine

Poplar (sapwood)

Poplar (sapwood and heartwood)

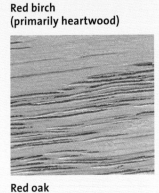

Red birch (primarily heartwood)

Red birch (sapwood)

Maple

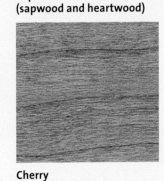

Cherry

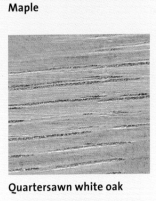

Red oak

White oak

Quartersawn white oak

Ash

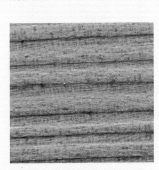

Vertical-grain fir

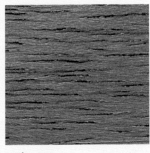

Mahogany

Aromatic red cedar

White cedar

Appearance Lumber Grades

B & BTR SELECT	
C Select	Only slightly lower quality than B & B BTR; only one sound, tight pin knot (max $1/2$ in.) allowed per 4 surface feet
D Select	Still a premium grade; only one sound, tight pin knot allowed per surface foot
COMMON GRADES	
No. 1 Common	Sound, tight round knots allowed
No. 2 Common	Often 1 Common and 2 Common are sold together as 2 & BTR Common
No. 3 Common	Used for siding, let-in bracing, and spaced sheathing—sometimes referred to as "Construction" grade lumber
No. 4 Common	Used for fencing or concrete forms—sometimes referred to as "Standard" grade lumber
No. 5 Common	Used for crating and pallets—sometimes referred to as "Utility" grade lumber

*The appearance grades of finish lumber are determined on one "better" face of each board. For stain-grade work, C select is often good enough. But even for paint-grade trim work, choose a No.1 Common or better. It's not worth the time to prepare No. 2 Common for paint, and the knots will inevitably bleed unless treated with a minimum two coats of shellac.

Finish lumber is graded by appearance only. Graders look for the shape, size, and frequency of knots, and the presence of the defects described above, including checks, pitch pockets, shake, and stain. The actual grading rules vary, depending on whether it's hardwood or softwood.

Softwood lumber grades

In general, softwoods fall into select and common grades. These grades are then divided into categories. As shown in the chart above, the premium, or "select" grades have fewer defects, while the lower "common" grades have more.

Hardwood lumber grades

Most hardwood is delivered to a millwork shop rough-sawn into general thicknesses, which are designated as 4/4 (about 1 in.), 5/4 (about 1¼ in.), 6/4 (about 1½ in.),

8/4 (about 2 in.), and so on. Typically, hardwood is sold in this rough form in random lengths and widths and usually in a green condition.

Grading is done when the lumber is in this rough condition. The most common hardwood-grading rules used in the United States are those established by the National Hardwood Lumber Association (NHLA). These rules specify the percentage of the total board surface (called surface measure, or SM) that can be cut out in the form of rectangular, clear-faced pieces (called cuttings). Here, "clear faced" means free of knots, wane, shake, and checks.

Hardwood lumber may also be specified by how it's milled, as follows:

• S2S: Planed on both surfaces of the board.

Hardwood Grades

FAS	The best grade commonly sold is firsts and seconds (FAS), which must be 83% clear (or better).
No. 1 Common	When price is considered, this is the best all-around grade unless you need very long, clear lengths. To qualify, the material must yield 67% clear material.
No. 2 Common	Must be 50% clear.*
No. 3 Common	Must be 33% clear.*
No. 4 Common	Must be 24% clear.*

*These three lower grades have some defects but generally not as many as softwood materials of similar designation. FAS-graded hardwood is the most reliable option if you are looking for a uniform surface for stain-grade work. However, FAS material is also pricey, and may not be necessary unless you need long lengths of perfectly clear stock. If you have the option of cutting out, or otherwise avoiding, small defects, No 1 Common is a good choice.

- S1S: Planed on one surface of the board.
- RGH: Rough-sawn lumber.
- R1E: Straight line ripped one edge.
- R2E: Straight line ripped two edges.

Millwork

As the name implies, millwork is any lumber milled into specific profiles for different uses. This can include molding pieces with a variety of curves, such as those found on most base caps, coves, and crowns. Or it can be simple square-edged, thin pieces intended for such uses as lattice and doorstop. Larger pieces, such as profiled casing and one-piece base stock, also fall into the millwork category. These days, however, not all millwork is made from wood. Many profiled trim pieces come from composite wood materials, such as medium-density fiberboard (MDF), or from pure synthetic materials, such as urethane foam and cellular PVC.

Wood millwork

The selection of solid wood moldings at most lumberyards is seldom very extensive, and more frequently it is upstaged by a grow-

More often than not, paint-grade trim stock today includes MDF and finger-jointed materials.

ing selection of MDF and composite profiles. Generally, a lumberyard buys wood moldings from just one millwork and then stocks only the most popular profiles from that supplier. As a result, if you want solid wood, you may be faced with only one choice of profile in each category. If you need stain-grade solid wood, it's worth doing some investigating. Different yards may carry different profiles. And reach beyond the usual lumber outlets to find the hardwood and millwork suppliers in the area, which often have a wider selection of wood moldings. Even if the profile you want is not in

Sorting Out the Pines

Carpenters who have been in the trade for a while can remember clear pine as an affordable standard for interior trim. Today, most lumberyards still carry pine but a clear, premium-grade material is often the most expensive option by a wide margin behind MDF, finger-jointed stock, and poplar. The relative scarcity is due to the devastation of Western forests by blister rust, pole blight, beetles, and overlogging, which altogether have eliminated about 90% of North American pine forests over the last 70 years. Eastern white pine has proven slightly more resistant to blister rust and, because Eastern stands are managed on a smaller scale, foresters have been able to respond more quickly to keep the disease at bay and to plant resistant varieties.

White pine Most pine used for trim is in a subgenus known as the white or "soft" pines *(Strobus)* that tend to grow quite large (with trunks in the range of 4- to 6-ft. in diameter or larger). These include:

- Eastern white pine (*Pinus strobus*), the tallest tree in eastern North America, grows from Newfoundland to Minnesota, and from southeastern Manitoba to northern Georgia.

- Western white pine (*Pinus monticola*) grows throughout the mountains of the western United States and Canada. An estimated 90% of the Western White Pines in the Cascades were killed by the blister rust west of the Cascades.

- Sugar pine (*Pinus lambertiana*) grows primarily in the mountains of southern Oregon and northern California. It fairs better in areas with dry summers where blister rust doesn't flourish as well.

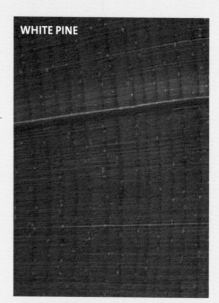

Eastern white pine: Transverse cut.

Eastern white pine: Tangential cut.

Radiata pine: Transverse cut.

Hard pine The "hard" pines represent a distinct subgenus, which includes smaller pines, such as the Scots pine and Jack pine, that are not often harvested for dimensional lumber but are sometimes harvested for fiber. Larger and better-formed hard pines suitable for trim stock include:

- Red pine (*Pinus resinosa*), which is native to northeastern U.S. and Canada, from Manitoba to Newfoundland down to West Virginia. It is sometimes known as "Norway Pine" thanks to our Minnesotan friends who adopted it as their state tree.

- Ponderosa pine (*Pinus ponderosa*) is a widespread native to western North America.

- Radiata pine (*Pinus radiata*) is a relatively recent import, typically plantation-grown in South America and New Zealand.

This "hard" pine group is sometimes called "yellow pine," which should not be confused with the "Southern yellow pines."

Southern yellow pine (a commercial timber designation) consists primarily of four species:

- Loblolly pine (*Pinus taeda*)

- Shortleaf pine (*Pinus echinata*)

- Longleaf pine (*Pinus palustris*)

- Slash pine (*Pinus elliotti*)

These grow to be substantially denser, and have a high resin content, which makes it naturally rot resistant. Most of the companies producing preservative-treated wood use southern yellow pine.

HARD PINE

Radiata pine: Tangential cut.

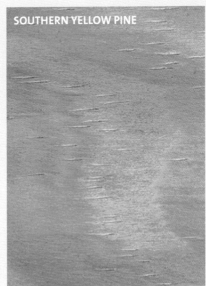

SOUTHERN YELLOW PINE

Longleaf pine: Transverse cut.

SOUTHERN YELLOW PINE

Longleaf pine: Tangential cut.

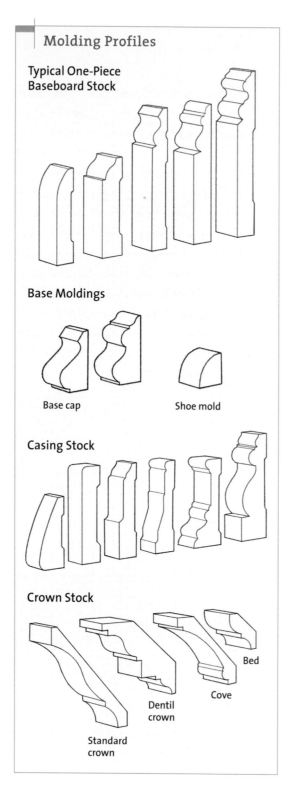

Molding Profiles

Typical One-Piece Baseboard Stock

Base Moldings

Base cap

Shoe mold

Casing Stock

Crown Stock

Standard crown

Dentil crown

Cove

Bed

stock, they will make available catalogs of their products, often on CD. Chances are good that you can find or order what you want to use.

Finger-jointed stock More and more "wood" moldings at lumberyards are made from finger-jointed stock. A finger-joint (sometimes called a comb joint) is a method of joining small blocks of wood to create a longer or wider piece of wood. It's an efficient way to make use of offcuts and usable scrap from processing lumber. Often the "culls"—the misshapen and defective lumber selected out during the grading process—are remilled into short blocks and processed for finger-joint material.

It's surprising how much paint-grade trim stock and molding is finger-jointed these days. Make sure you inspect any wood moldings, so you know what you have, as it can affect the performance of the job. Because finger-jointed material is processed from culls and offcuts, each block that makes up a single run of lumber or molding can have a widely different grain structure and will behave very differently as the wood shrinks and swells with climate changes. As each block expands and contracts at a different rate, the glue joints tend to open. It's not uncommon to come back to a trim job after the first heating season and find all the glue joints have cracked the paint.

At this point, there are no grading rules that take into account the dimensional stability of this material. Avoid using standard finger-jointed material wherever the climate conditions will fluctuate (such as in sunrooms, sauna dressing rooms, bathrooms, or on the exterior). And, even when using finger-jointed trim in a stable environment, check the moisture content prior to installation. If it's too

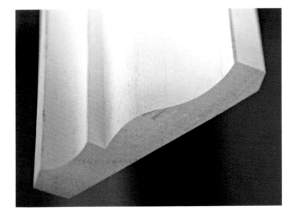

It's a safe bet that any pre-primed stock these days is finger-jointed. If the moisture content is below 8% to 12%, it should perform well in a stable environment. But avoid finger-jointed material that's either too wet or that will be installed in an area where the seasonal climate conditions fluctuate.

high before it goes in, you may experience finish problems.

Not all finger-jointed stock is created equal, however. Windsor Mills, a supplier of premium primed trim stock and millwork, maintains that its finger-jointed stock is more dimensionally stable than most solid-sawn lumber. In theory it should be; small pieces of wood will shrink and swell less than large pieces. But the overall stability of a large piece made out of short pieces can only be maintained when all the short pieces are similar. For this reason, Windsor Mills keeps track of its timber stands and uses only kiln-dried blocks from the same stands to ensure that the blocks used in each run of millwork come from trees with similar growth patterns. The result is an exceptionally stable material that's suitable for both interior and exterior applications.

Custom-milled moldings

Between the whims of architects and the need to match molding profiles in existing buildings,

FSC-Certified Woods

In recent years, the Forest Stewardship Council (FSC) has called attention to the rapid destruction of tropical rainforests where many of today's hardwoods are grown. FSC has established an international standard that has become widely accepted as the most rigorous and comprehensive in establishing a clear "chain of custody" to track the origin of a piece of wood to a responsibly managed forest. Today, it's not uncommon to find the FSC label on a variety of trim materials in lumberyards and home centers.

While the FSC deserves enormous credit for raising public awareness about destructive timber harvesting, there is a common misconception that FSC-labeled material is a higher-grade material. The FSC label has nothing to do with material quality, and is not associated with dimensional stability, reduced defects, color consistency, or any other characteristics that we typically associate with a lumber grade.

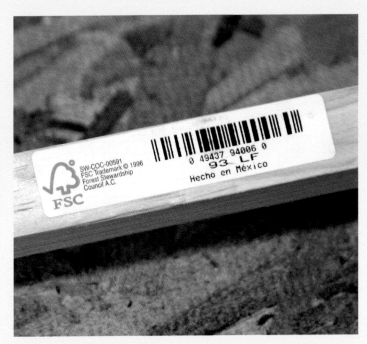

The FSC label certifies that the wood comes from a sustainable source, but it does not ensure the quality or durability of a wood product.

carpenters often have to turn to millwork shops for custom runs of a molding they can't find on any supplier's shelf or in any published catalog. It might be an unfamiliar profile, an extra-wide width, or a relatively uncommon wood species. Most good-size towns have at least one shop that can cut a custom knife for their shaper to match the drawing you bring in. There's a fee to cut the knife, and a smaller fee to set up the shaper, then you'll be charged by the foot for the lumber and for the milling.

Millwork shops save their knives from small custom runs, and many have large collections of custom profiles they've produced over the years for other customers. Unless you are aiming for historic precision or are actually tying into existing millwork, it's worth taking the time to look through the available knives or search the shop's catalog. Chances are you can find a profile that works for the job and avoid the charge for custom grinding a new knife.

The milling machines in a well-equipped millwork shop have one or more cutterheads. A series of "knives" are custom-cut from steel blanks to the exact dimensions of the molding profile you need; these knives are bolted into the cutterheads. The millwork shop will charge a fixed fee for cutting the knives, so the more trim you order in a particular custom profile, the cheaper it will be per foot. Typically, the cost of a knife is figured by the inch; a setup charge is usually added on, as well. The final cost of the trim also includes a linear price for the wood.

To order the knives, the millwork shop typically requires a full-scale drawing of the profile. If you are matching an existing piece of molding, bring a 1-ft.-long sample, if possible.

One-piece vs. built-up

Stock moldings on the shelf at a lumberyard or home center are usually narrow. The standard "large" width typically stocked for one-piece crown, for example, is 3½ in. Sometimes you may find a 5½-in.-width crown in stock, but rarely any bigger. For simpler trim treatments, these widths in dimensionally stable MDF usually perform well. But when made from solid stock, shrinkage and other dimensional changes can become a problem.

Think twice before you order extra-wide solid-wood moldings. The cost can be exorbitant, of course. But performance is an even more serious limitation. Wider pieces of

Built-Up Crown

Large cornices are typically built-up from several smaller pieces of molding, and the advantage is more than the availability of smaller dimensional stock. The individual pieces will shrink less and can shift independently with differential movement of the building.

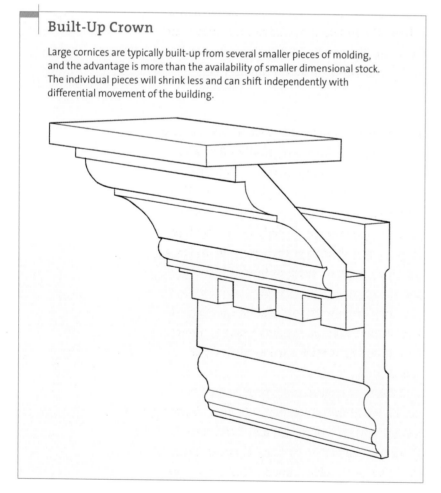

Wood Movement and Built-Up Trim

When multiple pieces are built up into a complex shape, any shrinkage in the individual pieces is spread over multiple joints. In most cases, an assembly built up from several moldings results in a treatment that looks just as good, and behaves better, than a large, profile milled from a single piece of wood.

wood are more likely to cup, twist, warp, and split than narrow pieces. And they're certain to shrink and grow in response to humidity changes. From a performance aspect, it's always better to build up custom profiles out of multiple narrow pieces.

Any piece of lumber of the same grade and species will shrink at the same rate regardless of its size. However, the effect of shrinkage on narrow stock will be proportionally smaller and cause less grief. The same logic that causes wide-plank wood floors to shrink, leading to the predominance of narrow strip flooring on the market, also applies to wood moldings: When one wide piece of wood shrinks, all the movement shows up at its edges. When many narrow pieces shrink, the movement distributes across all the joints between them—many small, and not so noticeable, cracks, instead of one big, glaring one.

When you stack up a multipiece assembly, you're basically repeating the same measuring, cutting, and joinery techniques you'd use to apply a single run of molding, over and over.

Composite Materials

Not all "wood" stock is from trees. In fact, with the decreasing quality of lumber in recent decades, composite materials have gained tremendous market share. Increasingly, materials made with wood fiber, such as medium density fiberboard, or MDF, have overtaken the market, while PCV and urethane have come into their own, mostly for exterior trim but occasionally for special interior applications, as well.

MDF

MDF is made from very fine wood fibers mixed with powered minerals (typically silica) and a urea-formaldehyde–based adhesive. The mixture is heated and compressed to produce a stable material with a super-smooth surface that takes paint exceptionally well. MDF typically doesn't shrink as much as wood, so it's less likely to warp, twist, or bow. If it does get soaked, however, it can swell. It must be protected from water and should not be used in a wet location (bathroom or sauna) unless a water-resistant MDF, such as Medex®, is specified.

Like most engineered products, quality varies. Premium MDF is typically made from a single species wood fiber, and the fiber is ground up and sifted by size—a process often described as "double refined" to create a more consistent material throughout. Examples

MDF is so much more affordable that it has now supplanted pine stock as a common paint-grade trim.

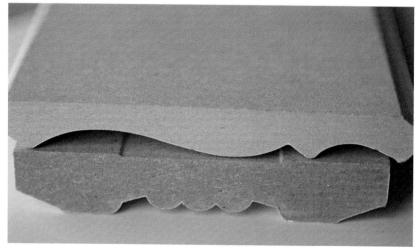

Not all MDF is created equal. Both of these moldings are made from MDF. The typical MDF uses a mixture of different-size hardwood fibers (bottom). The material on the top is made from Radiata pine fiber that is noticeably lighter and finer.

include Trupan®, a Chilean product made from Radiata pine fiber that is noticeably lighter than most MDF stock, and Williamette Premium MDF, made from southern yellow pine fiber. But there are literally hundreds of MDF manufacturers with products on the market, and it's often the available profile, not the substrate, that will determine what you buy.

MDF is rough on tools—it's high in mineral content and sometimes carries the odd bit of scrap metal that fell into a hopper at the manufacturing plant. When cut, the tiny fibers of MDF pulverize into a superfine dust that seems to defy dust collection systems. The formaldehyde-based adhesive used to bind the fibers is also irritating and possibly carcinogenic. (Notable exceptions are Medex and Medite® made by Sierra Pine, which use non-formaldehyde adhesive.) While it may seem impractical to wear a dust mask for chopping the material, it's strongly advised when ripping it. Plan to spend a lot of time vacuuming the dust as well.

As a panel stock, MDF usually comes in sheets measuring 49x97, which allows plenty of area to get lost to the kerf when ripping and still end up with whole-number increments. However, it's extremely heavy. A full sheet of ¾-in.-thick MDF weighs close to 100 lb. (compared to a sheet of hardwood plywood, which weighs about 70 lb.; Trupan weighs about 80 lb.), so you definitely need help handling full sheets. Although the homogenous thickness looks uniform, the edges drink paint. Any cut edges should be banded with solid wood. And just as the edges drink paint, they also absorb moisture, making the edges swell and, in extreme cases, crumble. Avoid using MDF in bathrooms or any location where it may get wet.

To bend an arched casing, PVC boards are first sandwiched between layers of "heat blanket" laid across scrap pieces of fiber-cement siding boards. When heated, the material has the consistency of cooked spaghetti and can be bent around a plywood form and then clamped in place to cool. (Photos courtesy Azek Building Products)

Cellular PVC

PVC trim stock is mixed with a foaming agent that injects tiny bubbles into the material. This creates more supple PVC than we associate with PVC pipe, which is brittle and would shatter if a nail were driven through it. Cellular PVC is pricey stuff and chiefly specified for exterior applications because it is impervious to water and will not weather or rot. But it is useful inside, too, for casing arched openings. Using the type of heat blankets plumbers use to bend pipe (available from plumbing supply stores), the material can be

softened and bent to a relatively tight curve around a plywood form.

While some attention needs to be given to control thermal expansion for exterior applications, the relatively even indoor temperature won't present enough of a temperature swing to make any difference. As a result, cellular PVC is very dimensionally stable, making it an especially good choice for forming long miter joints. Paneled interior columns are a good application for this material.

Not all cellular PVC is created equal. Some brands, such as Azek® (www.azek.com) and

Jeff Kent of Pawtucket, Rhode Island, uses cellular PVC to build interior columns. He begins by putting together a three-sided assembly in the shop (right), which gets slipped around a structural post on the jobsite and the fourth panel glued in place (far right). (Photos by Charles Wardell)

Cellular PVC can be cut and milled just like wood. If you plan to mill it, make sure the material has a uniform consistency, so that cutting into it won't expose any voids. When working the material, the only real difference is that the plastic dust created tends to stick to everything. (Photo by Charles Wardell)

Kleer® (www.kleerlumber.com), are made with a foaming process that evenly distributes tiny gas bubbles through the substrate, creating a dense, uniform consistency throughout the board. As a result, the material can be worked just like wood without exposing any voids. It's worth obtaining a sample to inspect carefully before you buy. A number of products are made by a "celuka" foaming process, which distributes smaller, tightly packed gas bubbles near the edges of an extrusion and larger bubbles toward the center. This increases the density near the surface and allows for a lighter product, but voids are common when the material is ripped or routed.

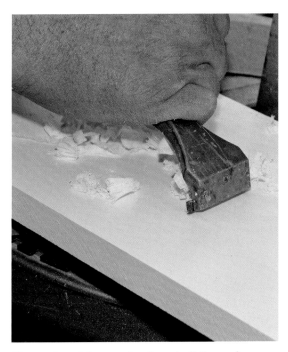

Glue and scratches can be shaved off the surface of cellular PVC with a sharp paint scraper. (Photo by Charles Wardell)

Cellular PVC can be joined with PVC plumber's glue. Not unlike joining PVC pipe, the glue fuses the two surfaces together into a single piece, so joints stay tight. Gorilla-brand PVC Glue®, a water-based product, works well: It's not quite as noxious as PVC cement, doesn't yellow, and doesn't set up as quickly, giving you a bit more working time. The glue should be scraped off. Scratches in the surface can also be taken out with a scraper.

A marked difference between cellular-PVC stock and wood is in its floppiness. Cellular PVC must be supported continuously when ripped in a tablesaw, for example, and long pieces are very difficult to handle without a helper.

Urethane

Urethane trim, frequently known by the brand-name Fypon®, has been around for decades, but it has come into its own in the last few years as the cost of clear finish-grade millwork has skyrocketed. Urethane is a dense, closed-cell material that resembles a hard rubber. It can be cut with standard woodworking tools and is a pleasure to work with. Taking a block plane to it is like shaving Gouda with a good cheese slicer, and there's no grain, so you can come at it from any direction.

Urethane trim must be joined with a proprietary adhesive, so inside corners are never coped. A full-contact surface of an inside miter is required. Manufacturers also make preassembled "miterless" corners that will work in (some) new construction, or wherever corners actually are right angles.

Urethane is often preferred for exterior work because it is impervious to water and won't rot. Inside, it is often used in place of large, ornate plaster and wood cornices. It's very expensive, but the labor savings (typically the largest portion of any job) often brings urethane in line with other alternatives. (This

Selecting Cove Molding

With its serene, swooping curve and deep shadows, a 6-in. or 8-in. piece of coved crown is one of the most impressive profiles around. Better millwork companies may offer two-piece coves (up to about 9 in. or more) joined with a spline or lap joint. MDF molding may also fill the bill, for paint-grade or (if veneered) stain-grade work: It will be as stable as any wood molding and generally more reasonably priced than stock milled from solid stock.

Urethane costs more than other materials but for an elaborate cornice (top right) or built-up architrave (below right), what you spend for material you will likely make up in labor savings. (Photos courtesy Fypon)

Urethane foam has the consistency of a dense cheese that cuts easily using ordinary woodworking tools (top) and can be joined with adhesive alone (above). (Photos courtesy Fypon)

savings is easier to realize in an exterior application because you can minimize the repeat costs of finishing it periodically.) The drawback is that urethane is typically a special-order item that may take you outside of the usual supply chain, requiring a new approach for receiving materials and handling warranty issues.

Appendix B: The Lost Art of Sharpening

C arpenters can only be as sharp as their tools. The true hack is one who goes at the edge of a board with a dull plane or attempts to mortise a hinge with a blunt chisel. But these days, sharpening is somewhat of a lost art. Many carpenters prefer to send out all their cutting tools to a sharpening service. While it certainly makes sense to send out saw blades and power plane knives, it's more convenient to touch up plane irons and chisels yourself. If you keep a true edge on these essential tools as you use them, you won't have to make a marathon session out of grinding and sharpening, which is what will drive you to the sharpening service.

Grinding and honing doesn't require numerous gadgets or fancy equipment. It does take some practice, but the techniques aren't hard to master.

Grinding

A bench grinder is a wonderful luxury but a belt sander will suffice. I use an 8-in. wheel grinder with a 36-grit wheel for all grinding. A 36-grit wheel will work to grind the finest edge, as long as it's honed afterward. Finer grit wheels heat up too quickly.

Grinding. To maintain a consistent bevel angle, grasp the chisel by the shank, using your forefinger as a stop on the grinder's tool rest. You don't want to grind too long at a time, or the heat of sustained friction will ruin the temper of the steel. But as you pull the tool on and off the grinder to keep it cool, keep the same grip. This will allow you to maintain a consistent angle.

When grinding, the most important thing is to maintain a consistent angle. Match the existing bevel on the tool by resting the edge on the wheel so the entire bevel surface contacts the wheel. Use the tool rest as a fence. With one hand, grip the shank of the chisel or iron, so your forefinger presses against the fence as shown in the photo above.

Find this grip with the grinder off, and then maintain it when grinding. You have to pull the blade off frequently to cool it in a water bath, but don't change the position of your hands on the blade. Just move your arms to a can of water. As long as you grip the tool in the same position, and rest the side of your first finger on the fence, you will automatically maintain the angle.

On-site, I do the same thing on a belt sander with an ordinary 80-grit belt to grind chisels and plane irons. If the sander is clamped on its back to a bench or stand, you can rest your finger on the back edge of the sander body, in much the same way you would

on the fence of a grinder. Keep a light touch on the blade or you will rip the belt. Klingspor® makes a very aggressive "Planer Abrasive" belt (available from The Sanding Catalog, www.sandingcatalog.com; 800-228-0000). Planer belts have a super durable cloth backing and zirconium abrasive that will grind a lot of steel before wearing out. (They are also terrific for removing paint or sanding rough surfaces, particleboard, and laminates.)

In all cases, cooling the blade is critical to keep the steel from overheating and destroying the temper. If you don't cool the blade frequently, you will see an obvious iridescent blue spot, which you will then have to grind past. Also, keep in mind that, over time, a grinding wheel begins to cut poorly and run hotter as it becomes "glazed," so it's worth using a dressing wheel to expose fresh, sharp abrasive. The restored wheel will cut faster and run cooler.

Honing

For honing, you need only two whetstones—medium and fine. You don't have to get too fancy. A block of wood covered with strips of 400 and 600 "wet/dry" paper (cloth-backed aluminum oxide) will do just fine, too.

Japanese waterstones, however, can provide very quick results. A 1000/6000 combination stone costs about $30 and lasts for decades. The 1000-grit side is slightly coarser than a soft Arkansas, so it works well to hone a freshly ground edge. The 6000-grit side is a bit finer than the Black Arkansas. This is finer than you need, but the stone cuts so fast, it's easy enough to put a razor edge on a chisel or plane iron with the 6000-grit.

As you work your blade across the surface of a waterstone, you will create a slurry of stone

Dressing. Waterstones create a slurry of water and stone particles that help polish the edge. Here the stone is prepared for honing using a special "Nagura" dressing stone to produce thick slurry. This dressing stone can also be used to flatten the waterstone's surface.

Honing. Maintain a consistent grip on the tool to keep the bevel angle true as you hone the edge. In this case, the forefinger running down the side of the blade acts as a guide. Lock your wrists and let your arms do the work.

Backing off. Keeping the blade at an angle to your backing-off stroke reduces the chances of bending the burr to the bevel side of the blade. If this happens, take a few more strokes on the bevel side, and so on, until the burr is gone.

particles and water. Don't wipe this away. The stone cuts faster and wears more evenly with this slurry.

You have to maintain a consistent angle on the stone, too, which takes a little more practice than it does for grinding, since you don't have a fence to guide you. There are numerous jigs to aid in this, but in our experience they limit the stroke, are difficult to adjust, or don't hold all blades. Instead, learn to maintain the angle by holding the tool, with the forefinger of one hand running down the side of the blade and the forefinger of the other hand acting as a guide just above the stone's surface.

Bend at the waist, with the stone at a comfortable height on the bench, and hold your shoulders and body in place. Maintaining your posture helps you keep the correct angle while the motion of your arms alone does the work. Your stroke should run the entire length of the stone, as you maintain constant pressure on the back of the blade.

Hone on a medium stone, holding the blade at the same angle as the hollow grind, and then hone a slightly steeper (35°) angle using both the medium and fine stones. With each grit, hone only until you feel a burr on the back edge. Then "back off" by pressing the back of the blade flat as you stroke across the stone.

As a final step, wood carvers often strop a blade on a piece of leather charged with rouge or a gray abrasive powder and mineral oil. But this is more than is required for a carpenter's straight chisels and plane irons.

Glossary

Apron The flat wall trim below a widow sill; the bottom piece of window casing.

Architrave In classical architecture, an architrave is the beam that extends across the top of the columns. It forms the lowest part of the entablature, and it is used to describe the trim across the head of a window or door, especially one built up to evoke a classical architrave.

Back band An L-shaped molding used to dress the outside perimeter of door or window trim.

Backer Any material used behind trim to provide a surface to nail to. With trim, it's used specifically to provide nailing for attaching crown molding and wainscot. The terms *backer* and *blocking* are often used interchangeably.

Backing out Cutting out the material behind the front mating edge of a miter or coped joint so that only the material at the front edges touch. If a cut is not sufficiently backed out, the joint may not close tightly.

Back priming Painting the back side of a board with a primer to seal it against moisture.

Banding Applying a strip of wood to the edge of a shelf to hide the plywood edge and create a thicker appearance at the edge. A solid wood band resists bending; the longer the shelf, the wider the band should be.

Base cabinet A lower cabinet that sits on the floor, usually beneath a countertop.

Base cap The molding applied to the top edge of baseboard.

Bead joint A raised joint between two pieces of trim created by applying thin, rounded molding between the two pieces.

Bed molding A molding placed between the ceiling and the wall similar to a crown, but typically smaller. The term *bed molding* traditionally refers to an exterior molding, but it can be used indoors, as well, as part of a built-up **cornice** or **architrave**.

Bevel The angled cut on the end, or along the edge, of a piece of material. An angled cut is referred to as a bevel when it is along the edge or end (through the thickness) of a board and as a **miter** when the cut is across the face (or width) of the board.

Bevel square A hand tool with an adjustable blade used to transfer a bevel or miter angle.

BF (board foot) A unit measurement for wood equal to 1 ft. by 1 ft. by 1 in. Rough-sawn lumber is typically sold by the board foot, whereas dressed lumber is usually sold by linear foot.

Bird's-eye Refers to the figure in wood grain that appears as a group of small ($\frac{1}{8}$ in. to $\frac{3}{8}$ in. in diameter) swirls or blisters thought to resemble little "eyes." Bird's-eye figure is most common in sugar maple.

Biscuit A football-shaped spline that fits in a slot in the edges of two boards to invisibly join two boards.

Block plane A small hand plane specifically designed to smooth end grain.

Blowout The mishap caused when a nail that is placed too close to an edge pushes out and mars a finish surface.

Bow Distortion in a board describing the curvature in the face of a board along its length. A bow is distinguished from a **hook**, which is a curve along the edge of a board, or a **cup**, which is a curve in the face running across the width.

Brad Small finish nail under 1 in. in length.

Brad-point bit Drill bit with a sharpened point used to precisely center the bit.

Butt joint The joint between two square-cut pieces of wood.

Capital The crown or top of a column. The term is often used to describe the top of ornate window and door trim.

Casing The trim used to "case," or surround, a window or door. Casing is applied between the window or door jamb and the wall.

Chair rail Horizontal molding applied to a wall about 3 ft. to 4 ft. above the floor.

Check A defect in lumber caused by the separation of the annual growth rings, usually at the ends, and most visible in end grain.

Chopsaw Common term for a power miter saw. In commercial work, a chopsaw specifically refers to a saw that uses an abrasive blade to chop steel channel and pipe, but it has been adopted for use by trim carpenters to refer to their miter saws.

Clamshell A small, inexpensive trim used for windows and doors milled with one thick edge that tapers to a thin edge.

Clear Wood without knots.

Colonial period The period in U.S. history used to describe a particular architectural style. The earliest colonial homes, dating to the 1600s, were Cape Cod style homes built by English colonists. More usual, colonial trim styles derive from Georgian Colonial homes built originally from the 1690s to about 1830 that attempted to imitate the stately, symmetrical homes of Georgian England. Georgian colonial trim styles came to the United States with pattern books, many of which are still available in Dover editions.

Conditioned wood Lumber that has been allowed to sit, or acclimate, to the temperature and moisture conditions where it will be installed. Using conditioned wood results in fewer problems due to shrinkage or expansion.

Coped joint A joint made by cutting along the profile of a molding, allowing the profile on one piece to mate with the profile on the other.

Coping saw A handsaw used to cut coped joints.

Corner block A square block used to join the top corners of window or door casing.

Cornice An elaborate crown between the wall and the ceiling, often built up from multiple pieces of molding.

Counterbore The hole drilled to allow a screw to be set below the surface of a board.

Countersink To set the head of a screw flush with or below the surface of a board.

Cove A molding with a concave, semicircular profile.

Craftsman style (Greene-and-Greene or Arts-and-Crafts style) An architectural style pioneered by Charles Sumner Greene and Henry Mather Greene in the early 1900s. Traditionally used in bungalow homes, the Craftsman style was inspired by Swiss and Japanese homes that celebrated natural wood, exposed structural timbers, and pegged joinery.

Crossbands The veneer layers in plywood that make up the core (distinguished from the face veneer).

Crown The trim between a wall and a ceiling. A smaller crown is sometimes made with **bed moldings**, while a

larger crown built up from multiple pieces is often called a **cornice**.

Cup (or cupping) Distortion in a board across the width of a board. Cupping is caused by the board absorbing more moisture on one face, so it expands more on one face than on the opposite face.

Cyma Molding of double curvature, combining the convex *ovolo* and concave *cavetto*. When the concave part is uppermost, it is called a *cyma recta* but if the convex portion is at the top, it is called a *cyma reversa*.

D & BRT A broad grade of pine lumber that includes all the select grades; may allow small tight knots (STK), but is usually free of defects.

Dado A wide groove cut across the width of a board to accept the end of another board. Often a dado is cut wide enough to receive the full thickness of the joining board.

Dentil A square block cut in series—said to resemble teeth—in a cornice molding.

Dimensional lumber (dressed lumber) Cut lumber planed to a finish dimension, usually measuring less than its **nominal size**. For example, a 1x4 measures ¾ in. by 3½ in.; a 1x6 measures ¾ in. by 5½ in.; a 1x8 measures ¾ in. by 7¼ in., and so on.

Double plate A second horizontal plate added to the top of a wall frame, over the first top plate. This plate is needed to tie the top of a stud wall together, but it may also provide good nailing for ceiling moldings and backer.

Egg-and-dart A common classical molding with egg shapes alternating with V-shapes.

Elevation view The geometrical projection of the vertical face of a building or interior.

Equilibrium moisture content A moisture level in wood that matches the moisture level in the surrounding air. The goal of acclimating wood to job-site conditions is to reach this equilibrium.

Face frame The frame surrounding the door on the face of a cabinet. In a face-frame cabinet, the doors and drawers are inset into the frame, as distinguished from a frameless cabinet, which has doors and drawers that overlay the edges of the cabinet box.

Face nailing Nailing on the surface that spans the width of a board.

Face frame The frame surrounding the door on the face of a cabinet. In a face-frame cabinet, the doors and drawers are inset into the frame, as distinguished from a frameless cabinet, which has doors and drawers that overlay the edges of the cabinet box.

FAS "Firsts And Seconds"; a hardwood grade that is typically free of defects but may include some very small imperfections.

Fascia The horizontal finish board installed at the ends of roof rafters. May also refer to trim used to tie together the top of a series of cabinets.

Federal period A Colonial period of architecture concurrent with the Georgian Colonial period, but marked by a more ornate style derived from Classical Greek architecture. Developed initially by the Adams brothers in England, the Federal period includes many more curved lines, such as fanlights over doors, and circle top, or Palladian, windows, differs from the square and boxy style of the Georgian style.

Finger joint A series of "fingers," or splines, machined on the ends of two pieces of wood. When the joint is finished, these fingers mesh together and are held firmly with an adhesive. Using this type of joint, it's possible to make a long piece of mill stock with many short pieces of wood.

Flitch Among lumber dealers, *flitch* refers to a section of a log cut on opposite faces, leaving two **waney** edges. It is also used to describe veneer. In this case, it typically refers to a bundle of sheets that are all flat-cut from the same section of a log. This type of veneer is distinguished from the curling spiral of veneer produced from rotary cutting.

Grade Rules used to sort the quality of lumber; lumber is graded according to the number and size of defects, including **knots**, holes, **pitch pockets**, and missing pieces on the edges or corners, called **wane**.

No. 1: Denotes a midgrade lumber, in which each board is at least two-thirds free of knots, but no large knots are allowed.

No. 2 & Btr.: Denotes a low-grade lumber in which each board is at least half free of defects; allows some large, red knots.

Clear select: Denotes the top grades of lumber; usually free of any defects.

Grain (texture) The growth patterns of the fibrous tissues in wood.

Close grain (fine grain): Wood with narrow, inconspicuous annual rings.

Cross grain: Any grain that deviates from the line parallel to the edge of a board. Often used to describe the direction of cutting or planing a board perpendicular to the grain lines on a board.

End grain: The ends of the fibrous cells that are exposed at the end of a crosscut board.

Flat grain: The grain in lumber that has been sawed parallel to the core (or pith) of the log and tangent to the growth rings. This results in the growth rings running at an angle of less than 45 degrees with the surface of the board. Flat-grain hardwood and specialty softwoods are often designated CMG, or clear mixed grain.

Open grain: A designation common among painters and finishers for describing woods, such as oak, mahogany, and ash, with large pores in the grain structure.

Vertical grain (edge grain, quarter-sawn, plain-sawn): Typically designated as CVG (clear vertical grain) by hardwood dealers, vertical grain lumber is cut from the log where the growth rings are running vertically, or close to vertical, through the thickness of the

board. The result is usually the most stable grain configuration in relation to the geometry of the board.

Greek-Revival period A period dating to the mid-19th century (19825 to 1860, predominately), which became popular first in public buildings during the Colonial period that were eventually adopted by homebuilders. Greek Revival homes usually have clapboard exteriors with plain, wide trim, a low-pitched gable surrounded by a large cornice and flat entablature, and a colonnaded entry porch (reminiscent of a very plain Greek temple). The interiors typically have wide, simple moldings, tall baseboard with plain, rectangular plinth blocks. Typically, the head trim is wider than the side trim around openings.

Grit The particle size of the abrasives used on sandpaper. The lower the grit, the rougher the texture of the paper (for example, 40, 60, and 80 grit); finer-grit papers (100, 180, 200) produce the smoothest surface but "cut" much slower.

Guilloche An interlaced pattern used to decorate molding in classical architecture. The center of the interlace may be empty or filled with a rosette design.

Header (head) Usually the structural horizontal beam over a window or door opening. Carpenters may also casually refer to the head trim over an opening as the header, or header trim.

Heartwood The darker grain in a board that is cut from the inner, central core, or pith, of the tree. The denser heartwood consists of dormant cells that ceased to carry sap at the time the tree was cut. Compare **sapwood**.

Boxed heart: Used to describe a board in which the pith falls entirely within the edges of a board, so there is lighter sapwood surrounding a section of heartwood.

Hook Distortion in a board describing the curvature in the edge of a board along its length. A hook (sometimes also called a "crook") is distinguished from a **bow**, which is a curve along the face of a board, or a **cup**, which is a curve in the face running across the width.

Jamb The vertical surrounding of a door, window or mantel opening. The jamb runs perpendicular to the casing, which it intersects.

Extension jamb: An additional trim piece that may be necessary to extend a window jamb so it ends flush to the wall

Jigsaw A power saw with a narrow, straight blade that runs up and down. Typically used to cut around curves and coped joints.

Joist The framing members in a floor or ceiling.

Kerf, or kerfing The path cut by a saw blade. When calculating the dimensions of pieces cut from a board or panel, it is necessary to account for the kerf, which will be turned to sawdust once the saw runs through it, but won't be included in the final dimension of the board.

Kick base The bottom of a cabinet that sits on the floor. Typically the kick base (often simply called the "kick") is recessed behind the front face of the cabinet above it.

Knot A dense cluster of cross-grained wood where a branch grew in the tree the board was cut from.

Loose knot: A knot formed by a dead branch of the tree. As the tree continued to grow around the dead branch it trapped the dead cells, which can make the knot prone to fall out. When a loose knot falls out, it creates a knot hole.

Sound knot: A knot that is solid across its face, at least as hard as the surrounding wood, and shows no indication of decay.

Pin knot: Very small, tight knot; defined by lumber graders as any knot less than ½ in. in diameter.

Spike knot: A knot cut nearly parallel to the long axis of a branch, so that the exposed section of grain is elongated.

Laminate Any product made by bonding two or more layers (laminations) of material. Specifically, it often refers to the thin plastic sheet material used as the top lamination on a countertop.

LF (linear foot) A measurement in feet along the length of the board, regardless of the board's width. May also be applied to the measurement of a run of cabinets, wainscoting, etc.

Long point The sharp end of a miter.

Luaun A type of mahogany used for making thin plywood. Standard lauan ply measures about ³⁄₁₆ in. thick (¼ in. nominal) and comes in 4 x8 sheets.

Lumber-core plywood A high-grade veneered panel stock with a core made of solid strips of wood (usually basswood).

MDF Medium density fiberboard; made from a fine wood flour mixed with an adhesive binder and heat pressed into panel stock, boards, or moldings.

MDO Medium density overlay; a high-grade fir plywood surfaced with a heavy-weight paper. Favored by sign makers, it takes paint extremely well and is rated for exterior use.

Melamine A thermally fused, resin saturated paper finish that's typically laminated over a particle board core.

Millwork Any wood milled to dimension for woodworking. Architectural woodwork refers specifically to wood milled for use in buildings. Often, millwork used synonymously with moldings to refer to profiled trim.

Miter A joint that forms a corner; usually both sides are chopped at a 45-degree angle to form a 90-degree corner.

Moisture content The amount of water contained in a piece of wood; usually expressed as a percentage of the weight of wood that has been dried in an oven to remove all the water.

Mortise A square or rectangular hole cut in wood to receive a tenon (a matching wood insert) or piece of hardwood.

Nailer (pneumatic) An air-powered tool used to drive nails.

Nail set A metal punch used to set nails.

Nominal size The size by which a piece of lumber is sold, but which may not reflect is actual, or dimensional, size. Example: A 1x4 measures ¾ x 3½ in.

Ogee A double curve that describes the molding shape commonly used in **crown** molding and **base cap**.

Open grain A designation common among painters and finishers for describing woods such as oak, ask and, chestnut with large pores in the grain structure.

Particleboard Panel stock made from small particles of wood, which are mixed with an adhesive and bonded with heat and pressure.

Picture framing (window trim) A way to trim a window with four miters, one in each corner, like the frame around a picture.

Pinch sticks Two sticks held parallel to each other. By sliding—in one direction and one in the other—it's possible to measure a space enclosed by two walls.

Pitch pocket An small defect in wood that consists of an opening, or pocket, that runs parallel to the annual growth rings and contains (or once contained) pitch.

Plan view A drawing of a building, room, or cabinet that shows the view from above; used to establish the layout of architectural elements.

Plinth The base of a pilaster or column. A plinth block is used as the base of the vertical side **casing** on doors to mimic the base of a column.

Plumb Perpendicular to a level line.

Ply A single sheet of veneer in the core of plywood.

Plywood Panel stock made from cross laminating several layers, or plies, of veneer. Often the core veneers are thicker than the finer, higher-grade face veneer.

Pocket Typically refers to a recessed cavity built to hold a sliding door in a wall or cabinet.

Pocket screw: A method of attaching wood pieces together by boring deep pocket holes from one side, running almost parallel to the face so they penetrate the end and can't be seen from the opposite face.

Preacher block A jig used to find the angle of a piece of baseboard that meets a plinth block or door casing.

Premium A broad grade of pine lumber (also referred to as #2 or #3) that allows for some knots.

Primer A low-solids paint used as a first coat to seal the wood.

Quarter measure Rough lumber size denoting thickness in quarters of an inch. 4/4 lumber is four quarters or 1 in. thick; 5/4 is five quarters of 1¼ in. thick, etc. When dressed, the lumber thickness is less. For example 4/4 lumber dresses out to ¾ in., 5/4 dresses out to 1 in. (or sometimes 1⅛ in.), etc.

Ray fleck In quartersawn wood, it is the figure made when a ray is cut. Rays are strips of cells extending radially within a tree that serve primarily to store food and transport it horizontally in the tree. In many woods, the rays are only a few cells thick and not always visible, but they are most prominent in oak.

Reveal An offset where two pieces of wood come together. A reveal is commonly used between the casing and jamb for window or door trim. The offset helps mask slight discrepancies in the squareness of the window and door unit.

S3S "Surfaced Three Sides"; denotes hardwood lumber that has been planed on the two faces with one edge ripped straight and the second edge left rough.

S4S "Surfaced Four Sides"; denotes hardwood lumber that has been planed on both faces and both edges.

Sapwood The lighter grain in a board that is cut from the outer portion of a tree. When the tree was cut, the sapwood was the living cells in the trunk that carried sap to the upper portions of the tree. Compare **heartwood**.

Sanitary base A small milled baseboard stock; the equivalent of **clamshell** for baseboard.

Scarf joint A splice made by overlapping two angled cuts in a piece of trim. The angle may be cut as a bevel or along the face of the board or both.

Scribing A method for transferring an irregular or contoured shape along the edge of a board. This line can then be cut so the board fits tight against the irregular or contoured shape

Section view A drawing that shows the relationship of parts in an assembly. It depicts what the assembly would look like if a slice had been taken through the assembly.

Shake A defect in wood that occurs when the grain separates along the annual growth rings.

Sheet goods (panel stock) Any type of laminated or pressed lumber sold in sheets. The standard size for one sheet is 4 x 8 ft.

Shim Any thin piece of wood used as a spacer. Typically refers to the thin, tapered pieces of cedar that are used to level a cabinet, or to fill the gap between a window or door jamb and the rough opening.

Shoe molding A small molding used to cover the gap between the bottom edge of baseboard and the floor. Shoe molding is typically rounded, and is a bit taller than it is wide.

Shoot board A jig made to guide a circular saw along a straight line; typically used for crosscutting panel stock or undercutting a door.

Short point The heel of a miter.

Sill The horizontal base of a window. The sill runs perpendicular to the casing, much like a jamb, but it typically projects into the room, past the face of the **casing**. An interior window sill is often referred to as a **stool** to distinguish it from the exterior sill, which is pitched to allow water to drain off of it.

Slip-matched veneer Veneer made from a sheet in a **flitch** that is slid across the sheet beneath and spliced at the joints without turning it.

Span The distance between two bearing points.

Splint A stiffener that spans a joint and helps hold it together.

Spring angle The angle between the wall and a crown molding. Crown molding is often defined in relation to its spring angle, because that determines the bevel on the back face of the crown molding.

Springwood (early wood) The portion of the growth ring that is formed during the early part of the growing season when the tree is growing the fastest. It is usually not as dense or as strong as summerwood.

STD (standard) A grade of pine lumber (also referred to as #4) that allows for large red knots, and some loose knots. This is the grade most often used in the manufacture of ship-lapped siding, and is *not* suitable for trim stock.

Stool A term used for the level interior window sill to distinguish it from the pitched sill on the exterior.

Story pole A stick used to transfer the height of architectural elements around a room. A story pole is typically held vertical and marked with the elevations of the baseboard, window sill, countertops, chair rail, picture rail, etc.

Stringer The diagonal framing member that supports the treads in stairs. The finished stringer runs parallel to the stringer but sits above the treads to provide a kick base that ties into the baseboard at the top and the bottom of the stairs.

Stud The vertical framing members in a wood-framed wall.

Summerwood (late wood) The portion of the growth rings in a tree formed after the earlywood, when the tree is not growing as fast. It is usually denser and stronger than earlywood.

T&G Tongue-and-groove boards have a groove along one edge and a tongue along the other; when installed, the tongue of one board mates with the groove on the adjacent board. Typically T&G is nailed only on the tongue side, allowing the boards to expand and contract with climate changes.

Tearout The splintered edges of a cut.

Tight grain A designation common with painters and finishers for describing wood grain that has small pores in the grain structure, which results in a dense, smooth surface.

Twist A deformation of a board that occurs when the edges warp in a twist, so part of the face curves one direction and part curves in another direction.

Veneer A very thin layer of wood. While veneers can be applied to almost any type of wood substrate it most often is used to face plywood.

Victorian period An architectural period extending from the late 1830s to the turn of the century. There are many different Victorian styles, including Italianate, Second Empire, Stick-Eastlake, and Queen Anne, but all are characterized by ornate interiors with elaborate ceiling cornices, pediments over doors, deeply carved moldings, carved rosettes, and fluted casing.

Wainscoting The decorative panels cover the bottom 3 ft. to 4 ft. of a wall. Wainscot typically sits on the baseboard and is capped by a chair rail.

Wane The edge of a board that is covered by bark or the outermost edge of the log from which the board was cut.
   Waney is used to describe the edges of a board

Warp Any distortion in a board the bends it out of its proper flat shape with square edges.

Index